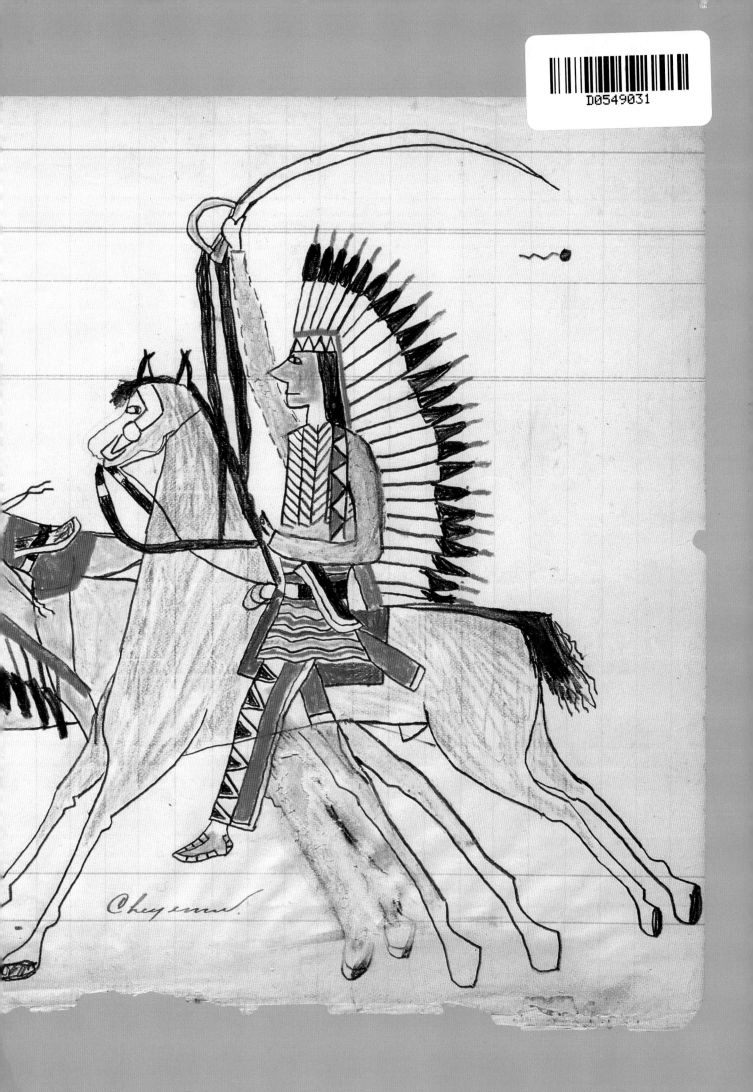

Cheyenne.

WARRIORS

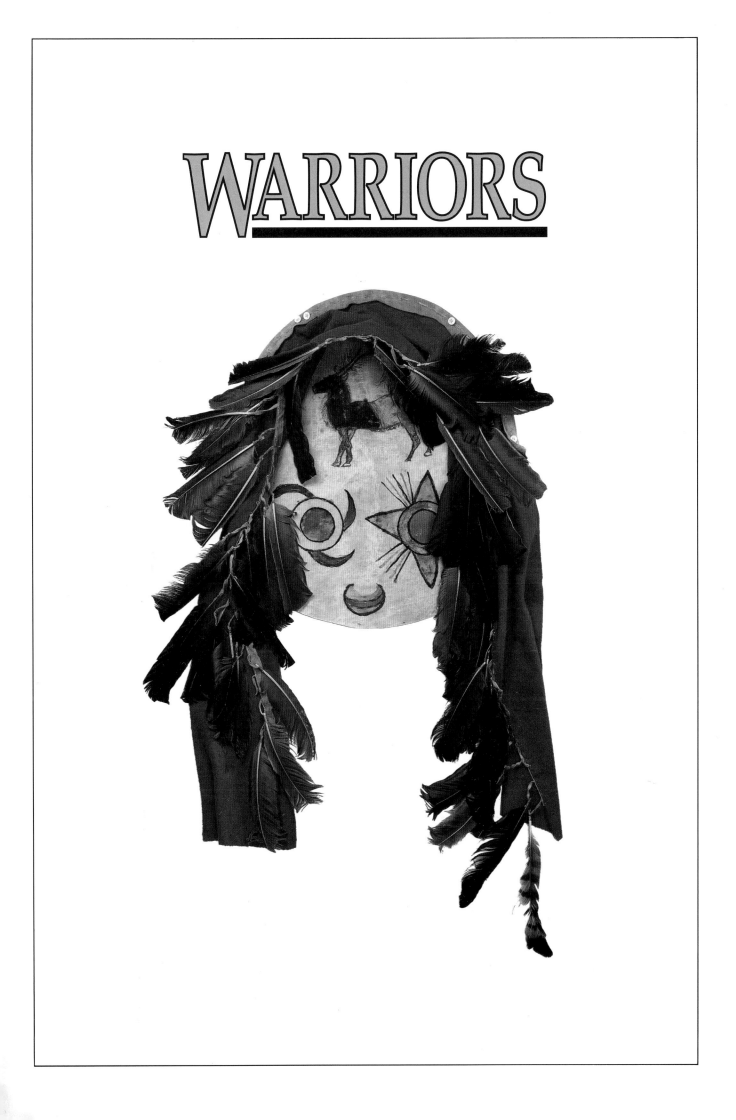

WARRIORS

WARFARE AND THE NATIVE AMERICAN INDIAN

NORMAN BANCROFT-HUNT

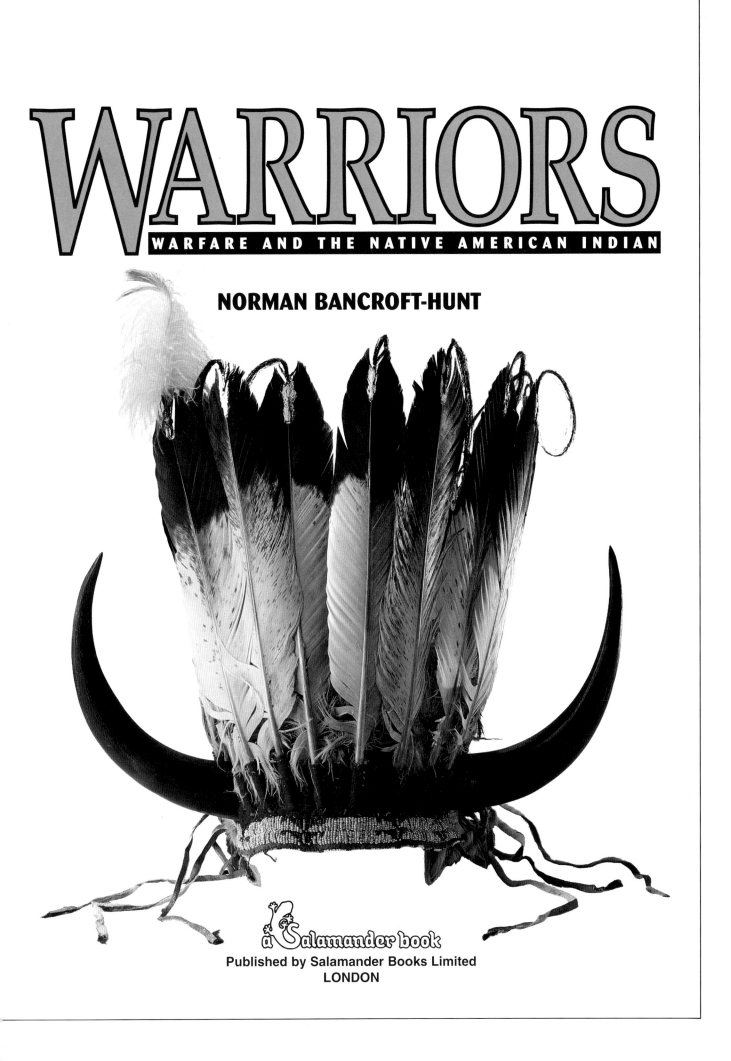

a Salamander book

Published by Salamander Books Limited
LONDON

A SALAMANDER BOOK

Distributed by Random House Value Publishing, Inc.
40 Engelhard Avenue
Avenel, New Jersey 07001

A CIP catalog record of this book is available from the
Library of Congress

Printed in England

ISBN 0-517-14033-0

All correspondence concerning the content of this volume
should be addressed to Salamander Books Ltd, 129–137
York Way, London N7 9LG, England.

CREDITS

Editor: Richard Collins
Designer: Mark Holt
Picture editor: Sylvia Bancroft-Hunt
Color photography: Don Eiler, Richmond, Virginia
(© Salamander Books Ltd)
Filmset: SX Typesetting, Rayleigh, England
Color reproduction: P & W Graphics Pte Ltd

*front endpaper: 'Pitched battle, Kiowa and Cheyenne', Kiowa ledger
book drawing*
page i: Southwestern shield, collected Arizona Territory
page ii: Omaha calumets
iii: detail from Cheyenne headdress
*back endpaper: 'Double coup, Kiowa and Ute', Kiowa ledger book
drawing*

CONTENTS

INTRODUCTION

Left: *Biróhkä, the Hidatsa warrior depicted in this painting by Karl Bodmer, wears a red buffalo robe painted with a 'sunburst' design which represents the feather war bonnet of an accomplished warrior and is used as a symbol of his high status and of battle honors he has gained. Such outward symbols of proven bravery and courage were important demonstrations of martial ability among all the semi-nomadic and nomadic tribes of the Great Plains.*

Below: *The use of exotic materials is apparent in the earliest of American Indian artifacts. This exquisite prehistoric banner-stone comes from Mercer County, Illinois, and is made from Huronian slate in which the pattern of the banding emphasizes its form and shape and attests to the skill of its maker.*

A T THE BEGINNING of his travels in 1832 into the interior of North America, where he was to make one of the most valuable records of North American Indian life and culture, the painter George Catlin wrote:

'No man's imagination, with all the aids of description that can be given to it, can ever picture the beauty and wildness of scenes that may be daily witnessed in this romantic country; of hundreds of graceful youths, without a care to wrinkle, or a fear to disturb the full expression of pleasure and enjoyment that beams upon their faces – their long black hair mingling with their horses' tails, floating in the wind, while they are flying over the carpeted prairie, and dealing death with their spears and arrows to a band of infuriated buffaloes; or their splendid procession in a war-parade, arrayed in all their most gorgeous colors and trappings, moving with most exquisite grace and manly beauty, added to that bold defiance which man carries on his front, who acknowledges no superior on earth, and who is amenable to no laws except the laws of God and honor.'

Catlin's description of these 'knights of the forests and prairies' is an enduring one that he was to find constantly reinforced during several years travel on the continent, and it has been underscored countless times since, in movies, novels, epic poems, and even in children's games of 'Red Indians'. It would be difficult to find anyone, anywhere, who cannot instantly conjure up a picture of such a warrior: eagle feathers streaming, mounted on a painted pony, riding off brandishing his gun and tomahawk and with his bow and quiver slung across his back, to meet, overcome, and scalp a distant foe; or to die honorably and bravely in the attempt.

But this heroic Indian is only part of the story, and his place in it stems from a recent period following the European introduction of the horse and gun. The image is that of the nineteenth-century Plains Indian, whereas Native Americans have lived on the continent for many thousands of years longer than that, and have occupied areas ranging from arctic to tropical, and from mountain pastures to deserts.

The diversity in habitats and lifestyles are reflected in attitudes to warfare and to the ideal of the warrior. The Hopi – the People of Peace – practiced only defensive warfare, and Pima and Papago aversion to aggression was so extreme that four hairs constituted a scalp, the taking of which required lengthy cleansing rituals and virtual seclusion from the everyday life of the community. Even the notoriously warlike Apache tribes did not consider the taking of life as a matter of little consequence, and one who had killed was considered to be contaminated and severely restricted in his activities until ritually purified.

On the Northwest Coast, in British Columbia and southern Alaska, the Kwakiutl had war seasons during which they slept on the roofs of their houses to avoid surprise attacks, and the Tlingit believed in overwhelming an enemy by presenting a ferocious appearance through the use of elaborate masks and body armor. In California, ideals of harmony prevailed, in sharp contrast to Plains practice where chiefly status was in part dependent on attributes that included war honors. Wars might even be fought at a spiritual level by the shamans, or medicine men, and not result in actual conflict, whereas elsewhere there was the extremely physical response of such groups as the Iroquois whose martial codes demanded displays of endurance and suffering.

War, however, was rarely waged for purposes of territorial gain, and was everywhere imbued with a sense that it was a sacred activity inspired by, and with warriors under the protection of, the various gods and deities that formed a supernatural pantheon. Appeals to these spirits frequently resulted in visions through which small charms and amulets, or 'medicines', were granted to individuals as tokens of their protection, and these were carried into battles to give warriors 'brave hearts' in contests with their opponents. Rivalry and feuding, rather than war, seem to have been the cause of much of the fighting that did take place, and this was frequently carried over into contests of skill which, to many tribes, were inseparable from warfare itself; since they employed the same songs and charms and derived from the same supernaturals as the war complex.

Dramatic changes occurred in indigenous patterns of warfare when tribal life was disrupted by the arrival of Europeans; since although initial contacts

Below: *Bannerstones, such as this example from Wapello County, Iowa , were originally thought to have served as clan emblems or totems, and it is from this that their name derives, although there was also much debate about their possible use as a weapon. More recent research has, however, revealed their true purpose as weights for the shafts of atlatls, or spear-throwers. The atlatl, a flat wooden platform with a knotch at one end to hold the butt of a spear, served as an extension of the thrower's arm, thus increasing the range and accuracy of the thrown spear. Better balance was achieved by weighting the end of the atlatl, and this also imparted greater velocity to the spear.*

Above: A stone-working technology was more highly developed among the Archaic Indians of North America than it was in the Old World, and was to prove so efficient that it remained in general use for manufacture of spear and arrow points until well into the historic period. The type of spear point shown above (top), known as Folsom, also has its place in the chronological dating of Indian occupancy in North America, since such points, found in association with the bones of extinct mammoth, established the antiquity of man in the Americas and proved conclusively that the Paleo-Indians of 8,000 to 12,000 years ago were big-game hunters. The Clovis spear point (lower) is even earlier. Both demonstrate the careful selection of rare flints and stones that impart an aesthetic value to such artifacts in addition to their practical function.

were almost invariably friendly ones, the vastly different attitudes expressed toward war by the Indians and the Europeans, and later the Americans, ultimately brought them into conflict with each other in bitter fighting on a scale that had rarely been seen previously on the continent. In addition, populations dwindled from introduced epidemics to which the Indians had no resistance, resulting in a death toll that was far higher than that caused by war; professional hunters destroyed the game animals on which the tribes were dependent; and a free, independent life was made impossible when wagon routes and railroads began crisscrossing the continent.

Yet in spite of this sad legacy, and of the tremendous differences shown in the practice of indigenous warfare, there remains a common ideal that formerly applied to all the tribes when honoring their young men as warriors and in defining the qualities they were expected to possess. These were bravery and courage, truthfulness and generosity, ideals that were demanded in both war and peace. Although the Indian wars are a thing of the past, such qualities live on among many Native American people who still follow the traditional values of their own cultures. This book is written in their honor as well as in memory of the old-time warriors.

FLORIDA, THE SOUTHEAST AND WOODLANDS

CHAPTER ONE

Left: *This drawing, by an unknown artist, depicts the Florida chief, Saturioua, performing a ritual in 1564, when the French witnessed him scattering water from a wooden platter prior to leading out a war party. It was explained that in the same manner as he now scattered the water so would the war party scatter the enemy.*

Below: *Engraved conch shell dippers, such as this one depicting a masked figure wearing an antler headdress and carrying a bow, were prized possessions of warriors of Florida and the Southeast. After death these shells were placed on the graves of their owners, where they served as memorials to their accomplishments and brave deeds.*

AMONG THE FIRST tribes for whom European explorers made written records are the village and town dwellers of the Eastern Woodlands and the Southeast. This immense area extends from the Great Lakes south to Florida, encompassing the entire region east of the Mississippi River. It is characteristically woodland, although this is by no means uniform in type or density. Hardy pines, mixed with birch, hemlock and maple, are dominant in the north; the temperate central regions are mixed deciduous forests, primarily of oak, elm and chestnut; the south is sub-tropical and includes the swamp-cypresses and mangroves of the thousands of islets and marshlands of the Florida Everglades.

The people living in these areas, though showing much variation in their customs, ideals and beliefs, have a warlike reputation. This is borne out by the first recorded instance of contact between them and Europeans. In the spring of 1513, the Spaniard, Ponce de León, arrived off the southern coast of Florida where his ships were stopped by a fleet of eighty war canoes manned by Calusa Indians with what he perceived as clearly hostile intentions. They prevented de León from setting foot on land and he tells us little about them; but it is on record that he turned his ships away marveling at the warriors' bravery and more than a little shamefaced that the might of Spain had been so readily repulsed.

Ponce de León had failed to understand the Indians, whose action was more probably a provocative display. This was to cost him his life a few years later, when in a similar misunderstanding and show of cowardice he was killed by a poisoned dart fired from the blowgun of a Florida Indian. French adventurers entering Florida in 1562 responded to similar provocation with a show of arms, upon which the Indians dropped their aggressive approach and welcomed the French with unprecedented hospitality; but one cannot help noticing the wry comment in the journals that in greeting them the chief 'did not rise up, but remained sitting on boughs of laurel and palm which had been spread for him'.[1] A second French voyage two years later was accorded

_14_

greater acclaim, when thirty arquebusiers at the head of a large war party of Indians who had befriended them faced down a superior force of their opponents, in spite of the shamans predicting defeat; yet it is again ironic that they were nonplussed when, before they could press home their advantage, the Indians hoisted the French on their shoulders and carried them back to the village with jubilant shouts of the great victory that had been achieved. Showing a remarkable lack of comprehension of native attitudes, the French then attempted to make peace with a number of different hostile tribes and immediately earned the enmity of them all for being 'faithless friends'.

It is apparent from these early interactions between Indians and Europeans that their conceptions of war were totally different and thoroughly misunderstood. But they also indicate the great emphasis placed on dramatic displays of power and strength by the Florida tribes, through which wars could be fought and won even though no blows had

Above: The Florida chief, Holata Outina, seen in the center of the square of warriors in the background of this engraving, conducted war parties as highly organized ceremonial occasions. The rich attire, weapons and tattooing of leading warriors are evident in the foreground figures, and it is clear from their demeanor that such 'war captains' occupied exalted positions.

Above: *After defeating an enemy, Outina's warriors took scalps, arms and legs as trophies which they severed with sharp reeds. Should the enemy have been routed and there was sufficient time to do so, such trophies were dried over small fires before being borne triumphantly back to the village. As a final act of humiliation, an arrow was driven deep into the anus of each corpse.*

Left: *Monolithic stone axes from the Southeast may have been used in war ritual rather than serving as actual weapons. The Mississippian example shown here was found in Georgia and carries incised markings depicting a human head with the characteristic forked eye motif employed by warriors who were active in the Southern Death Cult. Also shown is a hand, a widely used symbol for striking an enemy, and a scalp stretched on a hoop.*

been exchanged; the dignity of their chiefs who, while acknowledging French bravery, failed to rise in greeting these lesser mortals; and the importance of remaining loyal to one's friends by declaring open hostility to their enemies.

All these express attitudes that were part of the everyday life of the Florida tribes and which encompass values they saw no reason to question. Implicit in them is the fact that war, or the possibility of war, is always present. We are told that 'there is always some pretence for declaring war; and this pretence, whether true or false, is explained by the war-chief, who omits no circumstance that may incite his nation to take up arms'.[2]

Incitement often involved deliberate provocation of their enemies, conducted with a subtle understanding of the niceties of black humor and of the anger that could be engendered by mocking an opponent's beliefs. This was carried over into their contact with Europeans: the Timucua, while successfully resisting Spanish mission attempts at conversion to Catholicism, claimed that their own gods could only be placated at their annual renewal ceremony by the sacrificial offering of a Spaniard. This, undoubtedly, was said for the benefit of the Spanish, yet is characteristic of the mockery and taunting that marked aboriginal life.

War among the tribes was not only carried out at a rhetorical level, however, and fear of attacks and reprisals demanded constant vigilance. Villages were guarded at night, the importance of which is evident in the severity of punishments for negligence. Infractions, such as falling asleep while on duty, resulted in the breaking of the watchman's arms; but for more serious cause, if the enemy had evaded the sleeping guard and set fire to the town or killed some of the inhabitants, the punishment was death.

Such extremes enacted against a fellow tribesman indicate how real the threat must have been. The possibility of a surprise attack was in fact so prevalent that Timucua men habitually 'let their nails grow long both on fingers and toes, cut-

Above: Blowguns were generally used for hunting small animals and birds rather than as offensive weapons, but that they might also be used in this capacity is supported by the story that the Spanish adventurer, Ponce de León, was reputedly killed by a poisoned blowgun dart in the early 1500s after panicking when confronted by a war party of Florida Indians. The Cherokee examples shown here are more recent, but it is fairly certain that earlier ones would have been very similar. In the hands of a skilled user, such blowguns could deploy wooden darts with thistledown flights over an effective distance of more than thirty feet.

Below left: Not all war in Florida and the Southeast was conducted as open battle; a regular stratagem was to wait until nightfall and then attempt to burn the enemy towns. Specially prepared arrows tipped with dry moss were set alight and shot into the tinder-dry palm thatching of the buildings.

Below: A class of men, whom Laudonnière refers to as 'hermaphrodites', distinguished from the warriors by wearing their hair long and adopting female clothing, functioned as non-combatants in battle. In this engraving they are depicted carrying the wounded from the battlefield.

ting the former away on the sides, so as to leave them very sharp; and when they take one of the enemy, they sink their nails deep in his forehead, and tear down the skin, so as to wound and blind him'.[3]

It was to lessen the chance of being taken by surprise that the Calusa, Timucua and the other principal tribe of Florida, the Apalachee, formed their defensive chiefdoms, in which outlying communities created buffer zones between the main villages of the various warring parties. The extent and power of these is indicated by the fact that names have been recorded of more than seventy towns under the protection of, or paying tribute to, the Calusa chiefs. The chiefs of the Timucua could command forces of two thousand or more warriors. These often went out en masse, as is indicated in the comments of European observers who frequently refer to

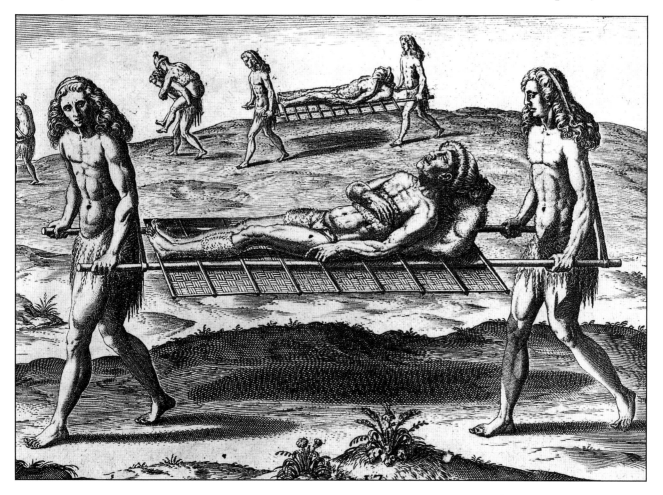

R. Holata Outina.

the Indian wars of the area as being fought by 'armies' and to their leaders as 'war captains', 'generals' and so forth. The sight of these must have been impressive. Warriors, gloriously tattooed with the emblems of their rank and martial achievements, carrying long bows, spears or heavy wooden clubs, with brilliantly colored feathers fastened in their hair or wearing the stuffed skins of raptorial birds to indicate their power to strike suddenly, marched purposefully out singing defiant war songs. Whatever military objective these may have had, it is clear their primary intent was to inspire their own warriors and to overawe the enemy.

An eyewitness account by the French commander, Laudonnière, describing a war expedition of Holata Outina in 1564, tells us 'he used to march with regular ranks, like an organised army; himself marching alone in the middle of the whole force, painted red. On the wings, or horns, of his order of march were his young men, the swiftest of whom, also painted red, acted as advanced guards and scouts for reconnoitring the enemy...they have heralds, who by cries of certain sorts direct when to halt, or to advance, or to attack, or to perform any other military duty...after encamping, they

Above: *Trophies secured on the battlefield were carried back to the village where, suspended from tall poles, they became the focus of a ritual exorcism by which the shaman drove away the spirits of the dead and laid curses on surviving enemy warriors.*

Above right: *At the death of a chief or shaman the entire village mourned, both men and women fasting and cutting off much of their hair. The chief's water dipper can be seen placed on top of his grave; this is surrounded by a protective ring of arrows.*

Right: *The incised figure on this Mississippian conch shell dipper has been described as a ceremonial dancer. But details of his costume are similar to those worn by the war captain on the right of the engraving on page 12, suggesting that a ritual in which the eagle figured served a war purpose.*

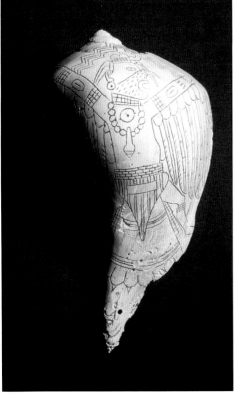

are arranged in squads of ten each, the bravest men being put in squads by themselves...the quartermasters place ten of these squads of the bravest men in a circle around [Outina]. About ten paces outside of this circle is placed another line of twenty squads; at twenty yards farther, another of forty squads; and so on, increasing the number and distance of these lines, according to the size of the army.'[4]

The march was certainly a grand display, staged for its spectacular effect, and the conduct of the army, the order of march, the formation of the war camp, as well as the presence of shamans predicting events, are more suggestive of a war ceremony than of a military expedition. In fact, the French were astonished to find when Outina's army came within striking distance of his rival, Satourioua, who had amassed an equally large force, that both sides immediately set up their elaborate camps within sight of each other without engaging in conflict.

From these camps they commenced a continual barrage of shouted taunts of defiance, challenge and insult, with parties of warriors stepping forward of the ranks to brandish their weapons and utter ear-piercing war cries. In the midst of this

uproar and clamor, the actual 'battle' was fought by small groups of warriors who attempted to slip away unnoticed and make secret incursions into the opposing camp or surprise any enemies who had become separated from the main body.

Killing was incidental and the light skirmishing resulted in few casualties; yet the reports relish in giving precise details of the treatment of any slain, and of the taking of scalps, arms and legs as war trophies, which would be dried over fires and then carried triumphantly back to the towns where they were set on tall poles. We should read these reports with caution, since it is likely they reflect the biases of their writers. In them we are treated to tales of the delight the Indians expressed on securing the limb of a foe, of the joyful wailing of the women when their men returned home carrying these symbols of their success, and their happiness at the display of these gruesome trophies. More probably they served a ritual function, and once this was completed were displayed as a typically provocative gesture.

In these chiefdoms war honors accrued to the group, and the status of the individual was established through membership in one of a number of elite warrior fraternities. These

Above: *Florida Indians, prior to taking important decisions, met in early morning councils at which the matter was discussed and where the stamina of participants was tested. During these councils the women prepared a drink called* **casina**, *of which only men who had proved themselves in battle were permitted to partake. Anyone drinking this was thrown into a sweat, and those who were unable to keep it down were considered unfit for military duty. It was believed that the use of* **casina** *during war expeditions strengthened and nourished the body and enabled warriors to survive privation.*

Right: *This Cherokee warrior displays a number of characteristic costume elements that date back to the earliest Southeast inhabitants, such as the engraved shell ear discs, a shell inserted in the septum of his nose, beaded straps or sashes which cross his body diagonally, the string of wampum beads he holds in his left hand, and the crescent-shaped silver breastplate. His shirt, turban and the 'peace' medal he wears are innovations introduced by Europeans.*

Below: *A collection of silver breast ornaments similar to that worn by the Cherokee warrior above, but dating from an earlier period. These were collected in Molino County, Mississippi, and are of a type that appears to have gradually replaced the wearing of incised shell gorgets after silver working techniques were adopted by the Southeastern tribes. Such ornaments depicted the status and achievement of a warrior and were highly prized family possessions.*

would appear to be 'the squads of bravest men' mentioned by Laudonnière. Personal accomplishment and proven bravery and courage were generally a requirement for admission and most men strove to achieve this recognition, but it is apparent that certain positions were hereditary ones which demanded no other claim than birthright.

This is almost certainly true of Outina and Saturioua, who held absolute and unquestionable control and authority and is a situation that prevailed among historic groups of the Southeast such as the Natchez and Taensa who occupied several villages in the Lower Mississippi Valley. Natchez hereditary power was of such paramount importance that the position of chief, which encompassed war and peace functions as well as making him the head priest, was vested in the 'Great Sun', whose position was equated with the gods and seen as a divine right.

So esteemed was the Great Sun that he could only be woken in the mornings by a respected member of the aristocracy, who whispered softly in his ear so as not to startle him, and when he left his house to tour the village he was carried aloft on a litter covered with swan skins, goose down

and bear hides so his feet would not touch earth that had been trodden by common people.

The same haughty disposition toward those beneath them was shown by an aristocratic class of Suns and Nobles, into which the principal war leaders and warriors were born. Below them were the Commoners, whom the aristocracy referred to as Stinkards, a term that implied near slavery and which was so lowly that it was never uttered in front of a Stinkard to avoid causing offence. The Commoners comprised the mass of the people, although achievements in war meant that ordinary warriors could rise to the status of Honored People, a rank just below that of the Nobles.

Some of these honored warriors developed their own specialist corps of militiamen with distinguishing insignia, marked by characteristic hairstyles and tattooed emblems, which made obvious their honorific positions. They are 'seen again and again [in the French accounts], heads flattened to a mitred point, hair cut in whatever bizarre fashion the wearer likes – shaved on one side, left long on the other, or trimmed to a single scalp lock, or tonsured like a priest's. They stroll the plaza, tattooed from face to ankle, negligently waving fans, or recline on their mats.'[5]

The superior attitude of the Natchez warrior is clear from an incident in which they killed the French commandant Chépart, who had provoked their anger by demanding the site of one of their principal towns for his plantation. It was left to a Stinkard to beat him to death with a stick. This was because Chépart, instead of standing boldly against his

Above and right: *European and American influence in the Southeast had a devastating effect on the political cohesion of many of the tribes, especially on the Creek where it gave rise to what was virtually a civil war. Some chiefs, such as Ledagie (above left), although opposed to American demands for removal from their ancestral homelands, were nevertheless submissive and gave in under pressure. Others warmly welcomed removal, seeing it as a progressive move. One of the first to do so was Yoholo-Micco (above center), who was known as the 'favorite narrator of the Nation', respected as an outstanding warrior, and who held a position as chief of the influential Eufaula Town. Others, however, bitterly opposed anything that interfered with traditional laws. The leader of this anti-American faction was Menawa (above right), the Great Warrior whose role in the execution of William McIntosh, a leading chief who sold lands to the Americans against the wishes of the Tribal Council, precipitated the internal feuding that was to lead to the division of the Creek Nation.*

Below: These silver armlets from Molino County, Mississippi, one of them etched with the figure of an eagle, are similar to those worn by the Creek chief Ledagie (above left) and were a popular form of personal adornment among all the tribes of the Southeast. Together with silver crescent breastplates, such as those shown on the preceding pages, they were important symbols of status and influence and reflected the individual wealth of their owners.

attackers as a warrior should, had cowered in a corner and pleaded for mercy. To the Natchez such behavior was contemptible, and to show their utter disdain they chose this method of execution as a demonstration that he was so unworthy that even touching him with their weapons would defile them.

Bravery was expected of the Natchez warrior, but the conduct of war and the behavior of the warrior were also determined to a large extent by ritual formalities and restrictions which show an obsession with the twin themes of death and status. For a warrior to die boldly on the battlefield by placing himself in a suicidal position while protecting others was an honorific act through which his wife, who by custom would be a Commoner, rose to social prominence. It was, however, important for his body to be brought back to the village for ritual cleansing of the contamination caused by contact with an enemy; if this was impossible, his fellow tribesmen would risk their lives to secure his scalp for this purpose. Contamination and the need for cleansing also affected those who killed an enemy. Returning warriors fasted and purged themselves by taking strong emetics, but 'one who had taken a scalp for the first time must remain away from his wife and eat no meat for the space of six months, living mainly on fish and broth. Otherwise it was thought that his destruction would be effected by the soul or souls of those killed.'[6]

Religious sanction of warfare was carried to the extent that Tonti, who traveled with De Soto's expedition in 1540, wrote of the Taensa, allies of the Natchez and living nearby, that 'there is a temple opposite the house of the chief, and similar to it, except that three [carved] eagles are placed on this temple, who look toward the rising sun. The temple is surrounded with strong mud walls, in which are fixed spikes, on which they place the heads of their enemies whom they sacrifice to the sun.'[7]

Through the display of heads the soul of the deceased could be released and warrior power or spirit accumulated at the site of the temple, where the enemy's strength could be turned back against himself; but there is also a power-

ful suggestive motive here by which an enemy is reminded that he can expect to meet a similar fate. A concentration of power at the temple is interesting, because many of the principal towns of the Southeastern tribes were religious sanctuaries as well as being combined military and administrative centers from which the chiefs and priests could exert authority over smaller outlying hamlets occupied by subject tribes.

The descriptions we have suggest these towns were protected by palisades, ditches and earth embankments, and sometimes even by moats, with the house of the chief, the temples of the priests and the dwellings of other dignatories raised on earthen mounds protected by secondary palisades or walls. By far the larger part of the population lived outside

Above: *One of the most essential items of equipment during a war expedition was moccasins, and each warrior carried several spare pairs tied to his belt, as well as a small bag containing rawhide, sinew and an awl for making repairs. The high sided type shown here, which have been smoked to darken and waterproof them and are decorated with porcupine quills, beads and tin cones, protected both feet and ankles and are similar to those worn by the Mohawk chief on the facing page. This style was common throughout the Woodlands area.*

Above: *This elaborately tattooed Mohawk man, Sa Ga Yeath Qua Pieth Tow, was one of a group of Sachems, or chiefs, who visited Queen Anne in London in 1710, where this portrait was painted. Although his costume has been highly romanticized in the painting, it is interesting to note the powder horn and flintlock musket with which he is armed. Such weapons were being traded widely by the English to the Woodlands tribes from an early period.*

these massive fortifications, and the only permanent occupancy was by an exclusive class of civil, military and religious leaders, who were guarded by warrior societies whose specific function was to protect the nobility and priests. Other people only came here when summoned by the chief or to observe and participate in ceremonies conducted at the temples.

This pattern of autocratic leadership did not extend to all the tribes of the Southeast. The Creek Nation, in the Carolinas, Georgia, and Alabama, was, for instance, an alliance of several unrelated groups who operated under an advisory council of chiefs and spoke a number of different languages, although the language used within the alliance was that of the principal tribe, the Muskogee. Membership in the alliance was fluid, since each tribe retained its autonomy and was free to act on its own; and the name 'Creek' is simply an abbreviation of the reference by the English to the 'Indians who live along the creeks'.

The Creeks separated out war and peace activities in an ingenious manner, by organizing their villages into White or 'Peace' towns with responsibility for administrative and civil affairs, and Red or 'War' towns which controled the ceremonials of war and from which their battle chiefs were chosen by a council of Beloved Men: elders with proven war records and who had gained the trust and respect of the people. Their Cherokee neighbors to the north used a similar system whereby each village had a white council that governed all village activity during times of peace, but which handed control to a red council if war was declared.

Any official function in these tribes, even that of the principal or peace chief, was determined by individual military ability, and a man rose in status through election to positions of increasing responsibility. Fierce competition existed among the Cherokee warriors for battle honors that would lead to election as a war messenger, ceremonial officer or scout. From here he could rise to become the War Speaker of the town, who announced declarations of war and tactics decided by the Seven War Counsellors, and who were themselves subservient to the Great Red War Chief and his second-in-command. There was even a group of Beloved War Women, with status above that of the Speaker, who judged the fate of captives. With the exception of the Beloved War Women, the Creek system paralleled these positions.

Highly organized, but intermittent, warfare broke out between the Creek and Cherokee, generally involving the members of one or a few villages rather than resulting in the entire alliance taking up arms. Yet these alliances might be

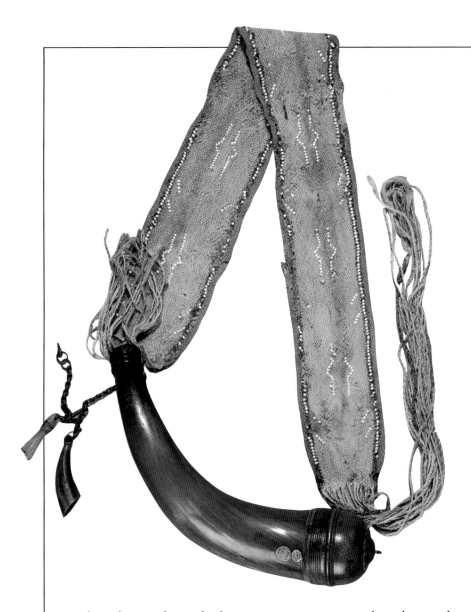

Left: *With the introduction of firearms, traditional skills were employed in the manufacture of new articles. The powder horn and measuring cap shown here are similar to that worn by Sa Ga Yeath Qua Pieth Tow (preceding page). The horn itself is of European manufacture, but the carrying strap is a traditionally woven yarn sash into which trade beads have been added to create a lighter pattern. Tribes in the close proximity of trade centers were able to acquire firearms and supplies of powder and shot more readily than those at a greater distance, and many of the power shifts that occurred between tribes in the region after the advent of Europeans stemmed directly from access to these sources.*

forced to work as a body on occasion, since south and east of them were the Choctaw and Chickasaw, powerful nations of allied tribes who aggressively defended their territories by sending out frequent war parties that could contain several hundred warriors.

If war seemed imminent, the War Speakers of the Creek and Cherokee encouraged the young men by lengthy speeches in which they outlined their grievances and spoke of the wrongs their enemies had enacted against the alliance; in such speeches the glory to be gained from brave acts in battle was emphasized. To show their willingness to go to war, warriors struck a post set up in the central plaza of the village to indicate they would similarly strike their foes. When organizing large war parties 'in town after town the red-painted posts were set up and hung with red feathers, red arrows, and red tomahawks, and after furious vomiting [as a spiritual and physical purgative], warriors danced and struck the post with their red-painted war clubs, with all their might, to signify their enlistment'.[8]

At times such as this, the battle chiefs of the various towns and villages vied with each other to bring other groups into the conflict under their leadership. The politics of the alliances favored those who attracted the most followers, and

Above: *The wooden ball-headed war club was widely distributed throughout the Woodlands area and among other tribes on the periphery of the region. It dealt a crushing blow and was a formidable weapon in hand-to-hand fighting, often being carried in addition to firearms for use in close quarters or for surprise attacks when silence was necessary. The nineteenth-century example shown here is from the Ojibwa of the Great Lakes area and has a characteristic small mammal, probably an otter, carved at the back of the club's head.*

Left: *Finger-woven yarn bags and pouches were used to carry all the vital subsidiary equipment an Indian needed to go to war. These included a small repair kit in case his clothing or weapons were damaged, a limited supply of dried provisions if caution was required and the trip was of any duration, his pipe and tobacco, personal war charms and paints, and, if armed, with a European trade gun, a supply of shot. Such bags remained in vogue even after extensive Indian–European trade contacts had been established.*

preparations for war invariably included the sending of emissaries to outlying settlements, particularly to those where the population was small and who had no highly respected battle chiefs of their own. At the same time the chiefs, often with the Elders of the village, met regularly in secret council to determine tactics and to interpret omens that came to them in dreams. For war to be successful it not only had to be carefully planned but spiritually supported, and in this the dreams gave indications of the intentions of the spirits.

Spirit power imparted confidence, since it was felt that if the power was strong enough it enabled warriors to defeat larger forces of their opponents. That greater power often resided with the Creek is indicated by their defeat of numerically superior war parties of the Chickasaw, Choctaw and Cherokee. If it failed, however, the function of the war pole might be inverted by their enemies as a sign of their own superiority and to indicate that the war pole held no fear for them. Thus, when the Luna Expedition of 1560 entered the Creek town of Coosa they found 'the town deserted, but in its plaza was a pole full of hair locks of the Coosans. It was the custom of the Indians to flay the head of the enemy dead, and to hang the resulting skin and locks insultingly on that pole.'[9]

Such an insult was a symbol of the defeat of the village's defenders but it also struck home psychologically, partly because it was felt the soul of an individual resided in the hair and through the implication that the spirits had withdrawn their protection and thereby permitted the town to be overrun. Warriors lost the confidence they needed for dangerous undertakings if they felt abandoned by this protective force, particularly since their opponents had already demonstrated how effective their power was in assisting them to gain victory.

Spirit protection was not, however, to prove sufficient to keep away a tide of unrest affecting the Creek and Cherokee in the late 1700s and early 1800s. Under pressure from white settlers to remove from their lands, factions developed within both nations. Pro-American groups, who were often

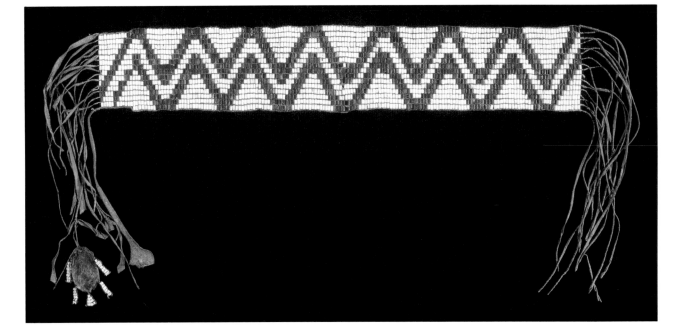

married into white familes, realized resistance was futile and that the future of the tribes would be better served by accepting compensation and moving to 'Indian Territory', a vast tract of country west of the Mississippi River that was reserved exclusively for the Indians 'until the rivers run dry'. Other groups were bitterly opposed to any policy that would diminish their power or take away traditional lands.

Similar divisions were also destined to occur in the central and northern Woodlands among tribes speaking various dialects of the Algonkian and Iroquoian languages. Political organization of these tribes varied to some extent from that of the Southeast. The Algonkians formed loose alliances with fewer formal controls than those of the Creek and Cherokee, since they were casual groupings of numerous small tribes each of which elected spokesmen to represent its interests. The more highly organized Iroquois-speaking groups were ultimately to form large confederacies in which authority was vested in ruling councils.

Warfare in these areas, if we are to believe the Jesuit Relations, was an unceasing activity carried out with a passionate vigor and considerable brutality, with the Iroquois inevitably named as the major cause of conflict. Adjectives such as 'horrific', 'barbarous', and 'devilish' are sprinkled liberally on the pages of these reports, and even though the priests undoubtedly exaggerated their tales of atrocity in attempts to have the Indians branded as 'heathen', the cruelty employed by the Iroquois in torturing their captives is notorious. The same impression of continual and highly aggressive warfare comes across in descriptions of Iroquois

Above: *Although many tribes of the Woodlands used small white and purple shells, known as wampum, in making sashes such as that shown above, it is from the Iroquois that they are best known. Wampum often served a specific function as a record of an agreement or treaty between rival groups or factions, and in this sense had a purpose which was as rigidly defined as any written treaty made between Indian tribes and the Colonial powers or the later Americans.*

villages as 'forts' or 'castles', surrounded by ditches and high defensive palisades.

Iroquois aggression did, however, enable them to establish themselves in the Woodlands. They had been pushed out of their original homelands and forced to the north and east by the centralized groups of the Southeast, and came into direct confrontation with the Siouan and Algonkian-speaking inhabitants of the country they entered. The Iroquois had no power base in these strange lands, and their survival depended on them striking harder and faster than the tribes they met. In this they were singularly effective. Some Siouan groups left the area entirely and others were pushed to its periphery, while many of the Algonkians were forced onto the coastal reaches. The Iroquois finally formed a stronghold in New York State – where they retained such distinctive southern traits as the Alligator and Turkey Dances – although there remained an Iroquois presence throughout Ohio, Pennsylvania, Maryland and Virginia.

Part of the reason for the successful incursion of the Iroquois tribes is that each had a strong central political organization which provided a means for co-ordinated action, whereas the more loosely structured Siouan and Algonkian peoples could not form a strong united front which would hold together long enough to resist these pressures. The Algonkians who had been pushed on to the coasts did fight back, but many tribes faced with well-organized and highly motivated Iroquois war parties defended themselves by the simple expedient of moving out of their way.

That the Iroquois were a warlike people is evident, yet the cohesion of their tribes which resulted in them being able to make their presence felt so forcefully rested in the hands of women and not in those of the war leaders. Descent was reckoned through the female line, with each communal 'long house' having a respected matriarch, known as the Clan Mother, who together with the Clan Mothers of the other households in the community constituted a governing body. Nothing took place without the permission and approval of these impressive women, whose rule was a firm one and to whom the war leaders and the warriors were answerable for

Above: A note attached to this artifact describes it as a 'prisoner's rope'. Although it would hav been admirably suited for the purpose of tying a prisoner, utilitarian ropes of this type actually served a number of different purposes. This particularly fine and very early example is made from braided vegetable fibers and is decorated with porcupine quillwork and tin cone dangles filled with dyed hair.

their conduct.

The control effected by these women helped prevent young men organizing war expeditions of their own without the active support of the entire tribe, but it also led to political autonomy which effectively prevented the Iroquois forming inter-tribal networks that were mutually supportive. This meant the different tribes in their move north came into competition with each other, as well as facing Siouan and Algonkian resistance to displacement. This ultimately lead to an internecine warfare which so weakened them that Iroquois power in the area came under threat. Faced with retaliation from the many enemies they had made and undermined by the bitter struggles among themselves, the Iroquois were forced to confederate.

They were reluctant to do so even though their strength was waning rapidly, as is evident in the story of the creation of the League of Five Nations. Inspired by the Medusa-headed Atotarho, a deity of immense power and influence in Iroquois thought, an idealistic reformer named Hiawatha (immortalized in Longfellow's poem, where he mistakenly attributes this tale to the Chippewa of the Great Lakes), traveled from tribe to tribe in the early 1500s, pleading for them to cease hostilities and to confederate for their mutual interest.

In spite of having supernatural sanction, and the support of the famed law giver Daganawe da and of a wise and highly respected woman chief known as Jogan sasay, Hiawatha met resistance everywhere he went. The strength of feeling against him ran so high that his own tribe banished him and he was forced to live elsewhere, but he eventually persuaded five tribes, the Seneca, Cayuga, Onondaga, Oneida and Mohawk, to join together as the League of Five Nations. This treaty was recorded on a wampum belt of white and purple beads, which was considered a binding contract, and placed in the hands of the Onondaga, the Keepers of the Central Fire.

Hiawatha's vision was of a peaceful union which would resort to force only in self-defence. Under the terms of an unwritten constitution, the Clan Mothers of the individual

Above: *Pipe tomahawks were a trade item in which a combined metal axe head and pipe bowl, usually manufactured in Europe, was fastened to a wooden stem through which a hole had been bored to facilitate smoking. In this they show a curious blend of war–peace symbolism, since sharing a pipe conveyed feelings of trust and bound the smokers in friendship whereas the tomahawk itself is clearly an aggressive hand-to-hand weapon. The contradiction may be explained by the fact that these were obtained in trade. By smoking with the trader a pact of friendship could be made through which a weapon might be obtained that was intended for use against other adversaries.*

households selected spokesmen who met in council, after canvassing opinion from their own tribe, to discuss and vote on any issue affecting the League. Each tribe cast a single vote, and for war to be declared the vote had to be unanimous. In this way the individual opinion and interests of every member of the League could be considered, a system that so impressed European settlers that the constitution of the Five Nations was later written into the State Laws of Connecticut and Pennsylvania, and eventually enshrined in the Constitution of the United States.

The dream of peace Hiawatha had sought so hard to achieve was destined to fail when the council voted to consolidate the League's position by subjugating their weaker neighbors rather than waiting for signs of hostility before taking defensive action. It was the old Iroquois policy of strike first and strike hardest, made more effective by combining the forces of what had previously been five separate tribes. Under the threat of large war parties and hopelessly outnumbered, many smaller tribes offered no resistance. These were adopted into the League where they became fully

Right: *There was an almost universal belief among North American Indians that the soul of a person resided in the hair, and many tribes felt that if the hair, or scalp, of someone who was recently deceased could be obtained this would also secure the soul. With few exceptions the scalp was thought of as a ritual object rather than a war trophy, was treated with respect and dignity, and was felt to be an object of both significance and power. The scalp shown here, which was probably taken by the Huron, has had the skin side painted red and is stretched on a wooden hoop decorated with porcupine quills and split roots.*

fledged members, thereby increasing Five Nations dominance in the region.

It is clear that the Five Nations preferred a policy of adoption, and it is estimated that the Onondaga contained twenty immigrant tribes with a population three times greater than that of the Onondaga themselves; but not all their neighbors were content to relinquish self-rule nor to acquiesce readily. The Huron, Neutra, and Susquehanna formed confederacies of their own strong enough to challenge the League's claims to supremacy, and the entire Valley of the Mohawk was turned into what has been described as 'one bloody battlefield'. Warfare, though not constant, was frequent, resulting in heavy casualties and confrontations between large forces. Records made at the time indicate the extent of this, with reports of the Huron capturing and burning 113 members of the League in 1639, and of a later fight in which three thousand Neutrals were attacked and beaten by a force of eighteen hundred Five Nations warriors.

Typical of the wars that raged among the Iroquois groups were ones in which an initial exchange of taunts and insults led to retaliations and reprisals, often escalating to a situation where war parties attempted to lay siege to the towns of their opponents. Temporary 'forts' were erected in the vicinity by the war party, and small groups of warriors went out from these to disrupt town life by continually harassing the occupants and stopping them from working their fields or gaining access to water. The town itself was relatively secure, since its fortifications prevented it from being stormed. Stout tree posts driven upright into the ground completely encircled it, leaving an easily defended narrow passageway as an entrance that would permit only two or three people access at a time. But they had a disadvantage in that the entrance passage created a prison for its occupants, since a few men could easily prevent warriors in any large number from leaving the town to counter-attack. This made the siege doubly effective. Not only was access to water denied, but the town's inhabitants had to be constantly vigilant whereas their opponents needed to keep only a minimum force in the field. Secure in their temporary forts, most of the attacking party could relax in relative comfort, sending out fresh warriors from time to time to replace those attacking the town, and simply wait for their opponents to be worn down through lack of water and sleep. Although many sieges ended because the plight of the defenders became known to other members of their tribe living close enough to send help, the burning of towns and the killing of entire populations is also on record.

During a siege, daring warriors attempted to prove their

Right: Thayendanegea, or Joseph Brant, was a Mohawk war captain who grew to fame as a statesman, orator and implacable fighter for the rights of his people. To achieve these he studied at Dartmouth College, achieving a level of literacy far in advance of most of the European colonists of the period, and traveled to England in 1786 to petition King George on behalf of the Mohawk. In England he refused to bow before the king, considering him his equal, but gallantly kissed the queen's hand. At home he mingled with generals and diplomats, preferring fine china and Irish linen to the rudimentary provisions of a Mohawk lodge; but he also earned his reputation for being fearless and capable of throwing a tomahawk with unerring accuracy. Always pro-British, Brant's decision to side with the Lords of the Valley rather than support the Dutch peasant farmers or the French, against the wishes of other Iroquois factions, was one of the factors that led to the dissolution of the Iroquois League of Nations and broke their power in the region. His last words, whispered on his deathbed, were 'Have pity on the poor Indians'. The portrait shown here is of Joseph Brant as a young man.

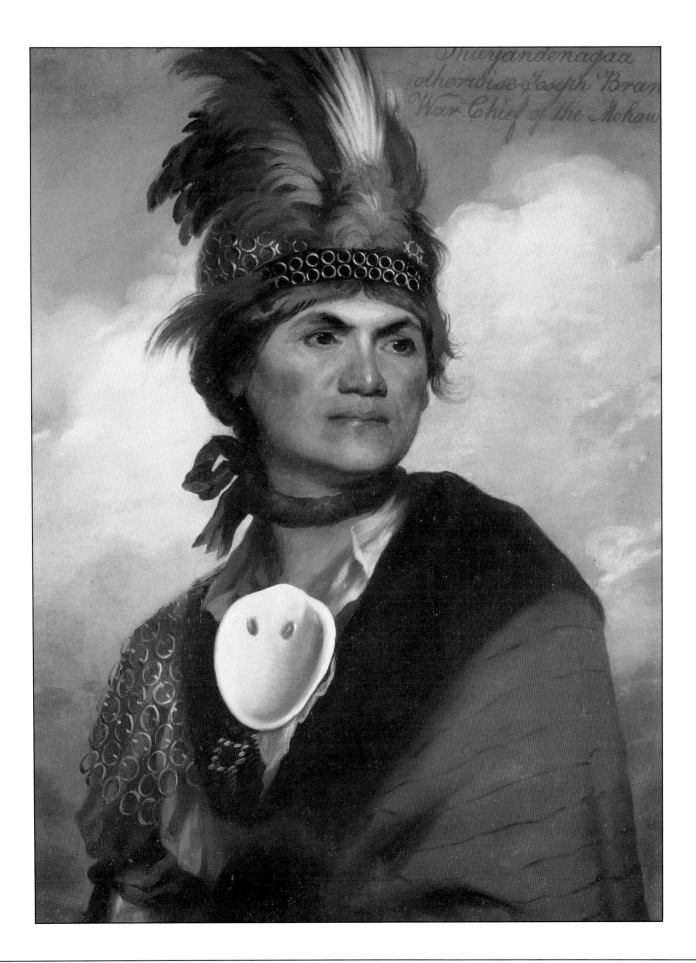

bravery by slipping out from the fortifications to catch an opponent unawares or to capture a prisoner who would be brought back for torture. Much has been written about this, and many wild speculations made as to its reason. Throughout these comments the impression is that the Huron were particularly adept at prolonging the agony of the victim, often over several days, while he sang derisive songs at his tormentors, inviting them to amuse themselves while killing him. The 'prisoner was expected to display the primary virtues of a warrior: courage and the ability to suffer without complaining'.[10]

It has been suggested that the captive became a 'hate object' on which vengeance could be exacted; however, the completely unemotional manner in which torture was carried out, since it was done in an orderly fashion with no display of anger or hatred, and that all members of the tribe were under taboo restrictions during this period, suggests a ritual function. There was none of the 'frenzied excess' some of the more sensational reports imply, and if several enemy warriors were captured only one or two would be selected for torture while the others were adopted.

The conclusion we must draw is that this was neither occasion for blood revenge nor a sadistic game, but was of a ceremonial order relating to the destruction of an enemy's spiritual, rather than physical, power. The prisoner had already been physically defeated through capture, when he could easily have been killed, and torture can only have been a test of spiritual strength, demonstrated by a refusal to break under pressure and an ability to 'stand above' the torments of his captors. Because spirit protection guarded the war party and not only the individual, the breaking of one man's power would symbolically strike at the group as well. This is supported by the fact that 'if the Huron could not make a prisoner weep and plead for mercy, this was believed to indicate misfortune for them in future wars'.[11]

Misfortune was, however, to strike from an unexpected direction. The French and Indian War brought massive European armies into the Ohio Valley and surrounding districts between 1754 and 1763, all of them keen to enlist the aid of the Iroquois League and to use them as a buffer between the war zones of the region. Many of the Iroquois became pro-British, for the simple reason that their Algonkian adversaries sided with the French. There was thus a continuation of the old tribal rivalries expressed through battles initiated by European struggles for supremacy.

But a legacy of European warfare and intrigue was to lead to bitter internal disputes and fights between the members of

Below: Joseph Brant's most ardent supporter was the Duke of Northumberland, whom he had fought alongside during the wars for the American colonies. The Duke introduced him to the House of Lords on his visit to petition King George, when Brant made an impassioned speech that was all but ignored. The Duke, in an attempt to confirm his friendship, had a pipe tomahawk made from the finest Sheffield steel with an English oak shaft bearing the plaque, dated 1805, shown here. The pipe is, however, unsmoked and it is uncertain whether the Duke had a chance to present his gift before Joseph died on 24 November 1807, in an estate house granted him by the British government on the shores of Lake Ontario.

the League during the American Revolution and the War of 1812. At an acrimonious meeting, one of the fundamental principles that had kept the League strong – that a unanimous vote was required for them to declare war – finally broke down under pressures and tensions being placed on the different tribes by the British and the Colonists. The Mohawk insisted on maintaining loyalty to the British, the Oneida claimed the Americans were stronger, and other groups decided to remain neutral.

Thayendanegea, or Joseph Brant, the famous Mohawk chief who had supported the English in the French and Indian War, was leader of the pro-British faction. Commissioned as a colonel in the British army, he led numerous campaigns throughout the Valley of the Mohawk for eight consecutive years. It is said that 'burned-out farms, pastures, and the scalped dead were grim testimony to the successful guerilla war Brant had brought to the New York frontier'[12] and that during this period of fierce fighting the dreaded cry of 'Brant's in the Valley' was heard over and over again.

One of the reasons for his successes was that he was a brilliant military strategist, but he was also well-educated, having been sent in his early youth to Moor's Indian Charity

Below: *This Ojibwa chief's headdress of red-dyed feathers, with a headband of porcupine quills, is typical of the honorific emblems worn by Indians of the Woodlands and through which the status and war honors of their chiefs and prominent warriors were made public. Such headdresses were also made by the Iroquois, and the portrait on page 31 of Joseph Brant, a leading war chief of the Mohawk, shows him wearing one of very similar type. The example shown here, which dates from 1780, corresponds closely to Joseph Brant's active years as a warrior when outward manifestations of war prowess were considered important.*

Left: *This pipe tomahawk has an iron blade with an inlaid piece of silver in the shape of a bowie knife which is fastened to a beechwood handle. It is of a type referred to as 'English' and was collected in Greenbriar County, West Virginia, about 1873.*

Below: *Cornplanter, also known as HandsomeLake, was the war captain of the Seneca whose forces fought beside Joseph Brant during the Revolutionary Wars. In later years he became a spiritual leader who advocated a return to the traditional ways and initiated the Handsome Lake Reforms or Longhouse Religion which brought him into bitter dispute with the Seneca chief, Red Jacket.*

School in Lebanon, Connecticut (later Dartmouth College), by Sir William Johnson, who had married Brant's sister. Unlike many of the European and American farmers and soldiers in the region, Joseph Brant was literate and erudite, more at ease in the company of dukes and generals than of others, and thinking of himself not only as a military officer but as an ambassador for his people. In later life, under the patronage of the Duke of Northumberland, he was to travel to England to plead the Mohawk cause before the British Parliament in the House of Commons.

These wars pitted members of the League against one another as allies of the contesting sides, but also created divisions within the different tribes. Although President George Washington was anxious to secure the support of Joseph Brant, Brant refused to attend a council in Philadelphia in 1792 with what he perceived as lesser chiefs, arriving the day after the other chiefs had left. At this council, Red Jacket, the great Seneca orator, acted as the spokesman for fifty Iroquois chiefs when Washington persuaded him to act as a reluctant mediator between the United States and the warring tribes, a move that was to be bitterly opposed by Cornplanter (Handsome Lake), the Seneca war leader, who in 1799 began urging the Seneca to stop all contacts with the Europeans and Americans and return to the old ceremonies.

Even though the history of the Iroquois has been one of fighting and division among themselves, in their early move to the north they had driven a wedge between the original Woodlands inhabitants, pushing Siouan-speaking tribes out or rendering them relatively ineffective in the tribal politics of the area and forcing the Algonkian-speaking groups further east; a displacement that is suggested by the fact that the culture of the most easterly Algonkians was a forest rather than coastal one and they made little use of the abundant maritime resources. The Algonkians lacked confederacies, but in spite of Iroquois strength were never defeated or subjugated. In fact, it is likely the presence of Algonkian tribes prevented further Iroquois expansion, since they held the entire eastern seaboard from the Carolinas to the far north, with relatives outside the Woodlands region both to the north and east of Iroquois-held lands.

While less aggressive than the Iroquois, the Algonkians were far from submissive. They consisted of perhaps one hundred or more small tribes acting independently of each other and with little political cohesion; but when threatened they formed temporary alliances in which groups that might

Below: Tenskwatawa, The Prophet, younger brother of the Shawnee war leader, Tecumseh, traveled from tribe to tribe after 1805 in support of Tecumseh's plan to unify the tribes as a confederacy against the incursions of the white man, a plan that failed when General (later President) Harrison destroyed the Prophet's village and precipitated a war before the confederacy was formed.

Right: This early nineteenth-century Shawnee bag is made from red-dyed leather, and is decorated with porcupine quills and tin cone dangles filled with dyed deer hair. The strap of coarse red wool has been trimmed with black silk. Such bags, as among the Iroquois, were an essential part of every warrior's equipment and remained in use after many other traditional details of dress had been superseded by trade items.

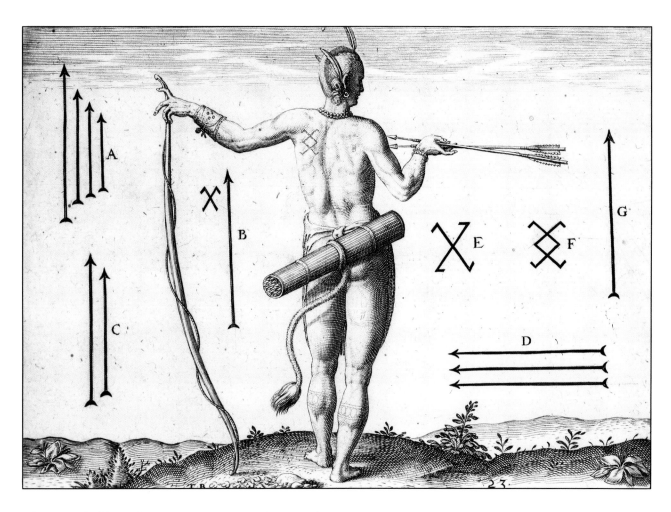

otherwise hold grudges against one another acted in concert for their mutual defence. These alliances had no permanent members, and the ties that held them together were those of social obligation established at annual summer gatherings through the exchange of gifts, feasting, 'friendship dances', and through inter-marriages. So important were these that the Algonkian word for their summer councils, 'pow wows', has passed into modern usage for any large gathering of American Indians at which dances, feasting and displays of friendship are a prominent feature.

Many of these alliances were held together by the presence of charismatic leaders who gained respect, rather than demanded it, from those who chose to follow them. Chief Powhatan is typical of the tribal leaders who could depend on the strength of their own personalities to rally support, and at the height of his power he was able to rely on the alliegance of approximately two hundred villages from thirty different tribes; but the so-called 'Powhatan Confederacy' only ever consisted of tribes who were free to come and go as they pleased, and there was no centralized authority such as that of the Iroquois.

Above: *John White noted that the Algonkian Indians of Virginia in the 1500s bore tattooed marks indicating the village to which they owed alliegance. In this De Bry engraving, made after White's original watercolor, the letter A depicts the mark of Wingino, chief of Roanoke; B is that of Wingino's sister's husband; C and D indicated prominent men from Secotan; and E, F and G were used by war chiefs from Pomeioc and Aquascogoc.*

Right: *Even though Algonkian warriors traveled on foot along forest pathways and might wear out as many as twenty pairs of moccasins in a single year, each pair was carefully and elaborately decorated. Those shown here, which are possibly Delaware, are embellished with dyed porcupine quillwork.*

Above: Many of the Woodlands villages consisted of bark longhouses located inside a protective palisaded wall, with cleared plots of land beyond the village perimeter where crops were grown. This engraving shows 'The Indian Fort of Sasquesahanok', one of the Delaware villages, and is typical of the Indian settlements of the area.

With the encouragement of such strong individuals, the alliances could enlist warriors from several villages over a large area when faced with crisis. Runners went from village to village asking for support, where they would meet in council with the chiefs and war leaders who would deliberate on whether to send warriors. The village leaders had to decide if it was in their own interests to become involved in a war that might not immediately affect their territories; but at the back of each man's mind was the certain knowledge that if his village failed to respond positively to a request for help from a powerful chief, then that chief might very well refuse his assistance to them when they needed it in the future.

The pattern of Algonkian warfare is very apparent in the relationship between Powhatan's village and the Jamestown settlement of European Colonists in Virginia. When they arrived in 1607 they found the Indians amiable and friendly, even to the extent of supplying them with food and, in the absence of a physician in the Colony, by

treating their sick. In fact, it is certain the Colonists would not have survived their first winter without chief Powhatan's support.

During this period of dependency the Europeans treated Powhatan as an equal and as an honored guest, a courtesy he responded to with equal vigor, so that they in turn became regular and welcome visitors at the pow wows, where they were feasted and given valuable gifts. To all intents and purposes Powhatan treated them as he would any respected ally. But when they were settled and able to manage on their own resources, the Colonists started ploughing Indian hunting lands. Powhatan ordered them to stop and they ignored him, clearly under the impression they were dealing with the pompous leader of a local village.

Powhatan's response was immediately to send runners to the other villages, and before the Europeans fully understood the gravity of the situation Jamestown was besieged, and would certainly have been completely destroyed had its defenders not been remarkably fortunate in capturing Powhatan's daughter, Matowaka (who has come down to us in legend and tale as the Indian 'princess', Pocahontas, and

Above left: *This view of a Woodlands village clearly depicts the upright posts set deep in the ground as a palisade for the town. The entrance to the village is shown at the bottom left, where the rows of posts overlap to form a narrow passage that prevented an enemy from entering in force.*

Above and right: *Paul Kane painted Kitchie-ogi-maw, a Menominee chief (right), in 1845 at an annual distribution of treaty money. Of interest here is the characteristic manner of wearing the knife sheath around the neck in a quilled sheath similar to that shown above. Although the sheath is traditional, the knife carried by Kitchie-ogi-maw is probably of English manufacture, as is the pipe tomahawk he is holding. Metal items of this type were important trade goods of the Hudson's Bay Company.*

who was later to marry the Colonist John Rolfe). Powhatan called off his forces but the Colonists' status as allies had been broken, and intermittent raiding, together with some wholescale uprisings in which several hundred Europeans were killed, was to mark the Indian–White relationship for the next forty years.

This episode is instructive in that it makes clear the ability of the alliances to respond quickly without a centralized authority, and the fact that warriors from several tribes would work co-operatively under the instruction of war leaders from a different village. It is also apparent that the disrespect shown by the Colonists and their affront to Powhatan's pride, dignity and authority was felt to be an insult of such magnitude that, even though he later stopped fighting them out of respect for the family tie established through

Above: *Intended purely as a weapon and without the ritual function of the pipe tomahawk, the tomahawk shown here has a hatchet blade opposed by a spike. It is of a type that was popular as a trade item in the northeastern regions of the Woodlands among tribes such as the Ojibwa.*

Left: *Thunderbirds, or Thunderers, were deities of great importance to the tribes living in the region of the Great Lakes, and were often depicted on pouches such as that shown here. Although Thunderbirds were considered to be associated with fertility, and in particular with storm clouds and rain, they were believed to be in a constant state of war with the deities of the Lower World such as the Underwater Panther. In these continual battles the weapon they deployed was Lightning, which flashed from its eyes to strike its foes. Although warriors did not derive power directly from this supernatural being, its strength and assistance was invoked through ritual and in dance.*

Pocahontas' marriage, he harbored a burning hatred for the white people until the end of his life. Although this example is from the Powhatan, other Algonkian alliances, such as those of the Abnaki and Pequot, showed an equal ability to rally support and retaliate in force under an organized leadership if they felt a wrong had been done to them.

Among themselves, most Algonkian tribes did not wage large scale warfare but fought only in self-defence or as a response to slights or injuries. Disputes between alliances did occasionally occur, and these could be 'of critical importance and cataclysmic dimension for all parties concerned [but] a meeting between strangers was more likely to be peaceful, even open and hospitable, than warlike'.[13] Most aggression appears to have stemmed from family and village rivalries, with vengeance and revenge being the prime cause. This could readily lead to retaliatory feuding which could last for years as a series of frequent, but generally small-scale, conflicts.

Algonkian alliances could be volatile, and much of this was because of the power held by individual families and the prestige associated with positions of influence. Other families might readily be drawn into these arguments, since it was not difficult to interpet an insult to an important individual as carrying an implicit denigration of that person's village; and if the village was one of some standing in the tribe, then that negative feeling could carry over as a suggestion that the whole tribe was unworthy. Among such proud people as the Algonkians it took little provocation of this kind before angry verbal exchanges led to bloodshed.

One of the greatest insults was to burn down a family's house while they were away in retaliation for a slight that had been received at a 'friendship dance'. This would set in motion a string of reprisals that might lead to retaliatory killings, when small war parties, sometimes of only two or three warriors, would secretly enter a village and lie in wait to make a surprise attack. The structure of Algonkian villages, where garden plots of corn, beans and squash were planted beside widely scattered individual houses made from pole frameworks covered with rushes, enabled the warriors to

Left: *George Catlin painted the Ojibwa warrior, The Ottaway, in 1835, commenting merely that it was 'a portrait of a warrior with his pipe in his hand'. The painting, however, clearly shows The Ottaway's use of facepaint and war exploit feathers by which his status as a prominent warrior was made evident and publicly asserted.*

make their escape before reinforcements had time to arrive from the other houses. This structure favored the small war party, since a large body of warriors would be detected long before they caused any real damage and the occupants could scatter, either to regroup and defend the village or to take their own revenge at a later date.

Feuds might also be initiated, not through rivalry, but by the activities of young warriors eager to gain war honors and to prove their courage. Without honors a man had little status, and it was an important social aspect of the pow wows that individuals were able to exhibit their power through dances that mimicked their acts of bravery on a war expedition. Other dances invoking the power of the Thunderers and other deities with war-like characteristics were regular events, although this should be understood from the

Above: *This collection of Chippewa (Ojibwa groups living in the United States) feathers demonstrates markings by which the war honors of an individual were made public. Different cut marks indicated specific war honors, since they represented, for instance, that the warrior had killed an enemy, rescued a fallen comrade, charged the enemy alone, and so forth. In this manner, and in the way in which the feather was worn in the hair, a complete record of any warrior's achievements was immediately evident. The actual meanings of the cut feathers in this photograph have not, unfortunately, been recorded.*

Right: Calumet pipes with fan-shaped feather pendants were important war–peace symbols. Bonds of friendship were established by mutual smoking and they featured prominently in rituals intended to promote harmonious inter-tribal relationships. It is significant, however, that the decorative elements on the pipes usually refer to birds or animals that are more generally associated with war. In this manner the pipe was imbued with the strength and courage of the warrior to defend the community by warding off danger of attack.

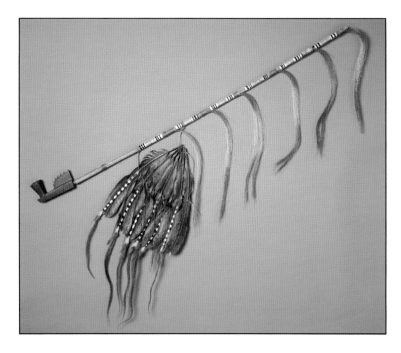

Below: This small but exquisite skin pouch, decorated with horizontal bands of quillwork and quill-wrapped fringes, is a type that was used in the northern Woodlands specifically for carrying shot after the introduction of firearms in European trade.

Algonkian viewpoint that such powers could be used for either offensive or defensive purposes and were relevant in contexts of war and peace.

One major alliance was that of the Ojibwa, Ottawa and Potawatomi, in the region of the Great Lakes. Known as the Three Fires Confederacy, their social organization was similar to that of other Algonkians of the east but they were too far north for agriculture, depending to a greater extent on hunting and on gathering wild rice, and carried aggressive raiding beyond their territories, at times to the tribes of the upper Mississippi and on to the Plains. In the mid-1600s they began a war with the Siouan tribes of the area which was to last for 100 years; eventually the Sioux were forced to the west and on to the grasslands of the Plains.

Of particular importance in the war–peace rituals of these northern Algonkians was the Calumet Dance, named after the French word for the long pipestems decorated with feathers, bird skins and with whole bird wing pendants, that were used to establish 'blood' ties between villages through creating a kin relationship of unrelated individuals. Once made, these ties could never be broken, and the people were pledged by a bond that united them in life and death. At the close of the ceremony, the sacred pipestems were held forward to symbolize the peaceful unification of opposites in creating a blood relationship where none had existed, but also to emphasize the immense power of the pipes in warding off enemy attack.

44

ALONG THE
MISSISSIPPI–MISSOURI

CHAPTER TWO

Above: *This Mississippian stone effigy pipe, found at Spiro Mound in LeFlore County, Oklahoma, depicts a warrior beheading a captive. The practice of decapitation among the tribes of the Woodlands and the Southeast may have been introduced along the Mississippi–Missouri by groups migrating from these areas.*

Left: *George Catlin painted Haw-che-ke-sug-ga (He-who-kills-the-Osages) in 1832 at Fort Leavenworth. This former war chief of the Missouri was then a highly respected Elder, whose outstanding prowess as a warrior in his youth was indicated by his necklace of grizzly bear claws. Note too the turban-like headdress of the Missouri, surmounted by exploit feathers.*

WOODLANDS INFLUENCE and the use of the pipe in sealing bonds of trust and friendship spread far beyond the eastern areas, following old trade routes that had been established by the ancient Adena-Hopewell people. Their large villages surrounded by complex earth embankments were centered in the Ohio Valley, but they had many smaller outlying communities and at the height of their power, in about AD 400, had established a trade in such items as obsidian from the foothills of the Rocky Mountains, silver from Ontario, shark teeth and shells from the Gulf Coast, copper from northern Michigan, and grizzly bear claws from Wyoming.

This continent-wide trade was not the result of an expansionist policy, but derived from itinerant traders following regularly used trade routes in order to exchange items of Adena-Hopewell manufacture for raw materials that were unavailable in their own country. Yet in spite of the individual level at which trading was carried out, Adena-Hopewell influence was widespread and allowed for the rapid dissemination of smoking rituals. These were a fundamental aspect of their trade, since by sharing a pipe the smokers became subject to a mutually binding oath to refrain from violence, thus enabling the pipe-bearer to travel unmolested even among tribes that may otherwise have been hostile.

The importance of smoking rituals to the Adena-Hopewell is evident from the abundance of stone pipes found at their village sites. Many of them are exquisite depictions of birds of prey or animal figures, carved with an unerring understanding of animal characteristics and behavior and with a vibrancy that denies the fact they are made of stone. These are almost certainly conceived as messengers of the various deities through whom the spiritual forces manifested themselves in the human realm. Although this great trade network declined after AD 800, the use of the pipe that had been introduced to other tribes continued as the focus of war–peace ceremonial and in making supplication to the spiritual forces for assistance in both war and peace activity.

Hopewell communities established village settlements along the Mississippi River, extending from the Minnesota–Wisconsin border to the mouth of the river on the Gulf Coast. During the later part of this period, after AD

700, the bird of prey was given additional significance by people living in the more northerly villages, where burial mounds were elaborated into massive bird effigies, one of which, near present-day Madison in Wisconsin, has a wingspan of over 600 feet. As well as bringing religious ideals from the Woodlands of the east, early Plains–Hopewell populations introduced maize growing to the region and began to depend to some extent on big game hunting, since buffalo skulls are frequently found during excavations of the burial mounds; it is thus among these tribes that we see the beginnings of a mixed farming–buffalo hunting economy that was to be characteristic of the lifestyles of the historic semi-nomadic tribes of the area.

While there is no evidence to suggest hostility between the various Hopewell groups, more aggressive traits did enter the region after AD 900 with a new wave of influences from the Mississippians of the Woodlands and Southeast that radically altered the Hopewell pattern. Palisaded towns suggest that war was frequent, and also indicate large centers of population. One of their towns, Cahokia, on the site of modern St Louis, is the largest archeological site north of Mexico, containing over 100 mounds and encompassing an area of five square miles. It is estimated that Cahokia may have had a population of as many as 10,000 people, among whom ritual sacrifice appears to have been important. The tomb of one wealthy individual contained six sacrificed male retainers, and close by and associated with it was another mass grave containing the bodies of fifty-three women.

Even the sacred bird symbol acquired new meaning as part of the Mississippian Southern Death Cult. In this politico-religious movement, warriors used distinctive regalia including facepaints depicting birds of prey, especially of the peregrine falcon which is reputed to strike swiftly and accurately, as well as woodpecker and spider emblems as distinguishing marks of status, and characteristic roached hair styles or partly shaved heads; all of these are engraved on shell gorgets and other artifacts excavated at sites within the Plains–Mississippi area.

The ideals of the Death Cult spread throughout Kentucky, Tennessee and Arkansas, and parts of neighboring southern states, with Mound Spiro in Oklahoma representing the

Above: The carving on the heads of this shell gorget from Mound Spiro is unusual, but the arrangement of four divisions with a central motif is similar to the gorget shown below; each head is marked with the typical forked-eye motif on the earspool at right.

Above: This shell disc gorget contains a summary of Mississippian belief. Divided into four parts, it represents the four world quarters, which encircle a central disc for the sun marked with a cross which symbolizes the sacred fire kept burning continuously in their temples. Each of the four world quarters is guarded by a crested woodpecker, the Mississippian symbol of war.

Top and above: *The characteristic fork-eyed face painting of the Mississippians is clearly shown on this clay earspool from Etowah. Earspools were a regular part of a warrior's costume, and can be seen on the carved pipe shown on page 45. A groove backed by a smaller disc is shown in the side view of this example; it held the earspool in place when passed through the slit in the ear.*

western limit of direct expansion, since the river valleys of the Plains would not support the intensive agriculture necessary for the Mississippian townships. In fact, it is very possible that climate changes along the Mississippi made it difficult to continue to maintain towns as large as Cahokia further to the north and forced a population dispersal to occur here at the same time as the Death Cult expanded in the south.

Speakers of Caddoan and Siouan languages were members of the Death Cult, and since migrations into the Prairies were by both language groups it is likely that modified elements of Death Cult practice were brought across the Mississippi and further to the west after the partial abandonment of the large central and northern towns. Although patterns of movement into and within the area are complex and poorly understood, we can assume that the ancestors of the Caddoan-speaking Pawnee, Wichita and Arikara, and of the Southern Caddo groups, were associated more closely with Mound Spiro and areas west of the Mississippi whereas the origin of the Dhegia and Chiwere dialect Siouans lies to the east.

The villages of these tribes were formerly numerous and scattered along both sides of the Mississippi, but by the early nineteenth century their populations had already been decimated by smallpox epidemics and they had coalesced into compact communities located primarily along the rich alluvial river valleys on the western side of the Mississippi–Missouri and its tributaries. This population decrease is evident from Arikara traditions that state they formerly had forty-two villages spreading over a large area of South Dakota; but when Lewis and Clark visited them on the upper Missouri in 1804–5 they reported only three villages, commenting that several dialects were often spoken in a single household so that members of a 'family' sometimes had difficulty understanding each other. George Catlin, twenty-five years later, noted there was one village for the entire tribe.

In the recent historic period the Mandan, Hidatsa and Arikara villages were located on the upper Missouri in North Dakota, where they served a function as a northern trade center between the various tribes of the area. South of them, on the Missouri and Platte rivers, were the Skidi and South Band Pawnee (Chaui, Kitkehahki and Pitahuarata), the Dhegia-speaking Ponca and Omaha, and the Chiwere dialect Iowa, Missouri and Oto. Other Dhegia-speaking Siouans, the Kansa, Osage, and Quapaw, lived further south in Kansas, Missouri, and Arkansas, with the Wichita on the Red River in northern Texas and Oklahoma. These tribes are sometimes referred to as the semi-nomadic Plains Indians, or Plains villagers.

Closely associated with them, since they shared a number of culture traits as well as made regular raids and forays into territories held by the Plains villagers, are the Algonkian-speaking groups of the upper Mississippi and southern Great Lakes, the Illinois, Kickapoo, Sauk and Fox and Potawatomi, as well as the Winnebago, linguistic relatives of the Iowa, Missouri and Oto, and the Santee, or Eastern, Sioux. In the far south, below the Wichita and again raiding against or being raided by the semi-nomads, were a number of scattered but large and influential Caddoan tribal groups.

With the exception of the most southerly tribes, villages consisted of large communal houses – elm bark lodges in the north, earth lodges among the upper Missouri and central

Right: *Meach-o-shin-gaw (Little White Bear) is depicted in this painting by George Catlin, who refers to him as a 'distinguished brave'. Catlin also comments on 'the hair being cut as close to the head as possible, except a tuft the size of the palm of the hand, on the crown of the head' and refers to the long braid, or scalp-lock, being 'scrupulously preserved … and offered to their enemy if they can get it, as a trophy' (Catlin: **Letters and Notes**, vol. 2, pp.23–4). Little White Bear also wears a roach headdress of red dyed deer hair, which was secured in place by passing the scalp-lock through a hole in the base of a carved bone or antler roach spreader, which was placed inside the roach, where it was held in position with a wooden or bone peg. Both the shaved head and the roach headdress were part of an ancient tradition that linked the semi-nomadic tribes of the Plains to the occupants of the Woodlands and Southeast.*

Above: *This cut and pierced shell gorget depicts two costumed dancers with feathered fans and rattles. Gorgets often contain a wealth of data concerning costume, and of interest here is that both Mississippian dancers appear to be wearing roach type headdresses similar to Little White Bear's.*

groups, and grass lodges in the south – surrounded by extensive garden plots of corn, beans, and squash; although the Great Lakes tribes, living too far north to rely on farming, often depended on wild rice as a staple. Most of them also spent a large part of each year living as nomadic hunters in a seasonal pursuit of migratory herds of buffalo.

The importance of corn and buffalo in the economies of these tribes is evident in the fact that rituals emphasize both, and is explicitly stated in a tradition of the Arikara referring to their origin. In this myth 'Mother-Corn encouraged the animals to help her get the people out of the ground … the

Above: Pottery vessels featured prominently in the rituals of the Southern Death Cult and, as in the example shown here, were often made in the form of an effigy head. The fact this portrayed a dead man was shown by the closed eyes and the line of vertical markings on the mouth to indicate that it had been sewn shut. Markings showing facial tattooing or painting are also apparent here, as are perforations in the ears from which ornaments were suspended.

Above: *The spider shown in the center of this gorget from Mound Spiro was an important Death Cult symbol, as was the hand which is repeated seven times. Although Mound Spiro is generally associated with Caddoan-speaking peoples, that the Siouan groups were also linked with it is suggested by the fact that the spider, the hand symbol and the number seven all had importance among the semi-nomadic Siouan-speaking Osage.*

Right: *The tattoos of Osage men, as in this photograph from about 1880–1900, were stylized symbols of war. According to the Osage tribal historian, Louis F.Burns, the tattooed lines can be interpreted as follows. 'Running vertically from under the chin to the abdomen is the sacred knife. Slanting from the knife point, on each side, and then over the shoulders, is [sic] the sacred pipes. Representations of the thirteen sun's rays are two diagonal designs which also run from the knife point and over the shoulders'* (**Osage Indian Customs and Myths**, *p. 133). Although not apparent in this photograph, it was also customary for Osage men and women to tattoo the emblem of the spider on the back of the hand.*

people now came out from the ground and stood outside. They saw other pathways, where other people had gone out from the ground, by the help of the Buffalo.'[1]

Although their populations had been decimated in the early epidemics, these were a proud and powerful people, and when the Duke of Württemberg visited the Grand (Chaui) Pawnee in the 1820s he described them as living on the edge of a large flat plain over which roamed their herds of hundreds of horses and mules. From the richness of their lives and the abundant animals they possessed, and notwithstanding the permanence of the village, he gained the 'impression

Left: *According to Catlin's notes, when he painted the famous Omaha warrior, Om-pa-ton-ga (Big Elk), he stood for his portrait 'with his tomahawk in his hand, and his face painted black for war'* (**Letters and Notes**, *p.28). Big Elk's importance is indicated by the fact that in two treaty signings, in 1830 and 1836, his name appears first.*

Above right: *Monolithic replicas of actual weapons, made from carefully selected and highly prized stones, were used regularly in the rituals of the Death Cult and were deposited as offerings in the mounds they built. This ceremonial mace from Mound Spiro has been made from a single piece of jasper and shows particularly fine workmanship.*

Right: *Figures such as this appear regularly on Death Cult gorgets, and have generally been referred to as 'flying shamans' due to their leaping pose and the fact they appear in ritual contexts. The shaman shown here carries a ceremonial mace similar to that shown above and a death's head in his right hand; although it has also been interpreted as a warrior dancing with the severed head of his victim.*

Right: *The Wichita, living along the Arkansas River and with access to extensive stands of reeds and grasses, used thatched techniques in their house building that were similar to those employed by Mississippians for the temples they erected on top of their mounds. Unlike the Osage and Omaha mentioned in captions on this and the preceding page, the Wichita were one of a group of Caddoan-speaking peoples who can be linked with the Mississippian culture.*

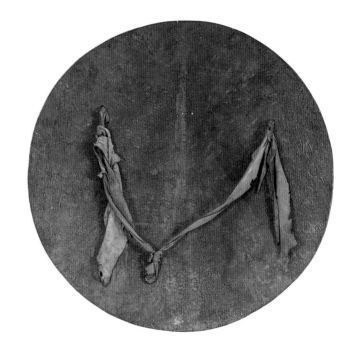

Above and left: *These photographs show the front (above left) and back (above) of a Pawnee shield collected by Duke Paul of Württemberg in the 1820s. It is made from the shrunken skin of a buffalo's neck and painted red. Shields offered physical and spiritual protection, and were imbued with the power of their owner's supernatural protector. When not in use they were placed inside soft buckskin covers, such as that shown to the left. This cover, although the fact is unclear from Duke Paul's notes, may belong to the shield shown above. It, too, dates from the 1820s, is the correct size, and depicts a pictographic battle scene in which one of the warriors, possibly the shield owner, carries a plain red-painted shield identical to this Pawnee example.*

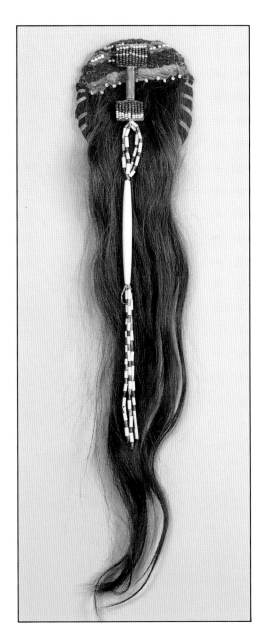

Above: *This beautifully decorated scalp, collected by the Duke of Württemberg from the Pawnee, is variously described as being that of an Omaha, a Sioux, or a Padouca warrior. Since the Pawnee fought against all these tribes any of these is possible.*

Left: *This photograph of the Pawnee village on the Loup Fork of the Platte River was taken in the winter of 1808–9. The lodges are built from brush and sod heaped over with earth on a timber framework. The narrow entrances to the lodges provided a means of defence if the village was besieged.*

of a nomadic prairie folk' and was told they had a population so large that 'there were as many people as there are stars in the sky'.[2] George Catlin, ten years later, spoke of them as formidable and warlike, with a temperament that matched that of their neighbors and with whom they were constantly at war, and as 'Lords of the Prairies' who knew no master and feared no foe, a term repeated almost exactly by John Treat Irving, also in the 1830s, when he commented about the 'wild, free air of the warriors ... the proud rulers of the prairie'.

Irving was impressed by the reception he received at the Grand Pawnee village, which was a conventionalized greeting he found repeated among the Oto and which was common to all the village tribes that had adapted fully to a Plains environment. It is not difficult to imagine the emotions of Irving's party, only thirty strong, when he comments that on their approach to the village the hills surrounding it were 'black with masses of mounted warriors to the number of several thousands' who sat motionless on their horses, watching.

At a signal from their chief this 'whole mass of warriors were rushing towards us ... it was a moment of intense and fearful expectation. On they came; each mad horse, with erect mane and blazing eye, urged forward by an Indian master ... the speed of their horses was unchecked, and the powerful tramp of their hooves rang like thunder upon the sod of the prairie. At a signal from the chief, the band separated to the right and left, and commenced circling round us, in one dark, dense flood. Their whoops and yells, and the furious and menacing manner in which they brandished their bows and tomahawks, would have led a person unacquainted with their habits, to have looked upon this reception as anything but friendly. There is something in the fierce, shrill scream of a band of Indian warriors, which rings through the brain, and sends the blood curdling back to the heart.'

He describes some of the Pawnee as having 'closely shaved heads adorned with the plumage of different birds. Others wore an ornament of deer's hair, bound up in a form resembling the crest of an ancient helmet, and a plume of the bald eagle floated from the scalp-locks of the principal warriors. Some few wore necklaces of the claws of the grizzly bear, hanging down upon their breasts. The bodies of some were wrapped in buffalo robes, or the skin of the white wolf; but the most of them wore no covering, save a thick coat of paint.'

Their principal chief was 'a tall, powerful Indian. A fillet of the skin of the grizzly bear, ornamented with feathers, was bound round his head. Over his shoulder was thrown a large mantle of white wolf-skin, also adorned with feathers. His legs were cased in black leggings of dressed buffalo hide, worked with beads, and fringed with long locks of human hair. These were taken from scalps won in his various war expeditions, and hung down over his knees, trailing upon the ground as he walked.'[3]

The Pawnees' impressive show of strength had the desired effect, and Irving's small party proceeded to the village 'in trepidation', escorted by the chiefs who rode in front to clear a path while the warriors dashed recklessly back and forth in displays of horsemanship. On entering the village they were taken to the principal chief's lodge where, in contrast to the

Below: *This William H. Jackson photograph, taken about 1868, shows four Kitkehahki Pawnee brothers. From left to right they are: A Man That Left His Enemy Lying In The Water; Night Chief; One Who Strikes The Chiefs First; and Sky Chief, who is wearing a bear claw necklace. Standing in the background is the half-Pawnee U.S. interpreter Baptiste Bayhylle who was also an active warrior. His Indian name translates as One Whom The Great Spirit Smiles Upon.*

Below: *This bear claw necklace, collected from the Iowa about 1820, is similar to that worn by the Pawnee on the right of the photograph opposite. Such necklaces were were symbols of highly respected warriors and were especially popular among tribes such as the Sauk and Fox living in the region of the Great Lakes, but were also used with some regularity among the semi-nomadic Plains tribes. The grizzly, being a formidable and dangerous opponent, was said to possess the character of a warrior and was, therefore, an appropriate adversary against whom courage could be tested.*

tumultuous reception they had received outside the village, they were feasted in total silence. A pipe was then prepared with a great deal of ceremony and offered to the four directions prior to being passed solemnly around this silent gathering, each man in turn inhaling from the pipe before handing it to his neighbor. When all present had smoked, and thereby pledged themselves to speak truthfully and to regard each other as friends, the chief broke the silence of the lodge and began his welcoming address.

The formality and dignity of the occasion, even though Irving and his men did not fully appreciate its significance, reflects the continuing importance of the pipe as a war–peace symbol. For the welcoming ceremony, which was used whenever a conversation of any significance was to take place, the

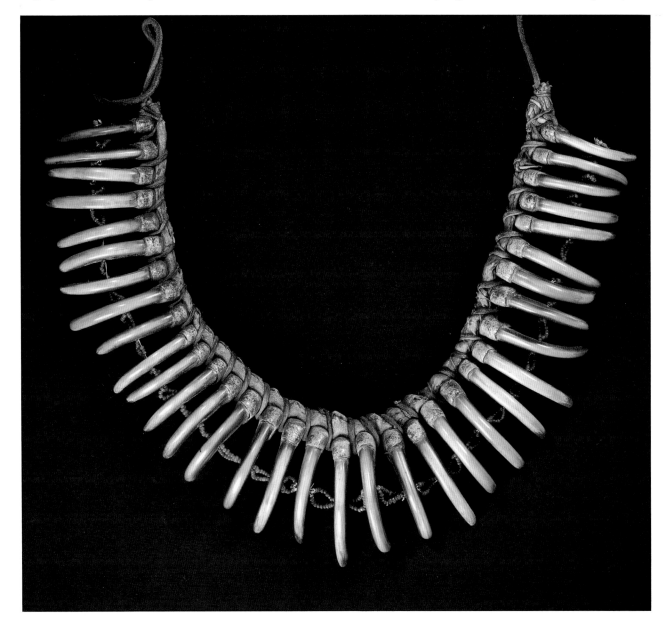

Left, and below: *In 1820–21 the Pawnee, Omaha, Kansa, Oto and Missouri delegation visited Washington under the leadership of Sharitarish (left), second chief of the Chaui Pawnee. Petalesharo (below), son of Knife Chief, represented the Skidi, while L'Ietan (right) was present on behalf of the Oto. Colonel McKenny, describing the White House reception, wrote, 'The copper-skinned chiefs and warriors walked into the crowded room with the air of ancient kings. The Pawnee wore buffalo robes, brilliantly painted with figures of birds and horses and battle scenes. The Omaha chiefs tinkled when they walked from the number of silver bracelets on their arms, and only the fierce dark eyes of the Kansa and Missouri warriors could be seen, so completely were they covered by robes and skins. Their faces, eyebrow to cheekbone, were covered with a thick red paint and the Oto half-chief stalked about the room in a weird headdress of a gold crown which dangled vermilion-dyed horsehair from which protruded two buffalo horns'* (**McKenny–Hall**, *p.46*).

chief used his ordinary smoking pipe. The symbolism of the pipe is, however, more fully explained by reference to the Chaui Pawnee Hako, or Calumet Ceremony, in which paired pipes representing the male and female principles are used to promote peace, well-being, brotherhood and adoption. These pipes are known as 'the stem with the white moving feathers' and 'the stem with the dark moving feathers'.

Fastened to the female pipe, which is painted blue to represent both the sky (the abode of the gods) and a clear, cloudless day (the symbol of peace), is a fan-shaped pendant of feathers from the mature golden eagle, or war eagle, and the head of a red-crested woodpecker. The Pawnee tell us that 'the red crest, which rises when the bird is angry, was here held down and tied in place' and that the woodpecker was favored by the spirits of the storm and could intercede with these war-bringers on behalf of the people. The pipe was also decorated with owl and duck feathers, the guides of the people, and a red line (the symbol of life) was the path along which the spirits of the birds travel to bring help. Dyed horsehair represented the sun and moon, day and night. The

Right: *The Oto half-chief, L'Ietan, bore this name as a war honor in recognition of the fact that a war party under his leadership had completely routed the Comanche, or Ietan, camp. It was customary among many of the tribes for the men to change their names at certain stages of their careers to reflect either brave actions or any unusual event in their lives or, as in L'Ietan's case, to be known by a popular name that reflected some worthy act. L'Ietan's young wife, Eagle of Delight, accompanied him to Washington where her grace and modesty created an impression equal to that of the chiefs and warriors.*

Below: *Pawnee war parties always left on foot, the warriors carrying long ropes with which they would secure any ponies they were able to capture. The one shown here, which was collected by the Duke of Württemberg, is made from a mixture of buffalo hair and hemp which, in addition to giving the rope strength, was also employed for its decorative effect.*

male pipe, painted green for the earth, had a pendant of white, or immature, eagle feathers and was said to stand for 'the father, the warrior, and the defender ... its place was always on the outside [where] it could do no harm, could rouse no contention, but would serve to protect and defend.'[4]

The principle of the Hako was shared by the other village tribes, and similar symbolism is found on the peace pipes of the Omaha. These are associated with the power of birds that 'were thought to be in close relation with the storm and the storm cloud, the abode of Thunder, the god of war'.[5] Their pipes were also decorated with 'the feathers of the fantail eagle, the owl and the woodpecker', and in spite of the close association of these birds with warfare and with death – the owl, in addition to its connection with the shamans and wisdom, is also thought of as the harbinger of death, since it is said to haunt the graves of the recently deceased – the pipes 'were to be used in establishing friendly relations with other tribes'.[6]

It is clear from the symbolism of the pipes that the forces which controled war, if approached correctly, could be persuaded to use their powers for the promotion of peaceful relationships, and it is appropriate that the 'war birds' which were in close communion with these forces should be expected to have an intercessionary role. These beliefs in smoking rituals that will appease the gods of war have a definite connection with the use of the pipe by the Adena-Hopewell to ensure peaceful trade; yet it is clear they have additional meaning linked with the aggressive war birds of the Mississippians.

In a Pawnee tale recorded by Murie the culture hero, Poor Boy, 'saw a red Hawk sitting upon a limb. The Hawk made a screeching sound and the boy thought that the Hawk was calling him. He followed the Hawk. Whenever he looked at the Hawk, he thought he saw a scalp hanging down from its claws. The Hawk also seemed to carry a war club.'[7] Poor Boy inherited these gifts from Hawk, and thereby became a great warrior through whose efforts the four monsters that threatened the people were defeated so that peace could be ensured. Myths and tales of the history of other semi-nomadic tribes often refer to villages that are on lake shores and in forested country, indicative of the fact that tribal knowledge recognizes an origin from outside the Plains region.

Archeological records also indicate a continuation of diverse Mississippian and Woodland practices. Villages were defended with stockades and ditches constructed on a pattern they brought with them from their former homelands, and although these were rarely as extensive as those of the Southeast it is clear that defensive measures were necessary. Hostility between the various village groups was caused by competition with each other for the occupation of fertile river lowland areas, since they were reliant on flash-floods to irrigate their crops, and there was an ever-present threat from the other tribes in the vicinity who raided the villages in attempts to gain war honors or to capture women and horses.

Above: *This riding quirt was obtained from Pawnee Indians living near Columbus, Nebraska, in 1870. The elk-horn handle is incised on both sides with quarter-circles representing feathers. Riding quirts were frequently used in battle for touching the enemy in a system of counting coup.*

Right: *Ah-shaw-wah-rooks-te (Medicine Horse) was one of the prominent Chaui Pawnee warriors whom George Catlin painted during his visit to Fort Leavenworth in 1832. The arrow passed through Medicine Horse's long hair is either a war medicine, or charm, intended to ensure success in battle, or commemorates a brave deed performed during a confrontation with the enemy.*

Mound burials too, though diminished in size from the great temple complexes of the Mississippians, were still being erected in the early 1830s. John Treat Irving commented on the 'large mounds' in the burial grounds outside the Oto villages[8] and George Catlin recorded the burial of a famed Omaha chief named Black Bird, who was interred on the back of his favorite war horse in a mound on a high bluff overlooking the Missouri River.

Catlin tells us that Black Bird 'owned, amongst many horses, a noble white steed that was led to the top of the grass-covered hill; and, with great pomp and ceremony, in presence of the whole nation, and several of the Fur Traders and the Indian agent, he was placed astride of his horse's back, with his bow in his hand, and his shield and quiver slung – with his pipe and his medicine-bag – with his supply of dried meat, and his tobacco-pouch replenished to last him through his journey to the 'beautiful hunting grounds of the shades of his fathers' – with his flint and steel, and his tinder, to light his pipes by the way. The scalps that he had taken from his enemies' heads, could be trophies for nobody else, and were hung to the bridle of his horse – he was in full dress and fully equipped; and on his head waved, to the last moment, his beautiful head-dress of the war eagle's plumes. In this plight, and the last funeral honors having been performed by the medicine-men, every warrior of his band painted the palm and fingers of his right hand with vermilion; which was stamped, and perfectly impressed on the milk-white sides of his devoted horse.'[9]

Black Bird's grave was large enough that it could be seen for several miles – in fact, it was shown as a landmark on the maps of the period – and Catlin's comments about this burial provide interesting details of the insignia and ornaments of the successful warrior. Many of these are of a generalized Plains type, such as the feather headdress and scalps which showed the war honors that Black Bird had gained during his lifetime. So, too, are the red hand markings made by the warriors. The right to do this was the sole prerogative of a man who had struck an enemy, and to place these on Black Bird's horse was a sign of the most unusual respect in which he was held by the fighting men of the tribe.

Respect shown to Black Bird and the recognition of his martial deeds as worthy and honorific reflect the warlike

Above: *This tomahawk was part of the ceremonial regalia worn by Washin-ha (who is generally referred to by the English mistranslation Chief Baconrind), a prominent Osage leader. The shaft of the tomahawk is covered with red felt and brass bells, a wool pendant, and eagle feathers are attached to its end.*

Left: *Wa-ho-béck-ee was credited by George Catlin as being the handsomest warrior in the Osage tribe. He is shown wearing a vast quantity of beads round his neck and holding a fan made from the tail feathers of a mature eagle. Of interest, too, is his hair style and the curious manner in which a war feather is worn at the back of his head.*

character of the Omaha and the village tribes, where the status and popularity of prominent warriors might at times rival that of the chiefs. Such men were feted and applauded wherever they went, and enjoyed a reputation for fearlessness which could be expressed at dances and other social gatherings, when they recounted their deeds of valor and courage on the warpath to exuberant shouts of approval and the trilling ululation of old women raising their voices in the victory call. Edwin James, traveling with the Long Expedition in 1819, was witness to such a recitation of deeds by the renowned Oto warrior Mi-a-ke-ta, or Little Soldier:

'After several rounds of dancing, and of striking at the post by the warriors [to demonstrate they spoke truthfully], Mi-a-ke-ta, a war worn veteran, took his turn to strike the post. He leaped actively about, and strained his voice to its utmost pitch whilst he portrayed some of the scenes of blood in which he had acted. He had struck dead bodies of individuals of all the red nations around, Osages, Konzas, Pawnee Loups, Pawnee Republicans, Grand Pawnees, Puncas, Omawhaws, and Sioux, Padoucas, La Plais or Bald Heads, Ietans, Sauks, Foxes, and Ioways; he had struck eight of one nation, seven of another, &c. He was proceeding with his account when Ietan [the Oto chief] ran up to him, put his hand upon his mouth, and respectfully led him

Right: Duke Paul of Württemberg acquired this feather headdress in St Louis in May 1823 from the principal chief Junaw-sche Wome who was there as the leader of a small delegation of Prairie Potawatomi Indians who had come to St Louis to meet the Indian Commissioners. Not only is it a superb and unusual example, it is probably the earliest complete feather headdress from the Plains and Prairies area in existence.

Below: The crow belt was worn by participants in the Dakota Heyoka ceremonies, a Thunder cult which is known as the Iruska among the Pawnee. The one shown here, decorated with a raven's head, porcupine quillwork, hair, downy feathers, owl feathers, tin cones and red dyed horsehair, is attributed to the Eastern Dakota and was collected by Friedrich Köhler in 1846, although the belt itself dates from 1820–30. In use the belt was tied round the waist with the raven's head at the man's back.

back to his seat. This act was no trifling compliment paid to the well-known brave. It indicated that he still had so many glorious acts to speak of, that he would occupy so much time as to prevent others from speaking, and put to shame the other warriors by the contrast of his action with theirs.'[10]

Yet in spite of their propensity for warfare, most of the village tribes defined war in terms of its defensive character. The Omaha say 'the warriors of a tribe were the only bulwark against outside attacks; they had to be ever ready to fight, to defend with their lives and safeguard by their valor those dependent on them',[11] and among the Osage 'peace was stressed as an ideal, symbolized by a cloudless day and the white swan ... they encouraged defensive warfare over aggres-

65

sive warfare [and] the highest honors were for defense of the village, women, and children. In short, for defending the survival of the tribe.'[12]

Defence, however, was understood to include deterrent and pre-emptive blows struck against an enemy in their own territories as well as revenge war parties. Among the Osage war parties were also organized for the 'Mourning-War Ceremony', which required the taking of a scalp so that the spirit of the enemy could accompany that of the deceased Osage on the 'lonely spirit path to spirit land'.[13] This seems to have been common practice; thus, among the Wichita a man would announce 'that within a short time he was going to lead a party on a war expedition, in which case, should he be successful in securing a scalp, he would give it to the mourners ... they continued to mourn [until] he returned victorious from a war expedition, with a scalp.'[14]

Most war parties were undoubtedly small and organized for the purpose of securing a single scalp to alleviate mourning or, more usually, to capture horses. Pawnee warriors actually left their camps on foot with the expectation of riding stolen horses back, a custom they shared with the Osage. Such raiding parties rarely consisted of more than about ten men and were intended as a means of economic gain or of raising individual status and prestige, but large-scale battles with a punitive character did take place on occasion.

In an horrific fight that took place in 1833, a large Osage war party came upon a Kiowa camp while most of the warriors were away hunting, and during the fighting that ensued the Osage decapitated the women and put their heads in the brass cooking pots the Kiowa had recently obtained in trade. Although this was obviously a challenging insult, the Osage later explained their action by saying they distrusted the white man and his trade goods, and that if the cooking pots had been of any value or interest they would have taken them home. Instead they chose to use the pots to indicate the disdain in which they held the Kiowa for trading with the white intruders.

The Osage were not always the victors in these encounters, and the desperate struggles that took place between them and the Pawnee – where there was a mutual antipathy and hatred which led to a continual series of raids and reprisals – are reflected in another tale in which a Pawnee war party attacked and destroyed an Osage village while they were away on their annual buffalo hunt. Women, children, the sick, and the elderly – in fact, all the people remaining in the village – were killed and the lodges burned to the ground. To add insult to injury, the Pawnee then rode their horses up

and down through the corn fields to destroy the ripening crop.

When the Osage returned they were in despair at the scene of destruction that confronted them, and the warriors seated themselves in small, silent groups, their blankets pulled over their heads to show their sorrow and resignation at the terrible fate that had befallen the village. Not even the bravest man was prepared to take up arms and avenge the deaths, until one of their chiefs went out alone and killed a Pawnee. He returned with the severed head, which he placed on a pole and paraded it through the ruins of the village, singing 'He's a Pawnee, are you afraid of him? Look at him. Are you afraid of him?'[15] Such was the rallying power of this chief's courage in going alone to the Pawnee villages that his song became a regularly used war song of the Osage to give 'brave hearts' to the warriors.

A similar tale of an attack on a village while the warriors were away on the annual hunt is recorded for the Skidi, or

Previous page: Having held the majority of the Sauk and Fox warriors neutral during the Black Hawk War of 1832, Keokuk, shown in a George Catlin portrait from 1835, was made principal chief after Black Hawk's arrest. The scalp attached to his horse's bridle and red hand painted on its flank are symbols of his war honors.

Below: Sauk and Fox houses were covered with elm bark over a wooden frame, and clustered in small permanent villages between the Great Lakes and the Mississippi–Missouri. They, with Potawatomi or Kickapoo allies and armed with superior weapons obtained in trade, made frequent incursions into territories held by the semi-nomadic Plains tribes.

Below: Collected in 1870, this Yankton Sioux war club bears a striking similarity to the ball-headed war clubs of the Woodlands tribes and attests to the movement of the Siouan groups to the grasslands from the east. The Yankton tribes occupied territory between the forks of the Mississippi and the Missouri and were feared raiders.

Wolf Pawnee, about whom Irving was told they possessed such bitter hatred for the Spanish that they 'would drink their blood', since they had driven them out of their original homelands on the southern Plains and forced them to the north where they came in conflict with the Siouan tribes. The Skidi village was beset by a war party of five hundred Sioux warriors. This attack, however, was repulsed under the leadership of Crooked Hand, said to have been the greatest warrior in the Skidi tribe. At celebratory dances Crooked Hand had the right to wear 'a robe made from the hide of a black and white steer, and fastened around the border of the robe were seventy-one scalps that he had taken.'[16] He was to become legendary for this defence of the village, which occurred when he was an old man.

The Sioux, realizing the village was almost deserted, 'advanced slowly in perfect order, the sun gleaming on their lances and guns, the fringes of their white war-shirts and the feathers on their warbonnets streaming in the breeze; as they came on at a slow steady pace, holding their excited ponies in, they were singing war songs.'

News of the advancing Sioux was brought to the aged Crooked Hand, who was lying sick in his lodge. 'He instantly sprang up, threw off his buffalo robe, and seized his weapons, issuing orders for everyone to prepare to fight. Mustering sick men, old men, boys of twelve, and even a number of women, Crooked Hand got a force of about two hundred together and mounted, some of the women armed only with iron hoes and similar weapons.' The Sioux, confronted by this motley crowd, burst into laughter, but a fierce charge led by Crooked Hand broke through their ranks, and after several hours fighting a battle which the Sioux had expected to be over in a few minutes, Skidi resistance remained unbroken. Seeing that the Skidi were not to be defeated so easily the Sioux began a slow withdrawal which 'turned into a panic flight with Crooked Hand and his old men and boys riding them down and killing them.'[17]

This pattern of large-scale war parties attacking the villages when the majority of occupants were absent seems typical of conditions faced by the semi-nomadic tribes, both from other village groups and from bands of nomadic raiders, since the permanent lodges and fields and the regularity of hunting seasons meant that any enemy in the vicinity knew exactly when the village was at its most vulnerable and where to find it. Throughout the year, however, there was a constant threat from small war parties lurking in the area. Waiting for an opportune moment, they would suddenly sweep out from a gully where they had been hidden, ride off

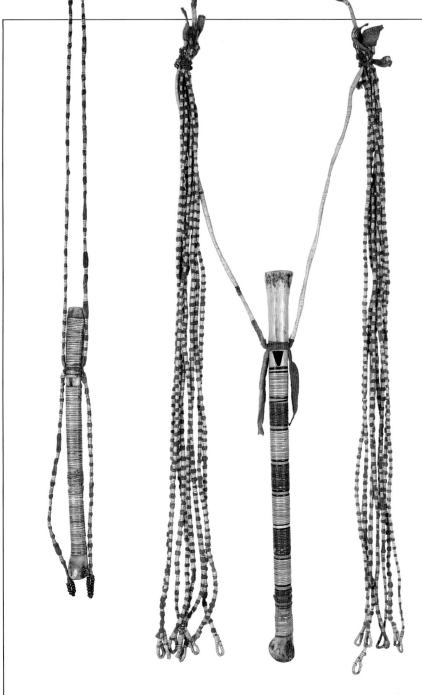

Left: *War whistles, or signal pipes, were used by many tribes living along the Missouri. Both these early examples date from 1820–30. That on the left is from the Assiniboine and was collected by Duke Paul of Württemberg, and the pipe on the right was given as a present by the Mandan chief Mato-Tope to Maximilian, Prince zu Wied. War whistles were used by members of the war party to maintain contact and were blown as they rode into attack, the Sioux generally fastening theirs above the ear so that wind rushing through it as they advanced at a gallop made the pipe sound.*

horses that had been turned out to graze or catch and scalp a woman or two working in the fields, and then quickly disappear before reinforcements from the village could arrive.

So regular were these attacks that women never left the villages alone but always worked in groups which were able to raise the alarm more effectively than a woman on her own. Armed guards often accompanied the working parties, especially if the scouts who continually roamed the surrounding countryside had reported signs of enemies. Look-outs, usually young men just starting to gain war honors, were also posted at nearby vantage points, where by waving their blankets or riding their horses in a circle they would instantly relay signals from each other and from the scouts to inform the village of the approach of strangers while they were still several miles away; this gave the women time to return to the safety of the lodges and for the warriors to drive in their horse herds and prepare to defend the village if need arose.

Right: *Prince Maximilian described Mahchsi-Karehde (Flying War Eagle) as the tallest of the Mandans and as a member of a distinguished band of warriors who regulated any matters of tribal importance. His richly decorated costume, as shown in this painting by Karl Bodmer, shows him to be a successful and prominent member of the community, and includes a number of references to his skill as a fighter. The wolf tails attached to the heels of his moccasins are a symbol of the scout, one of the most important members of a war party and a duty entrusted only to those with a proven record of courage, prudence and alertness, who could be relied on to report to the main body of warriors factually and truthfully.*

Left: *Mato-Tope, the Mandan chief, is said to have had a list of heroic accomplishments to hiscredit that was unmatched by any other warrior of the tribe, including defeating five other chiefs from awrring nations in single combat; but he was also admired for his faithfulness, good humor, and, above all, for his generosity.*

Below: *The wooden knife and painted sticks shown here are clearly visible in Bodmer's painting of Mato-Tope on the facing page and represent some of his war honors. The knife is a replica of the one he wrested from the hand of a Cheyenne chief after a fierce fight; the six wooden sticks each represent a bullet wound he received in battle.*

Not all warfare was defensive, and the organization of aggressive war parties was marked by burdensome formality and ritual since it required the sanction of the village priests. The Osage took this to the extreme that the leader of the war party, known as the Sacred One, had a function that was purely spiritual: although he accompanied the war party, he neither directed the activities of the warriors nor did he take part in the fighting. Actual leadership was in the hands of two 'officers', who appointed eight men as their representatives; they, in turn, asked for volunteers to carry the Hawk Wahope, or war medicine bundles, that gave the warriors the courage of the hawk and enlisted the powers of Thunder and of the Buffalo Men. Since the Wahope-bearers were supernaturally protected, it was they who led the charge against an opponent.

Among the Omaha, spiritual sanction of the war party by one of the Keepers of the four Sacred Packs of War was con-

sidered so important that a participant in an 'unauthorized' venture, even a successful one, was regarded as a murderer not a warrior. The leader of such a party, if he lost one of his own men, was likely to be put to death, and no act of bravery performed by any of the participants could be claimed as a war honor or recognized by the tribe. Sanction, however, absolved the leader from responsibility for the death of any of his party or for disasters that might befall them, since they were now under the authority of Thunder (the war god) and of the war birds contained in the Sacred Pack. He was nevertheless expected to think of the safety of his men before that of his own, and to be prepared to sacrifice his life in the protection of his warriors if circumstances demanded it. To think first of his own convenience and security incurred lifelong disgrace.

A memorable battle which confirmed the power of the Sacred Pack held by the Wazhiga division of the Omaha occurred in the eighteenth century. The Omaha and Pawnee were enjoying an uneasy peace, when a band of Pawnee warriors ran off several horses from outside the Omaha village. Wabacka, who was a prominent warrior but not a chief, lost his entire herd, and, not wishing to destroy the peaceful relationship, traveled on foot to the Pawnee villages where he asked the chiefs to intercede and secure the return of his horses. The Pawnee chiefs replied that their young men needed them, but that if Wabacka were to return to his village and make arrows (the Omaha being renowned as arrowmakers) then he might come back in the spring and exchange the arrows for his own horses. Wabacka replied 'he would go back and make arrows and return with more than the Pawnee would care to see'.

Wabacka went back and roused the Omaha to avenge the insult. In spring the entire village, men, women and children, set out for the Pawnee country, the women singing a song they had especially composed to give strength to the warriors on the battlefield and which became so famous that

Above: *This 'gunstock' club, which Duke Paul of Württemberg collected in the 1820s, has been labeled as 'probably Osage'. It is, however, of a type that was widely distributed in the Woodlands and which spread generally among the semi-nomadic tribes of the Mississippi–Missouri. The steel trade blade is inset into a carved and painted wooden handle. Snakeskin wrapping on the handle provided a firm grip for the warrior when wielding this weapon.*

Right: *Pachtüwa-Chtä, an Arikara, was a close friend of Mato-Tope who introduced him to Prince Maximilian and Karl Bodmer at Fort Clark in March 1834. He carries a 'gunstock' club similar to that shown above, on which the steel blade has been painted with red and blue pigment. His chest bears painted marks that represent bullet wounds and slash marks, and other war honors are indicated by the sticks in his hair. In return for posing for Bodmer, Pachtüwa-Chtä asked Maximilian for a drawing he had made of a bear. It is likely the bear inspired his personal war medicine: note the bear paws beaded on his moccasins.*

it has been used ever since, whenever warriors are away from their homes and facing danger. Half a day's distance from the Pawnee villages the warriors left the women and children and proceeded on foot. Reaching the Pawnee village at dawn, they leapt over the palisade surrounding the earth-lodges, tore the sods from the roofs of the buildings, and setting fire to the straw packed beneath the earth covering they slaughtered the Pawnee as they attempted to flee from their blazing homes. Wabacka, carrying the Wazhiga Sacred Pack, clubbed to death the chiefs who had insulted him. Although Wabacka lost his own life in this fight to preserve the honor of the tribe, the power of the Sacred Packs to 'strike the enemy in their own lodges' had been more than amply demonstrated.[18]

In addition to the conflicts among themselves, the villagers had to contend with other raiders who considered their vast herds of horses and mules as a rich source of supply. Because of their central location, the Pawnee, especially the Skidi, became both the instigators and the victims of much of the raiding. Skidi war parties seem to have been constantly traveling south into country claimed by the Comanche where even a small group of warriors might readily come back with two hundred head of horses; where, in turn, nomadic raiders from the north ran the herds off from their pastures outside the Skidi village.

Such forays obviously led to fights in which blood might be shed, which was justified in terms of the economic benefit of the horse and the value it had in being given away in demonstrations of generosity that might help lead to high status or chieftainship. They also provided opportunities for shows of bravery which could bring war honors. The Sauk and Fox, sometimes allied with the Kickapoo and Potawatomi, fought restless battles, initially with the tribes of the Woodlands and later with those of the Plains and Prairies, to such an extent that they suffered a population decrease. Among the Wichita death while in battle was held preferable to any other form of death; and the Iowa war leader, on return from a successful expedition, did not enter the village but waited outside to be joined by fresh warrriors and immediately led out a second party. To lead four successful war parties in immediate succession was the highest accolade a war leader could achieve, and to gain the courage that enabled him to do this it is said that the Iowa 'often' ate the hearts of their enemies.

Ritual, or token, cannibalism seems to have played a part in the lives of many of these tribes, as a means of assimilating the power of a defeated warrior. It is, however, most widely reported from the southern Plains and Texas and

Below: *According to the Duke of Württemberg's notes, the prisoner's rope shown here was used by the Pawnee in a ceremony of giving a captive his freedom and sparing his life by the unanimous decision of the people. This was symbolized by placing the rope on the body of the captive.*

Below: *Between the ages of two and eight, Omaha boys wore their hair in a fashion that indicated their affiliation to one of the ten kinship groups recognized by the tribe. Bodmer and Maximilian met this boy and his father when the steamer* **Yellowstone** *stopped overnight at Cabanne's trading post during their journey up the Missouri River.*

Louisiana, among the Southern Caddo, and the coastal fishing and hunting tribes of the Atakapa, Tonkawa and Karankawa with whom they came in conflict. To what extent this was actual practice, rather than a means of inciting young and impressionable warriors, is difficult to determine. An untrue rumor that the Tonkawa had been seen cooking a Caddo youth, for example, led to a massive reprisal raid by the Caddo which almost exterminated the Tonkawa. The

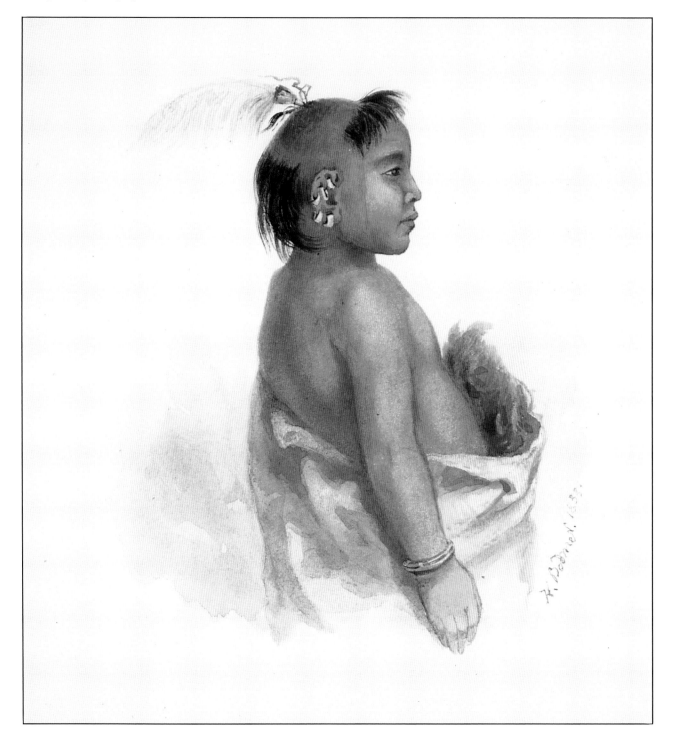

Caddo response was undoubtedly due to a widespread feeling among the tribes of the southern Plains that the Tonkawa were 'man-eaters', which, regardless of its actual validity, was nevertheless a firmly held belief.

This is supported in Comanche traditions which tell of a war party coming unexpectedly upon Tonkawas preparing to roast a captured Comanche warrior. The Comanche response seems equally cruel. Having defeated the Tonkawa, they severed their arms and legs and placed the bleeding torsos, still alive, on a huge fire about which they danced in celebration of their victory while their victims pleaded to be put out of their agony. Not all the tribes, however, viewed the Tonkawa in quite such a negative light. A Wichita warrior describing the bravest of their foes listed the Plains-Apache to the east, the Osage to the north, and the Tonkawa to the south.

The Caddo, nevertheless, seem to have thought of the Tonkawa as their principal enemy and used the excuse of cannibalism as justification for raiding their villages. Caddo raiders, if successful, took only one scalp – since this was sufficient to show they had been victorious – bringing this back to the village in a relay race where young men competed

Far left: *Although the drum shown here is attributed to the Dakota Sioux, this is not definite, and it is possible that it should be identified with tribes living further south. The drum is made from a wooden hoop over which tanned skin has been stretched.*

Left: *This ironwood club was collected from the Karankawa Indians of Texas by George Chambers in 1838. It is not a manufactured article, but utilizes a natural burl from the tree with part of a branch left attached to serve as a handle.*

Below: *By the late eighteenth and early nineteenth centuries, firearms had begun to supplement weapons of native manufacture, as in this print of Louisiana warriors. In some respects the bow and arrow, and the war club, were superior to early trade guns, since they could be fired more rapidly and could kill silently. This print, though arbitrarily colored, contains interesting details showing clan tattoos on the warriors' shoulders, and a tonsured hair style.*

against each other to be the carriers of the pole on which the scalp was suspended. They also went to great lengths to bring back prisoners whom the women would torture. Such prisoners were guarded carefully prior to their torture and encircled by a line of the bravest of the warriors, not from fear they might escape, but because if they could break through this line and gain access to one of the houses they would thereby be entitled to their freedom and to the rights and status of a Caddo warrior.

The extent of cannibalism is probably exaggerated, and accusations seem to have been used more as means of inflaming passions than as representations of fact. Yet is also clear that some cannibalism existed over a widespread area, probably as part of a whole complex of war activity that recognized bravery in an opponent and sought to acquire some of his courage and power as a warrior through the consumption of the vital organs that controled these forces. In this manner the more extreme war customs of the Mississippian Death Cult, in which it is apparent that fear of brutal reprisal, beheadings, dismemberments and other atrocities were used as a means of subjugating neighboring groups, became modified and assimilated into a pattern of warfare that, instead, recognized the individual achievements of warriors and in which fights over honor and status replaced battles waged for territorial gain.

PLAINS
GRASSLANDS

CHAPTER THREE

Left: George Catlin painted the Kiowa band chief Bon-son-gee (New Fire) in the Comanche village in 1834, when he described him as a 'very good man' and described the ornaments around his neck as a boar's tusk and a war whistle. The Kiowa–Comanche alliance had been formed in an attempt to present a united front against incursions from other tribes.

Below: This detail from a painting on hide, made for the ethnographer James Mooney in 1904, shows the hereditary decorated tipis of prominent Kiowa families as they would be set up in the annual circle-camp at which world renewal ceremonies took place. Such tipis were statements of family lineage and status, and the designs applied to them were traditionally handed down from one generation to the next.

THE STATUS AND honor of the individual warrior were of paramount importance to the nomadic Plains Indians, and took precedence over or strongly influenced every aspect of their lives. To simply call these people 'warlike' would be to under-estimate the significance that warfare had for them. This was, however, war that was waged under strict rules of conduct and which recognized only bravery. It was also something the Anglo-American pioneers and settlers, as well as the United States authorities, totally failed to comprehend. As Struthers Burt, a Western rancher, phrased it: 'One of the great tragedies of history is that the Indian and the white man had to meet. No two races could have understood each other less.'[1]

Plains Indians occupied the short-grass area lying primarily to the west of the village groups of the Mississippi River. This vast region of grasslands extends across the continent to the foothills of the Rocky Mountains, north into the Prairie Provinces of Canada, and south to Texas; it contained a remarkable quantity of plant and berry foods along its river valleys, in addition to the huge buffalo herds it supported.

Left: *In his youth Zepko-eete (Big Bow) was one of the most formidable warriors in the Kiowa tribe, although he was a non-conformist in that he usually went on raids alone or accompanied only by a Mexican boy he had adopted. Even so, his reputation was such that he had become a recognized war leader by the time he was only eighteen, later becoming one of the most prominent war chiefs of the Kogui tribal division.*

Right: *Big Bow's distinctive Tail Painted Tipi is shown here in a model made for James Mooney in 1904. A buffalo tail pendant was attached in the center of the back of the tipi and buffalo hair was used to tip the ears, or wind flaps, which are at the top center in this photograph. The tipi derives its name, however, from the fan-shaped tails painted in blue, and some red, lines around its bottom edge. They represent the tail of the water turtle, literally notched tail, a powerful water spirit.*

Tribes living here had a purely nomadic lifestyle, using skin tipis all year round and moving continually as relatively small hunting bands from one campsite to another, coming together as tribes only in summer for communal buffalo hunts and the celebration of annual Renewal Rites such as the Sun Dance.

All of the nomads were attracted by the open spaces of the grasslands and the unparalleled abundance of resources in what has been described as 'the largest natural game reserve in the world'. The lack of well-defined territories continually threw tribes into contact and conflict with each other, but the nature of Plains environments, whose vast spaces enabled the 'eye to travel as far as a thought', where huge skies might be rent asunder by dramatic storms in which all the elements seem to fight for supremacy, or where the endless grasses are continually set in motion by an ever-present wind that has no natural barrier to check its flow, encouraged a sense of freedom and of individual challenge and personal worth that was expressed by men through their martial successes.

Right: *The characteristic form of the Kiowa notched quirt is shown here. The Warrior Society to which Big Bow belonged used a similar quirt, with nine notches, as one of its emblems. During camps this was suspended above the door of the Tail Tipi with a fox skin pendant, painted green on the underside, attached to it.*

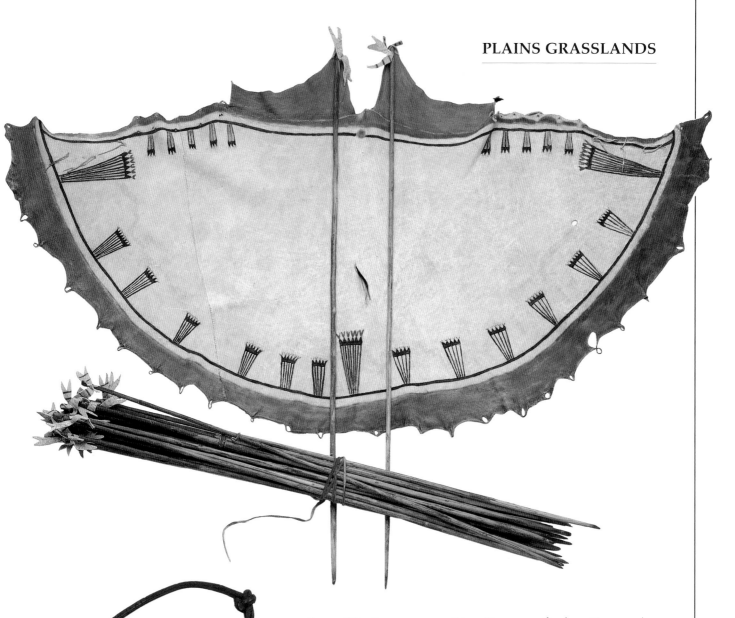

Parra-Wa-Samen, or Ten Bears, of the Yamparika Comanche, expressed this sense of space and freedom during a famous speech in which he said 'I was born upon the prairie where the wind blew free and there was nothing to break the light of the sun. I was born where there were no enclosures and where everything drew a free breath.'

In the northern grasslands, in Alberta and Montana, was the Blackfoot confederacy which Catlin considered 'the most powerful tribe of Indians on the Continent'[2] and with whom the Athapascan-speaking Sarsi allied themselves against the Plains Cree and Plains Ojibwa. East and southeast of the Blackfoot were the equally formidable Siouan-speaking Teton tribes, forming a confederacy known as the 'Seven Council Fires' which claimed a disputed territory centered on the Black Hills of South Dakota but extending south to the Platte River in Nebraska, east to the Missouri, west to the Teton Mountains of Wyoming, and north to the Yellowstone River. The linguistically related Assiniboine and Yankton were to the north and northeast, across the Missouri, while another Siouan division, the Santee, continued to occupy

villages in Minnesota between the Mississippi and Missouri rivers but regularly sent raiding parties deep into Plains country, where they considered the Pawnee a 'traditional' enemy.

South of the Blackfoot were the Crow, a small but proud and warlike tribe who separated from the village Hidatsa at the beginning of the eighteenth century and took up residence along the Yellowstone River in southern Montana and in the rich hunting grounds of Wyoming, where they successfully resisted Blackfoot and Sioux incursions. Below them were the Shoshone, who had migrated into the Plains from the western Plateau, and the Arapaho, whose movement into the area was from the northeast. Allied with the Arapaho, but maintaining an independent identity, were the Cheyenne. They had been settled farmers in Minnesota and North Dakota until the late eighteenth

Left: *Chief White man was head chief of the Kiowa-Apache, and represented his tribe in the delegation of Kiowa, Kiowa-Apache and Comanche chiefs who visited Washington in 1892 to negotiate the leasing of reservation lands. He was the owner of the powerful Bear Painted Tipi, which was erected near the center of the Kiowa-Apache section in the combined Kiowa and Kiowa-Apache annual circle camps. This tipi was considered to be such a powerful medicine object that only members of the hereditary family could stay in it overnight, and when the old cover was worn out and discarded it was staked out in the open and abandoned with the head of the Bear pointing toward the rising sun before painting began on its replacement.*

Left: *This Kiowa notched club was collected in Oklahoma by James Mooney in 1906. Note the similarity in form to the notched quirt shown on the preceding page. It is made from a single piece of heavy wood which has been painted and decorated with brass tacks.*

Right: *These twelve Comanche arrows date from the 1860s and have metal heads., either obtained in trade or cut from sheet metal, and are each fledged with three feathers extending almost a quarter of the length of the shaft. Painted marks on the shafts are recognition aids by which the tribe and the individual owner of the arrows could be identified.*

century but were fully equestrian nomads when Lewis and Clark met them in the Black Hills in 1804. Between them the Arapaho and Cheyenne controled much of Colorado and southern Wyoming. The southern Plains in western Texas were dominated by the Comanche, with the Kiowa and Kiowa-Apache in the Oklahoma area, the Jicarilla Apache in northern New Mexico, and the Lipan Apache in the Texas–New Mexico border area.

The Spanish met this last group in 1540, when they referred to them as *Llaneros*, 'People of the Plains', and commented on their nomadic lifestyle, use of buffalo-hide armor, and the fact that their shamans, or medicine men, were intrigued rather than overawed by the 'big dogs' the Spanish rode into battle. Instead of fleeing to safety at the sight of these strange white men mounted on even stranger animals, the Lipan Apache used their powerful sinew-backed bows to shoot the horses from beneath the Spaniards; their shamans

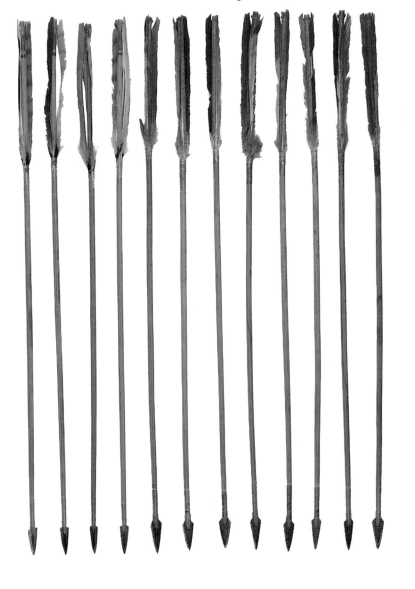

then dissected the animals and declared them 'mysterious' or 'wonderful', creating a demand for horses which the Apache satisfied by raiding Spanish settlements.

The Lipan Apache were probably the first mounted warriors, but the florescence of Plains culture did not occur until the eighteenth century, when the horse frontier moving up from the south and the gun frontier coming from the northeast met on the grasslands, transforming small groups of pedestrian hunter–gatherers into mounted and well-armed warriors seemingly overnight, and attracting numerous other tribes into the area from the north, east and west. Also participating in this whirl of tribal movements, many peripheral groups spent much of their time in the short-grass regions. Some of the Plains villagers virtually abandoned their settlements for half the year to hunt buffalo; Ute warriors rode in from the Great Basin of Utah and Nevada, while Nez Perce, Cayuse, and Flathead Indians came from the Plateau to hunt and trade, and sometimes to fight.

That they shared many of the Plains ideals and attitudes, while differing from them in other cultural aspects, is very clear. Ute warriors, after their acquisition of the horse, became virtually indistinguishable from Plains tribes in manner of dress and in their economy, although many of the bands retained brush shelters rather than adopting the tipi. Similarly, the Nez Perce kept their tradition of fishing, fish being considered 'poisonous' by most of the Plains tribes, but related to the land and the power it was felt to contain in much the same way as any of the grassland occupants. This is evident in an impassioned speech Chief Joseph of the Nez Perce made in an attempt to keep settlers out of his beloved Wallowa Valley, and in which he said 'the earth was created by the assistance of the sun, and it

Right: Prince Maximilian considered the Piegan chief Mehkskéhme-Sukáhs (Iron Shirt) as the most distinguished of several chiefs he met at Fort Mackenzie. When Iron Shirt posed for this portrait by Bodmer he wore a hide shirt trimmed with otter fur and decorated with trade beads and metal buttons. More significant, however, is the war medicine tied in his hair. This consists of feathers, a bear claw, and a small weasel skin on which blue beads have been inserted for eyes. His facepaint, as well as being a statement of tribal affiliation, is a powerful indicator of his own potential.

Above: This Arapaho carving was used by dancers during the first dance of the annual season of regulated ceremonies. It is pointed to enable it to be set upright in the ground and although carved as a horse is dedicated to the buffalo. The tuft of buffalo hair behind the head could only be trimmed by the man who had taken the scalp, and the lower end traditionally bore a buffalo tail, rattles, seven thongs wound with porcupine quills, and an eagle's wing feather. It is also said to stand as a symbol for the war club.

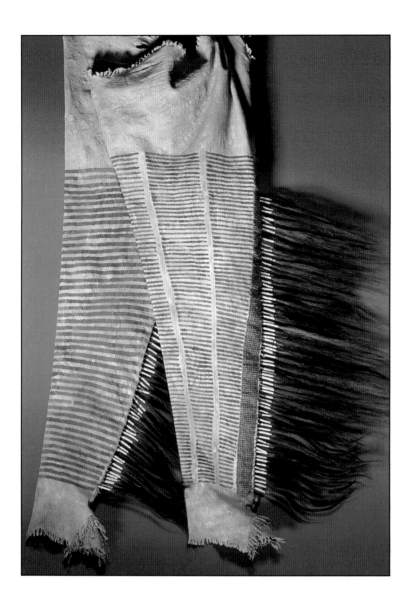

should be left as it was. The country was made without lines of demarcation, and it is no man's business to divide it. The earth and myself are of one mind. The measure of the land and the measure of our bodies are the same.'

Although Plains culture flared suddenly and splendidly, it lasted for little more than three generations. Before the end of the nineteenth century, in a series of bloody, often brilliantly led, sometimes futile, and eventually desperate attempts to protect their nomadic lifestyle and the buffalo from extinction, the proud warriors of the Plains had been crushed and confined by the superior weapons of the U.S. army, through devastating epidemics, and by the continual encroachment on their lands by farmers and professional buffalo hunters whose activities destroyed the great game herds on which the tribes were dependent.

The demise of this wild, free life and the atrocities, massacres, betrayals, and short-sightedness that brought it

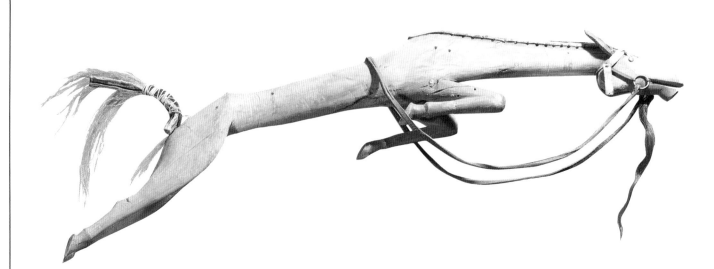

about, has been thoroughly, and frequently apologetically, documented by Western historians. Just as frequently the Indian attitude to war has been misrepresented through a concentration on fights between Indians and whites, rather than on indigenous patterns of warfare. The Native view is succinctly summed up by the Oglala. 'Call the enemy ground a testing place for daring, they had said, not a place for making killers out of warriors.'[3]

Above: *This beautiful Sioux horse effigy is the only example of complete equestrian sculpture known from the Great Plains. The tied-up tail and red horsehair pendant are accurate depictions of a pony prepared for battle, while carved holes painted red indicate the horse had been wounded in the fight. The carving follows in the tradition of other Horse Dance sticks, and would have been carried in honor of a valued pony which had gained its own war record.*

Left: *Alights on the Cloud, a Cheyenne, was given his name by his father, Medicine Water, who had one day seen a war eagle soaring high above the grasslands and seeming to land on the tops of the clouds. He also acquired from him an old 'iron shirt' that had been taken from the Spanish, and which Alights on the Cloud wore beneath his buckskin war shirt when in battle. In fall 1852 a Cheyenne war party he was leading engaged a party of Skidi Pawnee, and Alights on the Cloud rode in close counting coup, trusting to his armor to protect him. Riding close behind a terrified Pawnee boy armed with a bow, and keeping to his right so the bow could not be used against him, Alights on the Cloud was just about to touch the boy, who unknown to him was left-handed, when the boy suddenly turned and let fly an arrow. A great shout went up from the Pawnee and the boy turned to see his arrow deeply embedded in Alights on the Cloud's right eye, who was lying dead behind him. This daguerrotype was taken shortly before his death.*

Cheyenne. 19.

Below: *Plains Indians are well-known for pictographic representations of war records and decorative figures which were painted on tipi covers and linings, shields and other items, and occasionally beaded on clothing. Red and black horses painted on the flesh side are shown on this buffalo robe collected from the Cheyenne.*

A Blackfoot Elder defined the necessity of war at greater length as being 'so that the people would know the young warriors were there to protect them and so that the warriors would have the respect of the people because they were working for the people. This is why warriors were so important. Warriors learned to be responsible to the people. They used to do this by giving the people protection, and they showed how strong their protection was by challenging those who were in a position to suggest they were weak. This is why they went on the warpath. The bigger the challenge then, of course, the stronger the protection they could offer and the more they could prove their responsibility. They weren't interested in defeating the enemy, those warriors, they were just interested in proving how strong they were.'[4]

This same Elder, a wise man and highly respected for speaking truthfully and for his ability to clearly articulate the thoughts of The People, expanded on the concept of war as a challenge. 'Our enemies knew we would war against them,

just as we knew they would war against us. War was a challenge, a challenge to oneself and a way of proving one's own worth – to oneself and to others. But it was also a challenge to the enemy, to let them know we were there and to tell them that we were not afraid of them. They were doing the same thing to us.'

Similar ideas of challenging an enemy, and indeed of showing respect for the warriors they contested with, are found in Plains Indian tales referring to war and fighting. When reading these one is struck by the general absence of vindictive comment or expressions of hatred. The Santee Sioux, for example, in referring to their fights with the Plains Ojibwa, constantly mention the Ojibwa's daring, courage and ability to fight well and effectively. These are the qualities the Santee demanded from their own warriors and which they expected to find in those they fought. The Ojibwa provided the Santee with a foil against which their own warriors could test themselves, and the tales suggest that 'the Santee esteemed the Ojibwa for being as violent, as resourceful, and as nobly motivated as they'.[5]

Above: *Many war honors on the Plains demanded touching an enemy without attempting to cause any physical harm, and although this might be done with the hand or with any object held in the hand, a special category of coup sticks such as that shown here was developed to serve this purpose. The coup stick, which is clearly not a weapon, made it obvious that the warrior's intent was to gain honor rather than make a killing. This example, which has not been identified by tribe, consists of a wooden stick with black diagonal markings, and has a bunch of flicker and small feathers at the head with two pendant groups of eagle feathers.*

Left: *A frequently encountered form of a warrior's personal attire is the breastplate made from 'hair pipes'. Early examples were made from the long bones of a bird's wing, but manufactured hair pipes soon replaced these and became a sought-after trade item.*

Right: *This extremely rare and exquisitely decorated horse mask was collected by George Bird Grinnell among the Cheyenne, and dates from between 1850 and 1875. It is made from buckskin covered with dyed porcupine quills, with red stroud, beads and metal tacks along the lower edge. The entire mask is surrounded by cut and dyed feathers. Such masks were used during public parades and social gatherings, when both horse and rider appeared in their finest regalia, and when speeches, dances and displays of honorific insignia reinforced the warrior's status in the community.*

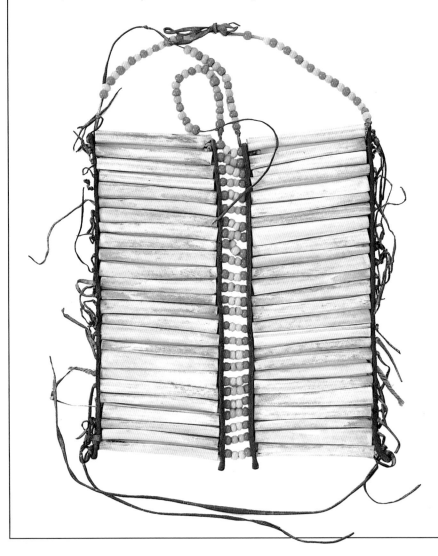

Noble motivation was encouraged by a system of war honors in which brave deeds were graded according to the courage required in carrying them out, and where each was awarded a token representing the deed. Thus, a red painted feather worn horizontally in the back of the hair might indicate a killing, horseshoe marks painted on a shirt represented horses captured in war, or a particular facepaint could be that of an honorific warrior society. A man's deeds were also recited and proclaimed both by himself and his supporters at virtually every opportunity. His claim to fame was through the acquisition of honors, by which he gradually rose in status and these, when combined with other qualities such as generosity, skills in diplomacy, and so forth, might lead to election to chieftainship.

Since every act had its individual merit, the gradings were not strictly fixed but judged according to the danger that had been overcome; with very few exceptions, however, the killing of an enemy or securing the scalp as a war trophy, although commendable, did not rank as a first class honor. Among the Crow the four war honors usually required for chieftaincy were striking an enemy with something held in the hand (not necessarily causing injury), cutting a picketed horse from in front of an enemy's tipi (which required entering the camp), taking a gun from an enemy, and successfully leading a war party. The Kiowa classed touching the enemy, charging the enemy while the party is in retreat, rescuing a fallen comrade, and charging the leading man of the enemy before the parties have met, as first-class honors; and the Blackfoot claimed that 'to ride up, jerk a gun from an enemy's hand and get away without injury to either party was the greatest deed possible.'[6]

The logic of this system was that all the honorific acts demanded daring which was not necessarily attendant on

Left: *Joseph was the undisputed principal chief of the Nez Perce living in the Plateau lands bordering the Plains; with the Cayusa they were the principal suppliers of horses through trade with the northern tribes.*

Below left: *Oscar Mark, a Wasco Indian from Oregon, is shown mounted on a pony which wears a trade cloth and bead decorated mask. Note the horned headdress with long trailer and the ermine trim on his shirt.*

Below: *The designs painted on shields protected their owners by association with the animal intermediaries in visions through which power had been granted. This shield is inspired by the spirit of the buffalo.*

either killing or scalping. It was, after all, possible to kill an opponent with a bullet or arrow fired from a safe distance without exposure to particular risk, and the scalp, though not necessarily fatal, was usually taken from the body of an enemy who was unable to offer any resistance. Warriors vied with each other to gain honors, to the extent that has led some observers to comment 'there is little doubt that the motives which led warriors into a life of warfare had some of the aspects of a game'[7] and 'fighting patterns ... are embellished with virtuosities that go far beyond the needs of victory. Display in bravery tends to become an end in itself. War has been transformed into a great game in which scoring against the enemy often takes precedence over killing him.'[8]

If war was a game played by virile young men intent solely on gaining battle honors, then it was a deadly one in which the stakes were high since 'the only game played between a warrior and his opponent was the gamble of life and death.'[9]

Left: *Medicine Crow shows the characteristic upswept hairstyle of the Crow Indians. The Crow were reknowned for their elegance and the richness of their costume, which is clearly reflected in the splendid shirt, beadwork and hair ornaments worn in this photograph taken about 1880.*

Far right: *Two views of the front and back of a scalp taken by the Crow. The very fine texture of the hair suggests it comes from the head of a child, and links it with the myth in which a child gave the Sacred Doll to the Crow which featured prominently in their annual renewal ceremonies. Such a scalp would have been highly honored and respected, and treated as an object of deep ritual significance. Talons from a small bird of prey, which also features in the myth, are attached to the leather strip on the front, while the reverse bears a beaded cross that represents the Morning Star. The contrast of black and white between front and back indicates the scalp's function as a symbol of both life and death.*

Such a view also overlooks the purpose of Plains warfare, which was never conducted under principles of conquest but was regarded as a demonstration of strength and of warrior power. In this respect the psychological effect of 'defeating' an armed opponent and showing his ineffectiveness as a warrior by riding up, touching him, and escaping safely without injury to either party was more demoralising to the enemy forces as a whole than might have resulted from a killing carried out at a distance.

The honor system nevertheless encouraged warriors to go to extreme lengths to engage in close combat where individual power over an opponent could be demonstrated, and also

Right: *This Crow recurved bow is made from Osage orangewood, a straight-grained timber ideally suited for bow making but only available to the Crow through trade in limited quantity. Such bows were highly valued and used only in parades or on occasions when power was an essential requirement. This example, although it has its original twisted sinew bow string, has been restrung incorrectly, since in use the bow would have been drawn to the right as shown in the photograph.*

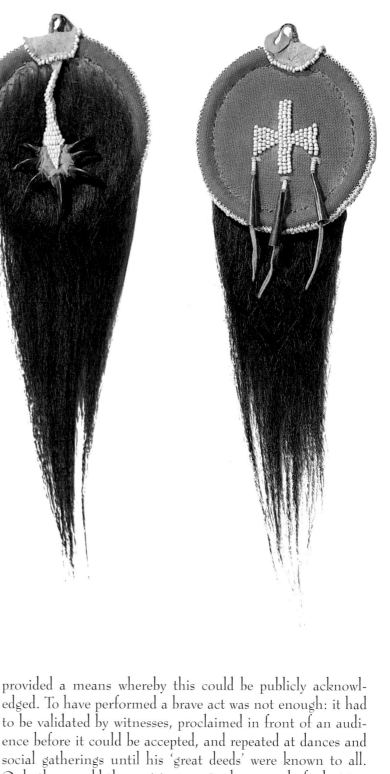

provided a means whereby this could be publicly acknowledged. To have performed a brave act was not enough: it had to be validated by witnesses, proclaimed in front of an audience before it could be accepted, and repeated at dances and social gatherings until his 'great deeds' were known to all. Only then could the aspiring warrior be assured of admiring glances and anticipate invitations to join one of the Warrior Societies. Some of these were age-graded, in that all members were of a similar age group, whereas others consisted of men who held comparable war honors; an invitation to join any of them, other than the children's societies that emulated those of the adults, was usually extended only to those

who had proven themselves worthy of membership.

Social pressure to be a member of one of these societies, and to progress through them from ordinary membership to prestigious ranks as whip-bearers, lance-bearers, pipe-bearers, and leaders was immense, but could also carry heavy obligations. Thus, the lance-bearer, in accepting this role, also made a pledge never to retreat before the enemy. The greatest pledge, however, was that of the 'No-Flight' warrior, whose vow committed him to staking the long sash emblematic of his rank to the ground in front of the enemy and to remain fighting regardless of the consequences. These were the bravest men in the tribe, since they were compelled to fight even against overwhelming odds, and they received immense respect and adulation from the other members of the community.

It was, however, rare for the societies to act in concert as a fighting group. The nature of Plains social organization mitigated against this, as the bands were separated for much of the year and society memberships crossed band obligations and alliegances; but even in summer, when the tribal camp circle was formed and the societies became fully functioning, it was considered unlucky for all the warriors of a single fraternity to venture out together. Tradition says that when this did happen on one occasion, all the warriors were killed.

Warfare was generally a matter of individual initiative, and anyone could lead a war party simply by announcing they intended to leave at a certain time and by inviting others to join them. This was entirely voluntary, so the leader's record

Far left: *Catlin painted this portrait of He Who Jumps Over Everyone in 1832–3, describing him as a Crow warrior displaying all the ornaments and trappings of this 'gentlemanly race of picturesque warriors'.*

Left: *Prince Maximilian obtained this Blackfoot bow in the 1830s. It is partly bound with sinew and buckskin to add to its elasticity, and has strips of porcupine quillwork and red cloth decoration.*

Right: *This war medicine shield belonged to the great war chief Arapoosh at the time of the Lewis and Clark expedition. The design represents the Moon, and if the shield was rolled along the ground and fell face up the war party was ensured of success.*

Below: *Duke Paul collected this magnificent knife and sheath from the Teton Dakota in the early nineteenth century. The knife blade is a trade item, which is set in a bone handle. The sheath is decorated with porcupine quills stained with vegetable dyes.*

of honors and, especially, his success at guiding previous war parties that had returned successfully and without loss were influential in deciding the number of men who would choose to follow him. Someone without honors wasn't debarred from leadership, but would be likely to find himself without followers and forced to set out alone! Usually the nucleus of a war party was a group of friends, perhaps numbering ten or twelve, yet war parties of only two or three men were quite

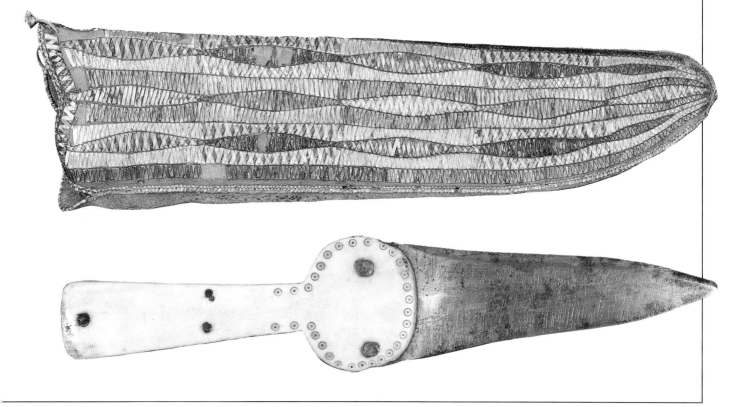

common, and those exceeding twenty were relatively rare.

The war party set out with a clear objective, either to seek revenge against an enemy or, with much greater frequency, to raid for horses. The disparity in types of warfare during the nineteenth century is evident from the Blackfoot, among whom it is estimated that as many as fifty horse raids would take place during a year compared with only one every three or four years that was organized specifically for revenge, although, of course, scalps might be taken during a horse raid if this resulted in fighting. Sanction for a raid was received by the leader in a dream or vision, through which spiritual protection was assured. This was given for a specific purpose and could not be extended to cover any other activity.

Revenge raiders therefore tried to strike quickly, kill an enemy and take his scalp, and then escape without thought for other plunder, whereas horse raiders attempted to capture ponies and to put sufficient distance between themselves and their enemies before they were detected to prevent pursuit. Indian skill in capturing horses was expressed by Colonel Dodge who, in writing about the Comanche, said that one of their warriors 'could crawl into a bivouac where a dozen men were sleeping, each with a horse tied to his wrist by the lariat, cut a rope within six feet of the sleeper, and get away with the horse without waking a soul.'[10]

With the exception that large scale raids were more frequent among the southern tribes, the organization and conduct of the war party is similar throughout the Plains area. Among the Blackfoot, for example, the warrior receiving the vision either canvassed support among his friends or, if still a youth, went to an older, more experienced, man and asked him to act as leader. Those wishing to join signalled their assent by beating time with sticks on a stretched buffalo hide, meanwhile singing wolf songs that gave them the strength of the wolf and his ability to hunt successfully in packs.

In horse raiding, three ritual war camps would be made during the expedition: the first, just out of sight of the main encampment, replaced the white road of peace with the red road of war through the ceremonial smoking of a war pipe and the imposition of war restrictions on the participants; the second, made immediately before the raid, was where warriors enlisted the help of personal spirit protectors by singing war songs, preparing amulets and war charms, and painting their faces and bodies with sacred images received in individual visions; and the third, made before re-entering the main camp on a successful return, was where the spoils of the

Left: *This superb club is both a weapon and a war medicine imbued with supernatural power that has been granted by an animal intermediary in a vision. In this example power derives from the eagle, which is able to strike swiftly, accurately and without sound. The eagle's assistance is recognized here by the claws attached to the handle of the club. The handle itself is made from the upper tail of a buffalo, leaving it flexible and thereby imparting a more serious blow against an enemy than if a rigid handle had been employed.*

Right: *After 1870, when the Plains tribes had been confined on reservations, a new art form developed in ledger pad drawings which recalled memories of a free life as nomadic warriors. This drawing, 'Man with Bird on Cheek Lances a Pawnee', shows a Kiowa wearing a war shirt with sacred hail designs and a long feather bonnet spearing a Pawnee armed with a flintlock musket. The bird figure on the Kiowa's cheek is a symbol of his war medicine. Note, too, the shield with a long feather decorated pendant, tied-up horse tail and bridle pendant.*

Right: *This ledger pad drawing, 'Head-on Charge', seems inappropriately labeled. Costume details of the lance wielding warrior suggest he is Kiowa and not Arapaho, and his opponent, although tribal identification is difficult, is certainly not a Nez Perce. The trade cloth blanket of the enemy is marked with a symbol indicating supernatural protection, and a similar function applies to the Kiowa's shield, with its streaming feather attachments, which is worn over his shoulder rather than being carried as a defensive measure.*

raid were divided, and the warriors applied victory paint preparatory to a triumphal entry.

At the first of these camps the war leader assigned two of the bravest and most experienced men to act as scouts. Wearing wolf skins, they traveled ahead of the party while in hostile territory and located the enemy villages, ascertaining the size of the horse herds and identifying any valued war ponies picketed beside the tipis. He also appointed the youngest members of the party as water-carriers. These boys, often on their first war experience, were expected to fetch fresh water and to obey the demands of the warriors, who used this as a way of testing their courage, staying-power, and future promise as fighting men of the tribe.

In one tale a water-carrier was sent out four times during one night, being told each time he returned that the water was 'stale', or that the water container was only half full (the warrior questioning this having taunted him by pouring most of its contents on the ground) He is said to have traveled without sleep 'twice the distance a fat man could walk in a

day', and was then expected to keep up with the party which, if travelling on foot, might cover a distance of twenty-five miles in the next day's travel.

It was also the water-carrier's responsibility to remain behind at the second war camp while the warriors went ahead. This camp afforded an opportunity for the warriors ritually to prepare for the raid by calling on supernatural protective power. Tokens of this power in the form of feathers, animal or bird skins, and other objects, with their associated songs and face paint, constituted the warrior's War Medicine Bundle, and an element from this, often in the form of an amulet, was worn for protection during the raid.

The second camp was used as a rendezvous to which the warriors returned after attempting to capture horses at dawn before the enemy camp awakened, and by not permitting the

Above: *This coup stick is probably Sioux. It consists of a straight wooden stick wrapped with trade cloth and fringed with red dyed horsehair. The feather pendants are those of an owl, widely believed to be the messenger of death and clearly appropriate in this context.*

Right: *Plains Indians regularly adapted trade items to suit new purposes. The Sioux club shown here, from the 1870s, has three knife blades removed from the hilts and set into a painted wooden handle with feather decoration.*

direct participation of the water-carriers to be extended beyond this they learned the trials and obligations of the war path, as well as the conduct of a war party, without being exposed to immediate risk. Later, when they had proven themselves reliable, they would join in running off the loose horse herds, until eventually gaining sufficient trust to be asked by the war leader to undertake the dangerous, but honorific, task of entering the camp and cutting loose the prized ponies picketed there.

Having captured ponies, the warriors made a headlong dash for safety. Traditionally they drove the captured herd non-stop for three days, changing mounts as they became fatigued, in order to put as much distance between them and any pursuers as possible, continuing thereafter at a more leisurely pace until they reached the third war camp. Here each man recounted his deeds, calling on a witness to corroborate his story, and each warrior claimed those ponies he had personally cut from a picket line. The war leader gave the less valuable horses to the warriors according to the bravery and courage they had displayed; but on driving the captured herd into the main camp, most of them immediately gave these away to relatives or to respected men they wished to honor. The war leader not infrequently disposed of all his gains in this manner, thereby gaining recognition for exceptional generosity.

Small scalp raids followed the same pattern, the only important difference being at the third camp, where the warriors blackened their faces to show they had taken a life and prepared the scalp by stretching it on a wooden hoop which was carried into the village on a pole. The larger revenge

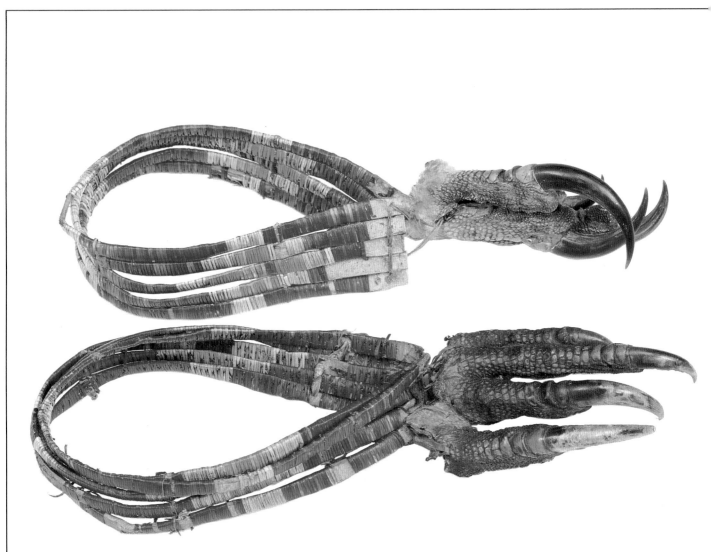

raids, however, were associated with much ceremony and ritual preparation and lacked the caution of the raiding parties. Prior to departure, and dressed in their finest clothing, the warriors made a mock attack on the camp, known to the Blackfoot as the 'Big Riding Dance', in which, after circling the tipis on horseback, they rushed upon the 'defenders' with all the startling ferocity of an attack on the enemy.

It was a spectacular event. Painted warriors, feathers streaming from war bonnets and tied in the ponies' tails, carrying long lances and firing guns into the air, raced into the camp from the four directions to converge on the mass of women, children and old men gathered in the center, all of them raising the 'war whoop' that was recorded by travelers in the Plains as the most terrifying sound imaginable. These war parties, sometimes containing several hundred warriors, rode out boldly against their foes. Their objective was not to run off a few horses or to surprise and scalp an enemy in a swift attack, but was to deal a damaging blow. It was on these occasions that warriors carried shields which were regarded as Medicine Bundles, attributing their power to the painted images they bore, the Crow being particularly renowned for the splendor of their shields. After the introduction of guns, against which the shield offered little physical protection, small models of the shield designs were often carried into

Above: These eagle claw armbands date from the middle nineteenth century. They are made from leather strips decorated with porcupine quills that have been painstakingly flattened between the teeth and dyed prior to being sewn in place.

Right: Plains Indian Warrior Societies usually had two members who were known as lance bearers. It was their duty to carry the long banners or lances into battle, such as this Arapaho example bearing hawk wing and tail feathers, and to plant them in the ground where the Society was to make its stand.

Above right: This Crow shield from the Schreyvogel collection was made about the middle of the nineteenth century. It is decorated with hawk and owl feathers and has a bird's head medicine attached to it which provided supernatural protection for its owner.

battles, when they were considered to have the same protective supernatural strength as the original. Even these large parties, however, after engaging in battle, immediately returned home to either celebrate their victory or mourn their loss.

Revenge raids were infrequent. The Blackfoot, as noted previously, conducted them only once every few years, whereas the Crow linked them with the annual Sun Dance, in which the pledger of the ceremony made a vow to lead a war party for the purpose of securing scalps that would ritually transfer mourning for the Crow's own dead to a rival tribe. Scalps obtained on raids were considered to be sacred objects endowed with warrior power, and not viewed simply as war trophies; and scalp dances which celebrated a victorious return were both joyous displays of triumph and a ritual transfer of power to the non-combatants of the camp. Women, dressed in the flowing feather war bonnets and quilled and fringed war shirts of their husbands, 'adopted' the soul of the dead warrior into their families, thereby releasing it from the earth and enabling it to travel as a spirit companion with the souls of their own deceased.

Revenge raids were almost inevitably a summer event, since this was the only time of the year when the bands gathered as tribes and large numbers of warriors could be recruit-

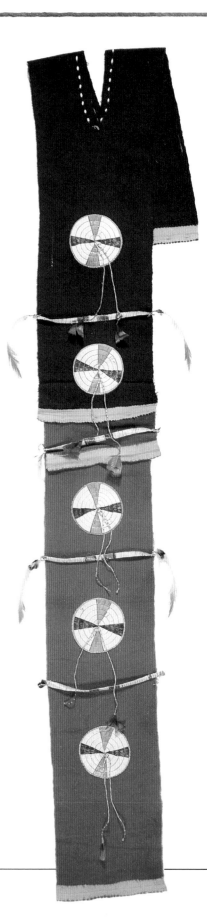

ed; although not directly linked with the Sun Dances or Renewal Ceremonies, they nevertheless became associated with them through vows to perform brave deeds if supernatural power was granted.

The Sun Dance of the Siouan-speaking tribes, from which the ceremony derives its generic name, was also a test of warriors' courage and endurance, since at the height of its performance young men had their breasts pierced, through which a stick was inserted and a thong attached to the central pole of the Sun Dance Lodge. By throwing their weight against the thong, they attempted to tear themselves free, falling into a faint on doing so. During this they were said to be 'like dead' and under the safekeeping of the supernaturals. A vision obtained at this time was believed particularly beneficial, since it occurred when power was being drawn into the camp circle by all the participants and was, therefore, far more potent than that an individual might attract on his own.

The village Mandan, also a Siouan-speaking group, held a similar ceremony known as the O-Kee-Pa, which George Catlin witnessed in 1832. It varies from the Sun Dance in that all men coming of age underwent the ceremony and not only those who had pledged a vow. In the O-Kee-Pa splints passed beneath the pectoral muscle so the aspiring warrior could be hoisted free of the ground on thongs pulled by men on the top of the lodge, when they remained suspended until they passed out and were lowered to the floor and the splints withdrawn. Another ordeal followed on their recovery. Buffalo skulls, attached to thongs in their backs, had to be torn free during the Last Race, a giddying dash in which they were literally dragged by two older warriors until the skulls broke free and the initiate collapsed. 'In this pitiable condition each sufferer was left, his life again entrusted to the keeping of the Great Spirit, the sacredness of which privilege no one had a right to infringe upon by offering a helping hand.'[11]

Catlin tells us the purpose of the O-Kee-Pa was 'to harden their muscles and prepare them for extreme endurance [and to] enable their chiefs, who were spectators of the scene, to decide upon their comparative bodily strength, and ability to endure the privations and sufferings that often fall to the lot of Indian warriors, and that they might decide who

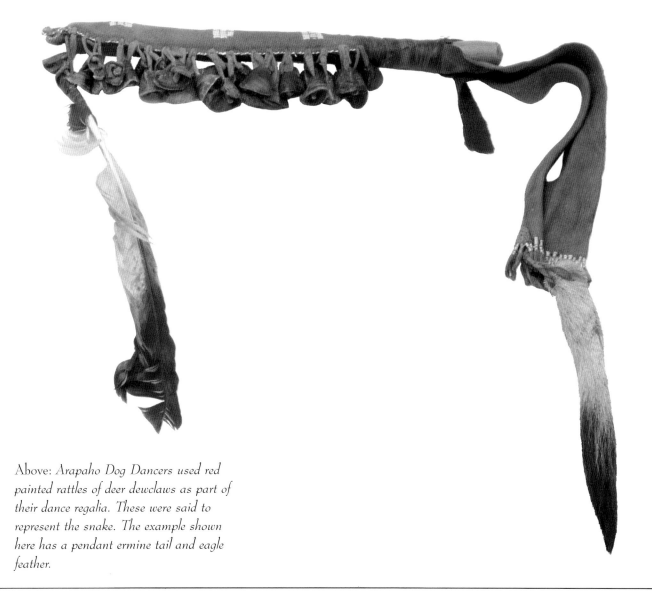

Above: *Labeled 'war bow, Arapaho', but Plains warriors seldom made this distinction; they did distinguish between high grade bows used in war and buffalo hunting, and inferior bows for more general use.*

Left: *A Warrior Society banner collected among the Mandan or Minnetaree by Friedrich Köhler before 1846. Sashes were pinned to the ground before the enemy, pledging the wearer not to retreat unless released from his vow by another Society member.*

among the young men was the best able to lead a war-party in an extreme exigency.'[12]

While this may be true in part, it fails to recognize the deep spiritual significance attached to the O-Kee-Pa, the Sun Dance, and to Renewal Ceremonies in which self-sacrifice was not practiced. All these were rituals whereby the power and strength of the tribe as a whole was renewed and in which a tribal identity was clearly established for the forthcoming year. Young warriors acting out vows of suffering, whether accompanied by the extremes of the O-Kee-Pa or not (among the Kiowa, for instance, the pledger danced to exhaustion without taking water, but the shedding of even

Above: *Arapaho Dog Dancers used red painted rattles of deer dewclaws as part of their dance regalia. These were said to represent the snake. The example shown here has a pendant ermine tail and eagle feather.*

accidental blood was a bad omen that brought the Sun Dance to an end) did so during a period of national rather than individual crisis, demonstrating their power, ability, and willingness to act as defenders not only of the local band or village but of the entire nation. The sacred nature under which these privations took place is also indicative of their role in protecting both the spiritual and physical unity of the tribe.

The 'good heart' displayed by these warriors is even more readily apparent in the Hunka ceremony of the Oglala Sioux, by which an individual was bound for life in blood-brotherhood to another, and by extension to all other Hunkas in the band or tribe. The origin of the Hunka lies with the Four Brothers who admitted a beautiful woman 'with the front part of her hair bound' into their tipi, and became suspicious when she refused to eat anything. Leaving their younger brother, Hakela, at home to watch the woman

Right: Mato-Tope (Four Bears), second chief of the Mandan, posed for this portrait by Karl Bodmer wearing a shirt of bighorn leather trimmed with ermine tails, locks of hair and panels of porcupine quillwork. A record of his war deeds is painted on the shoulders of the shirt, which also has red markings on the front indicating wounds he received in battle. The spear he carries bears the scalp of an Arikara warrior whom Catlin mentions as having killed Mato-Tope's brother, while the long feather headdress represents the deeds of the Half-Shorn Society to which Mato-Tope belonged.

Left: At the conclusion of the O-Kee-Pa, Mandan warriors who had pledged themselves to vows of endurance underwent the torments of 'the Last Race' in which they were dragged around the central plaza until buffalo skulls attached to their bodies by splints and thongs were torn loose. Unconscious and bleeding, they were left at the 'mercy of the Great Spirit' to recover from this ordeal, during which they might be granted a vision giving them supernatural power and protection.

Left: Prior to the last race, the warriors were subject to testing in the Medicine Lodge when they were hoisted aloft by thongs passed through the muscles of the chest or back. Note the buffalo skulls by which the warriors' bodies are weighted, the men with long poles who spin the hanging figures, and the masked shaman with a tomahawk at lower right. It was customary for the warriors, after being lowered to the ground and regaining consciousness, to go to this shaman where they sacrificed a finger of the left hand.

Right: *Little Bear, Steep Wind and The Dog, three Sioux warriors, were painted by George Catlin at Fort Pierre in 1832. Catlin's painting of Little Bear in profile (left) caused an argument in which all three warriors were to lose their lives. The Dog accused him of being only half a man, since only half his face showed, and in argument he killed Little Bear. The Dog fled but Little Bear's supporters, in a rage, killed Steep Wind, The Dog's brother. Some time later they found The Dog and killed him too.*

the three elder brothers went out to fetch wood, but she sent Hakela away on a false errand. Soon after going out he smelt something roasting in the tipi. Changing himself into a chickadee, he flew to the top of the lodge and peered in, where he saw the woman had taken men's heads from her bag and was cooking and eating them.

Hakela warned his elder brothers, and in a chase the woman beheaded them; but Hakela, being warned by the chickadee, shot an arrow at her forelock and killed her. He then gathered the remains of his brothers and built a small lodge, in which he sprinkled water on red hot stones and bathed the bodies in the steam, whereby they came back to life. The moral of the story is that the woman's hair style is that of a chief and shaman, which Hakela through his superior shamanic power is able to destroy, thereby removing a force for evil and replacing it with one for good. The power of the stones as 'life-givers' and their ability to unite and heal, as the Hunka unites two individuals and heals rifts between them, is also expressed.

'Stone-power' is explicitly named in the Hunka relationship between two warriors, since it was inspired by Inyan, the spirit of earth that dwells in the stone and which always speaks truthfully and with a 'straight tongue'; and a stone was painted during the ceremony because 'it pleases Inyan to

Above: *O-ke-hée-de appeared on the fourth day of the O-Kee-Pa. He represents pro-creative power; the rod he carries is attached to an artificial penis. By being defeated through the power of the medicine pipe this is wrested from him and given to the people.*

Above: *Central to the performance of the O-Kee-Pa were eight men, the Buffalo Bulls, whose dance ensured the fertility of the buffalo and the prosperity of the tribe. During their performance they used round rattles identical to this Assiniboine example.*

have red placed on a stone'. This gains even greater significance when linked to the myth of Stone Boy, in which the perfection of the Four Brothers, the original 'good hearts' of the Oglala, made them invulnerable to the trickery of Iya, the Evil Spirit, until she distracted them by sending a woman to live in their tipi. Eager to please their 'sister' the Four Brothers hunted a grizzly bear sent by Iya that led them to their destruction.

Stone Boy, born from a magic transparent pebble swallowed by his mother, tracked down Iya, slaying her and restoring the Four Brothers to life. In doing so he relied on powers given him by various people, and on which warriors would later depend in their battles against human foes. 'The shaman gave him a charm that would keep all harm from him. The old woman gave him a robe on which she had painted a dream. This dream made the robe magical so that it hid one who wore it from the sight of everything. The warrior gave him a magical spear that would pierce anything, a magical shield that would ward off anything and a magical club that would break anything. The hunter showed him how to find anything.'[13]

The significance of the Hunka was broader, however, since it could also unite individuals and bands from different tribes, even when they did not speak the same language. This

Above: Greater striking power was sometimes added to war clubs by incorporating a movable head consisting of a stone wrapped in rawhide and attached to the club handle by a flexible leather strip. Although the Sioux example shown here gives the appearance of being fragile, it was nevertheless an effective and deadly weapon in the hands of a skilled warrior.

*Left: When George Catlin painted this portrait of the Oglala Tchan-dee (Tobacco) in 1832, he described him as 'a desperate warrior, and . . . one of the most respectable and famous chiefs of the tribe' (**Letters and Notes**, vol. 1, p. 222). Tchan-dee is also shown, however, with the characteristic top-knot of a shaman, and therefore combined the roles of chief, warrior and shaman.*

*Below: In the ceremony to paint the red stripe of the Hunka and the black stripe of the Akicita, Oglala shamans dedicated a stone to Inyan (Rock), the primal cause of everything. During the dedication the stone was painted red 'in veneration of the Rock, for red is sacred and the Rock is pleased with this mark of reverence and may bestow perseverance and endurance on one showing it' (**Lakota Belief and Ritual**, p. 235).*

power came from a chief whose sons had been killed by the enemy, and who adopted a baby boy and girl he found abandoned in a lone tipi as his son and daughter. The boy became a great hunter and warrior so the chief's tipi is filled with enemy scalps to replace his lost sons; whereas the daughter, who is described as industrious and generous, has the ability to paint dreams (visions) on robes that even Iktomi, the Trickster, is afraid of. When the shamans asked the chief to tell them the last word that Whirlwind, the bringer of any events of a spiritual nature, had said to these magical children, he told them 'Hunka'. This was used as a name for the children and for anyone who desired to offer a great favor to another through the tie of blood-brotherhood.

Oglala warriors went to war feeling they were protected by the same supernatural forces that created the Hunka, yet at the same time were acutely aware their opponents drew on similar powers to resist them. Warfare, although apparently waged to raise individual status and to gain personal benefit through the acquisition of horses and war honors, was nevertheless conditioned by such tribal myths in which the relationship of the individual to the whole is expressed, and where any individual act of cowardice reflected on the entire community. In this context the Blackfoot belief that the 'warriors worked for the people' is more readily understood.

That the people also worked for the warriors is just as obvious, since warrior power demanded their recognition before it could be realized. This is abundantly clear among the Arapaho, where the safety of the individual and the tribe was vested in the Sacred Pipe, the most important and powerful Medicine Bundle, and through which an identity as an Arapaho was achieved. The Sacred Pipe, in fact, contained and represented the lifeblood of the entire nation.

The Arapaho, together with their close allies, the Cheyenne, were considered by neighboring groups as one of the strongest alliances on the Plains. An elderly Arapaho man, describing the enemies of the Cheyenne–Arapaho to Alfred Kroeber, said they 'fought most with the Utes because they were the strongest, and next with the Pawnees because they were the fiercest.'[14] In fact, all of Kroeber's

Cheyenne–Arapaho informants testified to fighting the Utes because they were the bravest after themselves; it is nevertheless apparent that the alliance regularly fought other tribes such as the Sioux, the Osage, and anyone else who happened to venture near their territories. The only tribes with whom they made a peace were the allied Comanche and Kiowa and Kiowa-Apache, although this did not occur until after 1830, when pressures from groups being relocated in Indian Territory or forced out of other areas through white expansion made co-operation vital to the survival of both the alliances.

Although revenge and horse raids were common among all the nomadic tribes and generally carried out with a similar belief in supernatural protection under a proven leader, some differences occurred in the southern areas. Both the Comanche and Kiowa commonly adopted brave opponents into the tribe. Berlandier tells us that 'sometimes in battle, when an enemy defends himself with courage and attracts attention for his bravery, the Comanches will try to capture him without harming him. They offer him hospitality, they say, to perpetuate the race of a warrior'[15] and among the

Above left: This powerful headdress of northern goshawk feathers is probably Dakota and comes from a region where Plains and Woodlands influences mingle. These aggressive birds, the largest of the goshawks, possess a temperament to which the warrior could relate in battle.

Above: Small talismans or amulets referring to an episode from the warrior's protective vision were often carried into battle. In this example from the Southern Cheyenne, a wooden snake effigy is coiled around a hoop filled with cord lacing.

Right: Wahktägeli (Big Soldier), a Yankton Sioux warrior, was about sixty when he posed for this portrait by Karl Bodmer. He told him the feathers bound to his hair with red cloth represented enemies he had slain.

Kiowa 'males ... are most commonly adopted into the tribe, and soon become the most expert leaders of war parties ... they sit in council with them, hunt with them, go to war with them, and partake of their perils and profits, and but few have any desire to leave them.'[16]

The dedication that might be shown by adopted members of the tribe is apparent from the famous fight when the Osage attacked the Kiowa and placed the women's severed heads in their brass cooking pots. In this battle 'a party of women was saved by a brave Pawnee living in the camp, who succeeded in fighting off the pursuers long enough to enable the women to reach a place of safety',[17] even though he could easily have escaped without putting his own life at risk.

Not all captives, however, reacted so favorably. Another Pawnee boy, captured by Sitting Bear in 1851 during a fight with visiting Pawnees who claimed to be friendly but carried concealed weapons, made a daring escape the following winter, taking with him the finest race horse of the tribe, a bay

Below left: Duke Paul of Württemberg collected this superb pair of leggings from the Yanktonai Sioux in the 1820s. They are made from the skin of the pronghorn antelope with very finely quilled side seams from which scalp locks are suspended. The privilege of wearing leggings decorated in this manner was reserved for proven warriors.

Below: Tokens granted to warriors as part of their medicine power were kept in bags made from the skin of the animal appearing in the vision. This Dakota Sioux medicine bag, collected by Prince Maximilian in the 1830s, is made from the skin of a badger and is decorated with beaded rosettes, quillwork and tin cone dangles. The neck of the bag has been sewn with red trade cloth.

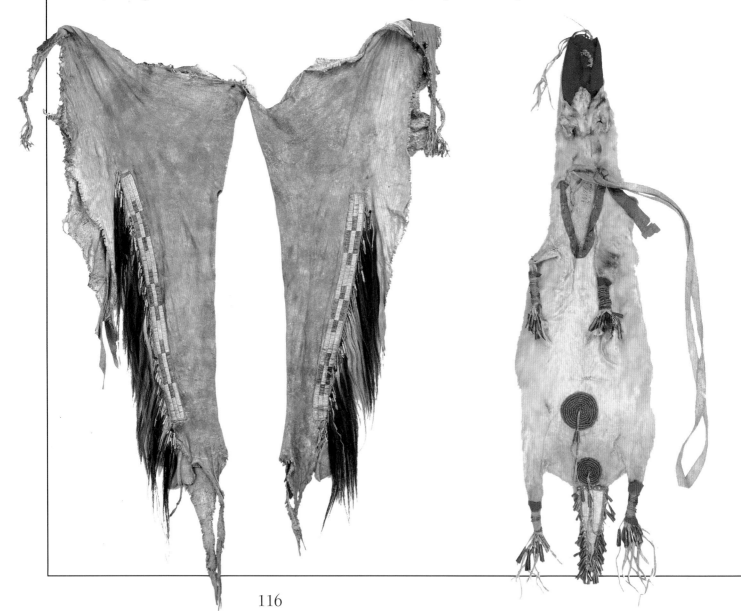

Above: *This small amulet consists of a string to which war medicines in the form of an incised bear claw and a small pouch have been attached, all of which has been painted red. It is typical of the type of object warriors used as protective talismans. Such talismans were sometimes worn around the neck, but just as frequently they would have been tied in the warrior's hair or fastened to the mane or tail of the war pony he rode into battle.*

pony known as Guadal-tseyu, or 'Little Red'. It is said the Kiowa felt the loss of this pony so severely that the whole tribe was crying, and regarded it of such signifance that it was recorded in their pictographic calendar depicting the most important event of the year. It may be that this particular horse represented a much deeper belief of the Kiowa, since having raced and beaten all the other ponies of the tribe it could be associated with the superior power of warriors who defeated every opponent.

The Comanche allies of the Kiowa placed an equally strong emphasis on the value of their horses. Catlin noted the Comanche, the 'lords of the southern Plains', spent so much of their lives on horseback that they were awkward when walking, but transformed into the most elegant of warriors when mounted. He describes young warriors showing off their riding skills; '[A Comanche] is able to drop his body upon the side of his horse at the instant he is passing, effectually screened from his enemies' weapons as he lays in a horizontal position behind the body of his horse, with his heel hanging over the horses' back; by which he has the power of throwing himself up again, and changing to the other side of the horse if necessary. In this wonderful condition, he will hang whilst his horse is at fullest speed, carrying with him his bow and his shield, and also his long lance of fourteen feet in length, all or either of which he will wield upon his enemy as he passes; rising and throwing his arrows over the horse's back, or with equal ease and equal success under the horse's neck.'[18]

Although the Comanche and Kiowa frequently sent out joint war parties, each observed its own ritual preparations and depended on different supernatural forces to guide them. Thus among the Kiowa the power of the Bear was highly respected and leading warriors often bore this honorific name. So strong was this power that other warriors were unable to address them by their personal names, since the mere mention of the word 'bear' was a threat to their own safety as usage had not been sanctioned. This respect for one of the great supernaturals may, in fact, partly account for the alliance between the Kiowa and Kiowa-Apache; the Kiowa-Apache, although speaking a totally different language, shared the same tradition, a belief they brought with them from the forests of the north where Bear Power was considered a potent and vital force.

The Comanche, however, considered the bear as a food source in much the same way as they thought of the buffalo or deer, and this almost split the co-operation between them and the Kiowa and led to the deaths of a number of Kiowa

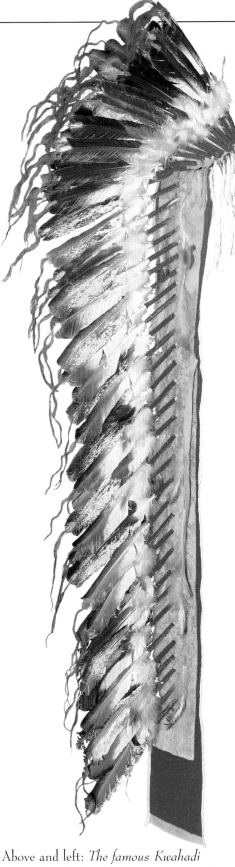

warriors. During a large combined revenge raid against the Utes in 1847, the war party camped with the Kiowa downwind of the Comanche and sent out hunters to secure food. The Kiowa hunters soon came back with two deer but in terrible anxiety, since they said the Comanche had killed 'that thing which can not be named'. The Kiowa war leader, Heap-of-Bears, together with Sitting Bear, trusting in their supernatural relationship with the animal to offer them some pro-

Above and left: *The famous Kwahadi Comanche chief and war leader, Quanah Parker, is shown left wearing a superb feather bonnet and trailer similar to that above. The bonnets, made from the black tipped feathers of the immature golden eagle, were honorific emblems of the most powerful warriors. One of the finest examples of these headdresses, this dates from about 1870.*

Far left and above: *The Comanche shield and cover shown here were collected by Jean Louis Berlandier in 1828. The cover (above, left) bears a stylized representation of a black bear, a black circle filled with black dots, a black line below this, and two black dots at the left. In common with many Comanche shields and shield covers, a medicine token, in this example consisting of fur feathers, has been attached. The shield itself (above, right) is fringed with red trade cloth to which are fastened seventy-three pelican feathers, and which has been elaborately painted in red and yellow. The central figure is difficult to identify, but may be either a man wearing a horned headdress or a representation of a buffalo. Two figures flank the central motif, painted in the characteristic black and yellow of early Comanche shields. When placed in their covers the feathers of such shields were folded back into the concave surface of the shield to protect them (far left).*

tection, crossed to the Comanche camp and asked them not to eat the bear because it was sacred. The Comanche, though sympathetic, insisted on cooking it anyway.

Throughout the night the wind carried the heavy, sweet scent of bear's grease across to the Kiowas, and in the morning Heap-of-Bears and Sitting Bear started back, not wishing to continue while they had 'power working against them'. A young Kiowa, Eagle Heart, who was known for his impetuous nature, persuaded many of the warriors of his own age who were eager to gain honors against the Ute to continue. Much later, when the war party was long overdue, four of these warriors straggled back into the Kiowa camp with the news that Eagle Heart and all the other young men had been killed when the Comanche, following their custom of leaving the battlefield if a Comanche death occurred, had abandoned them soon after the fighting started.

Although the Comanche never developed the strong warrior societies of the central and northern Plains, they nevertheless shared fully in the warlike characteristics common throughout the grasslands, and, according to some observers, excelled many of them in their proclivity to go to war. Newcomb wrote that 'among these peoples who have oriented their life around warfare, few have done so more thoroughly and completely than the Comanches ... in a very literal sense Comanche culture came into being through military prowess [and] blossomed through raiding, and nearly every aspect of life became intertwined in one way or another with the art of war.'[19]

THE SOUTHWESTERN DESERTS

CHAPTER FOUR

Left: Canyon de Chelly, Arizona, acts as a symbol for the cultures of the Southwest. White House Ruin, set in a natural cave on the canyon wall, was home to some of the ancestors of the modern Pueblo tribes, whereas in the historic period the canyon was the heartland of the Navajo, who raised their sheep and planted peach orchards in the canyon valley.

THE PLAINS APACHE were part of a group of linguistically related Athapascan-speaking peoples who had migrated from the north into the Southwest, where their cohesion was split by the Comanche in the 1700s. Migrating south from Wyoming, the Comanche drove the Kiowa-Apache before them and forced a wedge between the Apache groups, pushing the Jicarilla into the mountains further to the west, where they came under Puebloan influence, and leaving the Lipan, who had formerly been dominant in the area, to function as an intermediate group between the extremes of Plains and Southwest cultures.

The Jicarilla had many Plains traits, including the use of the tipi and a dependency on buffalo hunting; although they retained the northern Athapascan fear of the dead, they fully embraced the Plains ideal that a scalp could be used positively in securing the soul of an enemy to accompany one's own deceased on the spiritual journey to the 'other world'. This contradiction was resolved by reserving the privilege of taking a scalp to the ritually prepared leader of a raiding party. 'When anyone else killed a foe, he had to request the leader to remove the scalp for him [and] when a victorious war party returned home, the first action was to hold a ceremony over the warriors that the ghosts of the enemy might be driven away.' The scalps that had been taken 'were considered much too dangerous to entrust to the warriors; instead [the scalps] and all the possessions taken from the foes were put in the care of old men with the requisite ceremonial knowledge, to be sung over and cleansed.'[1]

Above: Apache caps decorated with turkey feathers and zigzag bead, button, or brass tack marked borders were worn during social dances and war preliminaries rather than on the war path itself. They might, however, be worn at dances held the evening before a war party left the camp on a raid.

Plains Apache groups were aggressive and warlike. John Cremony, in reference to one of their warriors, wrote 'all occupations unconnected with war or plunder are esteemed altogether beneath his dignity and attention ... but he is ever ready to take the war-path.'[2] This was clearly a response to the prevailing attitude of the Plains Indians, among whom honor and status could only be achieved through warfare, but other groups of the Southwest who held different ideals were to influence the Athapascans of the area.

Under these pressures the western Athapascans in New Mexico and Arizona, who had also migrated into the area as small independent groups, separated into the Mescalero, Chiricahua, Western Apache and Navajo, among whom cultural traits linking back to the rancheria tribes and the Pueblos are apparent in the adoption of limited agriculture and other culture traits. The Navajo developed this to the point where they became famed for their peach orchards in Canyon de Chelly – which led to their ultimate defeat by troops under the command of Kit Carson who spent five days destroying Navajo fields and forcing them into surrender – and for sheep-herding that provided wool for weaving their well-known blankets, a skill they learned from the Pueblo tribes.

In spite of these changes, the Apache groups kept many of their Subarctic traditions. With the exception of the Kiowa-Apache, none of them took over the highly organized Warrior Societies of the Plains or equated status with the acquisition of war honors and the boasting of war deeds; neither did they think of themselves as belonging to a 'tribe'. The local political, economic and military unit was the extended family, with distant relationships established with corresponding clan members in other groups. These sometimes united as small bands under the guidance of strong individuals but family ties frequently resulted in married couples moving to a different band to be close to relatives, which

Below: *Kiowa fringed and beaded moccasins.*

Below left: *Comanche fringed and painted woman's cape made from a single deerskin and collected by Jean Louis Berlandier in about 1840.*

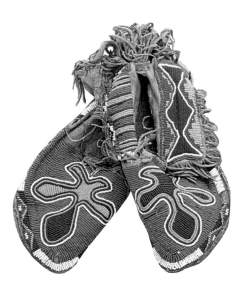

The region in which the Southwest and the Southern Plains meet saw a whirlpool of influences coming from every direction. Prominent among these, though rarely given the importance they deserve, were ideals introduced into the area by the Lipan Apache. It is very likely the Lipan were the first equestrian American Indians, and that other people moving into the area, such as the Kiowa and the Comanche, adopted many cultural traits from them. Cut fringe decoration, as on the Kiowa moccasins and Comanche cape shown here, are a typical form of Southern Plains decoration; but note the superb fringing of the Apache shield on the facing page. This early style of cape was worn on ceremonial occasions by the women of many tribes of the area, and it may be significant that it only appeared as a regular item of dress among the Apache.

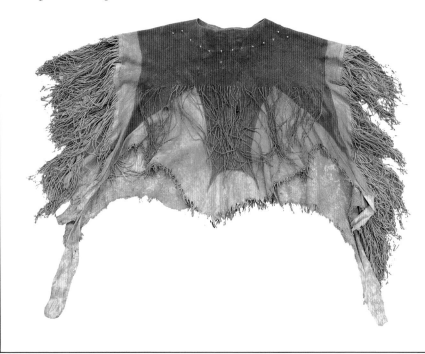

Below: *Double-layered shields were packed with absorbent materials to lessen the impact of a blow. Traditionally filled with either grass or compacted feathers, after European contact paper was often employed as a substitute. The heavy fringing replaces the feather decoration commonly associated with shields made by tribes of the Plains.*

prevented any form of tribal unity or of clearly defined roles for chiefs and war leaders.

Even today, the clan takes precedence over any other form of political or tribal organization. This is expressed most obviously in the annual Go-jii-ya of the Jicarilla, in which young men (formerly warriors) from the opposing red and white clans run a relay race to determine which clan will assume leadership of tribal affairs for the forthcoming year. That this is not purely secular leadership is evident from the

fact that shamans paint the runners, attaching feathers to the heels of their moccasins to give them the power of fast flight, and from the use of bowers, or clan houses, in which secret rituals are performed to denote the sacred character of the race.

Clan bonds and sacred power are expressed in the Fire Dances of the Mescalero, Chiricahua and Western Apache, in which masked dancers representing the Gans, or Mountain Spirits, race from their mythical mountain homes to attack a huge fire in the center of the camp, descending on it from the four directions. The relation between the Mountain Spirits and war is an evident one, since they gave a vision to the mythical Twins, Lame Boy and Blind Boy, from which the original warrior power descended, and the dancers wear headdresses painted with symbols of Lightning, the war arrow of Sun. The dancers were formerly prominent warriors of a single clan, and through the Fire Dance, as well as the Go-jii-ya race, the power of the clan, of brothers and cousins, and of warriors, is brought to the fore and demonstrated by the group.

Even though there was an almost total lack of formal organization beyond that of the family and clan, little true leadership in the sense of individuals having authority over others, and no fraternities of warriors, the Apache and Navajo nevertheless terrorized the Southwest and northern Mexico from their arrival in the area until they were finally starved into submission with the destruction of their horses, orchards, and fields, and from being denied access to hunting areas, by the U.S. army in the late 1880s. Prior to this they gained a reputation for being both elusive and fearless, and there was a grudging admiration for their ability to strike back effectively no matter what the odds against them. Captain John G. Bourke, who was General Crook's adjutant during his campaigns against the Apache and Navajo, wrote:

'No Indian has more virtues and none has been more truly ferocious when aroused. For centuries he has been pre-eminent over the more peaceful nations about him for courage, skill, and daring in war; cunning in deceiving and evading his enemies; ferocity in attack when skillfully planned abuscades have led an unwary foe into his clutches; cruelty and barbarity to captives; patient endurance and fortitude under the greatest privations.'[3]

But regardless of Bourke's comments the Apache and Navajo were not 'brave' in the sense of Plains traditions, since they regarded an unnecessary exposure to risk for the sake of gaining honors as the height of foolhardiness, and went to great lengths to avoid open combat with their ene-

Below: *Front and rear views of a nineteenth-century Apache cap made from white deerskin and decorated with owl feathers and paint. Although labeled 'girl's puberty cap' this identification is almost certainly wrong. Records of puberty ceremonies do not indicate use of such caps, although men are regularly shown wearing 'war caps' of this type and the owl is generally associated with warriors and with averting danger. The painting is directly linked with symbols of the Lightning Snake, the Stars, and the Sky, suggesting a relationship with the Gan spirits who inspired such powerful war leaders and shamans as Geronimo.*

Right: *This Lipan Apache warrior was painted in Mexico by the Italian artist Claudio Linati in 1828. Though it is a romanticized image, it nevertheless contains a wealth of ethnographic information. Of particular interest is the cut fringe decoration which can be seen beneath the shield and behind the rider's foot, and the feathered war cap he is wearing. The long lance, which was usually tipped with a blade taken from a saber, was a highly characteristic weapon of the equestrian Apache groups.*

mies; although if forced to do so they would, and did, fight courageously and without quarter. Stories are legion in which a lone and wounded Apache, cornered at a pass leading to one of their mountain hideouts, would hold vastly superior forces at bay while the rest of the encampment fled to safety; or of how bands of Apache warriors, sometimes numbering only twenty or thirty men, successfully eluded and inflicted punishing injury on thousands of U.S. troops, civilian volunteers, and Indian allies during the Apache Wars.

Although few of the white people involved in these wars knew the Apache character and temperament at first hand, frontier tales were rife with references to their ruthlessness and cruelty in torturing captives and the amusement they gained from doing so. Everyone knew 'authentic' reports of Apaches (there being no attempt to distinguish one band or group from another, regardless of the level of friendship or hostility) burying their victims up to their necks in the sand, covering their heads with honey, and then watching while the ants ate their eyes, lips, and tongues; of captives being tortured to death by women slicing off small pieces of their flesh; and of Mexicans, persuaded to give up their arms through promises they would be set free if they did so, being bound to wagon wheels in such a manner that their heads were suspended over small fires and their brains slowly roasted.

Many of these reports were fanciful exaggerations; some were true. Forced to the limits of their endurance by European atrocities – the Spanish, for example, garlanded the Palace of the Governors in Santa Fe with the severed ears

of their Apache and Navajo victims – the Indian warriors struck back in kind. More traditional was their adoption of enemy women and children. These are always referred to as 'war captives' or 'prisoners' in the early reports, but the kinder face of the Apache is reflected in the fact that many of them refused to return to the realities of life in white frontier society when the opportunity to do so arose.

The greater part of the fear with which the Apache were regarded stems from a situation in which few were free from their raiding. This, however, was considered by the Apache and Navajo as an economic necessity, since the raid was conceived as a means of obtaining 'the things men live by', and much of their economy derived from securing necessary items from neighboring groups. The distrust with which

Above: The Gan dancers posed for this photograph by Forman G. Hanna in 1925. Characteristic of the Gans are the elaborate headdresses and painted wands depicting symbols of powers, such as Lightning and Hummingbird, which assist the Gans. The Gans, or Mountain Spirits, were protectors of the people, but the fifth figure, standing on the other dancers' right, is a clown who burlesques their performance. His role is crucial, since by his antics he diverts any negative influence from interfering with the Gans.

their neighbors viewed them and the limited material products of early Apache and Navajo culture meant there were few opportunities to establish regular trade contacts. Thus they raided the Plains tribes, the Spanish and the early Texan and American settlers for horses and livestock, the Pueblo tribes for corn and agricultural produce, the Mexicans for guns and ammunition, and all of them for whatever plunder they could gain.

Such activity did not endear them to any of their neighbors, and they made few friends in the area; the Plains Indians tried to force them out, the Southwest Indians resorted to defensive tactics in order to keep them at arm's length, and the Spanish, the Mexicans, the Texans and finally the Americans all waged wars of extermination intended to rid the area of these marauders and render it safe from their raiding. In these attempts they were singularly unsuccessful, largely due to the Apache and Navajo habit of never willingly engaging in open battle, their superb qualities as guerrilla fighters, and their adeptness at concealing their presence until they were certain victory could be gained with minimum risk.

The Apache was said to be able to 'travel as invisibly as a ghost [and] appear or disappear as silently as a shadow'.[4] A legendary example of this comes from the Chiricahua, when a band of warriors was surrounded by a vastly superior force of U.S. soldiers. Realizing their situation was desperate, the war leader and shaman, Geronimo, pointed to a distant mountain, telling his men they should slip through the ranks of soldiers guarding their position and rendezvous on the mountain in four days. Using his shamanic power, Geronimo called on the spirits for help and a small sandstorm blew up, stinging the eyes of the soldiers and making it difficult for them to observe the movements of the Apaches. The warriors crawled from their hiding places, each holding on to the heel of the man in front, and in this manner passed between the soldiers, sometimes so closely that it is said they could hear their breathing. Geronimo's amazing feat is still commemorated today in a Fire Dance song of the Chiricahua.

Above: *Grenville Goodwin collected a set of Gan masks made by John Robinson, a San Carlos Apache, in 1901, of which this is one. Robinson may also have been the maker of the masks used in the 1925 ceremony shown at the left. Snake or Lightning symbols are very apparent on this example, which is attached to a hood dyed black with walnut juice. The form of the mask is a traditional which Robinson was taught by his father.*

Colonel John Cremony commented on their adeptness at seeming to 'disappear' when he wrote 'an Apache can conceal his swart body amidst the green grass, behind brown shrubs, or gray rocks, with so much address and judgement that any but the experienced would pass him by without detection at the distance of three or four yard' [5]and noted that 'they will watch for days, scanning your every movement, observing your every act; taking exact note of your party and all its belongings. Let no one suppose that these assaults are made upon the spur of the moment by bands accidentally encountered. Far from it; they are almost invariably the results of long watching – patient waiting – careful and rigorous observation, and anxious counsel.'[6]

The Apache and Navajo recognized this trait in themselves and deemed it a virtue, being completely bewildered by the American habit, when hearing a shot, of immediately rushing to the spot to discover the cause of trouble. Apache prudence and instinct would, in similar circumstances, cause them to scatter widely, the warriors making a long detour and finally coming up to the source of the shot on the 'by and by'; watching from places of concealment until they determined the cause, and only after carefully weighing every possibility deciding on an appropriate course of action.

Prudence was not, however, merely the result of caution and a sense of self-preservation, but stemmed from the deep belief that both raiding and war were supernaturally directed, and that the manner in which they were to be conducted had been determined by the gods who initiated them. When Sun placed the people on the earth, he instructed them as follows: '"When you reach the earth, don't do anything. Let me make the first slaying." Consequently, the first blow was struck at Big Monster by Lightning, sent by Sun, deafening the enemy, depriving him of sense, and softening him for the later blows of The Twins [Monster Slayer and Child-of-the-Waters, the offspring of Sun and Changing Woman].'[7] Because of this the Apache waited until the enemy was at a

Above: *In a photograph probably taken in the 1880s, the chief, war leader and shaman, Geronimo, is shown mounted in the center of a line of Chiricahua Apaches. The Apache dress of a shirt and waistcoat, breechclout and high moccasins and a kerchief or bandana tied around the head, with cartridge belts, is typical of the period.*

Above: *The Apache ranged widely on both sides of the U.S.–Mexican border, adopting some traits that clearly have their origin to their south. Among these was the use of the bola, a weighted thong that could be used to trip and disable an opponent's horse.*

Right: *The Apache inclination to wait and attack from ambush meant that shock weapons were used less frequently than among the Plains tribes. These early examples show, however, that the club was not unknown among Apache groups. The use of a red stone and horsehair relates to concepts apparent in Apache myth.*

disadvantage and considered the beginning of an event, or the first blow to be struck, as a sacred omen of the final outcome; it was not something to be rushed into headlessly, but required much thoughtful planning and ceremonial preparation.

Similarly, 'once the God People had put horses on earth, the Navajo and Apache sought them in the four directions. As their culture heroes had sought the horses of the gods [Monster Slayer had recovered Sun's favorite blue horse and restored it to him], now the people trailed the earthly models down with ceremony and song. Through every coulee and over every divide, they went on holy missions to capture and bring home horses.'[8] These were no ordinary animals, since they descended from the first horse made by Changing-Woman which had hooves of agate, mane from a rain cloud, and eyes from stars. Its teeth were of white shell and its heart of red stone, and it was guided by a bridle made from sunrays. When it spoke, it was with the voice of the black flute; and, they say, 'rainbow its gait was made'.

Apache and Navajo warfare was conditioned by this awe of the holy nature of all things, and by a religious outlook which demanded a cautious approach to anything where danger might be involved. The prevalence of raiding as a sacred quest meant that almost everything was carried out in a circumspect manner. Even village life was affected by this, since it was incumbent on the female relatives of a raider to observe strict ceremonial restrictions governing behavior, what foods might or might not be eaten, manner of talking, and so forth. 'Peace meant merely absence or end of war, not an ideal for which other values should be yielded. [Apache and] Navajo culture is built on the premise that war is necessary, that nothing esteemed can be achieved without it.'[9]

In addition, 'anyone whom they opposed was considered a monster and the enemy of all human life ... warriors sallied forth to engage no mere opponents but the would-be destroyers of their entire blessed race',[10] re-enacting in reality the mythical episode in which Monster Slayer and Child-of-the-Waters traveled the world destroying the enemies of the people. Monster Slayer was also the first to use 'enemies-against power', the real war power that guaranteed success but which could only be obtained by those who were ritually prepared.

To protect themselves in any dangerous undertaking and to ensure they took advantage of the disabling 'first blow' struck by Sun which would render their opponents vulnerable, war and raiding parties underwent spiritual purification before they set out, and considered the war path as a ritual act in which the powers of mythical heroes were sought as aids to ensure a successful outcome. Because Turtle and Green Frog, the two old warriors who started warfare between humans by leading Monster Slayer's forces in the first war party against Taos Pueblo, had spoken a language they called 'irritably they speak', raiding parties, on entering enemy territory, adopted 'not talking plainly', a war language in which circumlocutions were employed to indicate they were engaged in activities that involved war power.

Both Turtle and Frog were important deities. Turtle had a shield (his shell) that was impenetrable by any weapon, whereas Frog had helped The Twins acquire the first horses, and possessed a magic stone axe that would strike dead any enemy it was pointed at. They were assisted by Bear and Big Snake, the guardians of Sun's house, who both possessed the ability to travel invisibly among their enemies and to change shape as they willed. Bear, in addition, was able to frighten his enemies and send them into a trance, thus rendering them powerless.

Navajo and Apache raiders enlisted the power of Bear, Big Snake, Turtle and Frog on their expeditions, by painting symbols of them on their bodies and horses, thereby dedicating them to the gods and acquiring some of their characteristics as well as their protection. Hummingbird was also favored since he enabled a warrior to run fast and become like the hummingbird, which moves so rapidly that no one

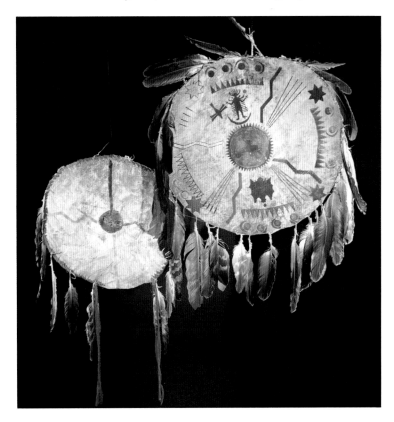

Right: The long arrow shown here is Mescalero Apache, the two shorter ones are from the Chiricahua. Even after the introduction and widespread adoption of firearms, many Apache warriors continued to carry bows and arrows which could be used in sudden and virtually silent ambushes when the report and flash of a rifle would have revealed their place of concealment.

Far right: This owl-feather decorated war cap was collected by Dr Washington Matthews among the Navajo in 1887, and is said to have been the last one used by the tribe. Its similarity to Apache war caps is evident. The eagle feather attached to the cap implies that it was worn only in war.

Left: These two Western Apache shields contain cosmological references to the Four World Quarters. The shield at left was made as a 'model' in 1932, but the larger shield dates well back into the 1800s. Its complex painting refers to a number of elements used in 'warriors against power'. Apart from its four divisions, the shield has a figure at the top which is a stylized representation of the culture hero Monster Slayer. To Monster Slayer's right is a hummingbird and on his left a lightning stripe, the bird used because of its ability to fly swiftly, and lightning as the weapon of Sun. The black figure at the bottom of the shield is a bat, since it was believed that bats were difficult to kill and were able to hide effectively. The dark green central motif is probably a representation of the Sun which, as the Giver of Life, served to protect a warrior.

can see him; so too was the black bat, because 'bat power' made a warrior elusive and unlikely to be hit. All these powers could be transferred to the warrior by a shaman who knew the correct songs and chants, and who would place sacred pollen – pollen which had been in contact with the animal intermediaries of the spirits and 'shaken off' in a highly ritualized procedure – in small war charms, or amulets, which were carried on the raid.

Raiding was an economic necessity and a spiritual undertaking, and both were firmly intertwined and entrenched in Apache and Navajo thinking; it is nevertheless clear that raids, regardless of their material value and importance, were conducted in a manner that emphasizes their sacred rather than secular context. Warriors became separate from secular life through the use of war talk, which it was believed might attract the attention of an enemy if used in the camps, they were also daubed with white clay on approaching hostile territory to disguise their human character, forbidden to eat salt while on the war path, because although this furnished strength and an ability to ward off danger it had proved ineffective when used by Water Sprinkler (whose role as a clown mitigated against the strengthening power of salt and reversed its effect), and desisted from the practice of smoking which in normal circumstances ensured communion with the spiritual forces.

These, and numerous other taboos and restrictions, emphasized the fact that the objective of the raid was a spiritual one. Through this the logic of the 'enemy-monster' can be explained, since if the Apache and Navajo were 'Dine', The People, then their opponents, who were decidedly 'non-Dine' since they were speakers of other languages, must accordingly be assisted by the Monster Gods who were the antagonists of Monster Slayer and Child-of-the-waters. In this sense, Apache and Navajo attacks, even though often carried out by only two or three warriors intent on capturing horses or other goods under the cover of night, had all the character and meaning of a crusade through which the 'evils' inherent in the world could be controlled.

But raiding could, obviously, meet with opposition in which blood might be shed, and such deaths needed to be avenged to prevent the monsters gaining ascendancy. Monster Slayer assisted avenging parties directly by throwing rainbow and lightning around the party to protect them during their attempts to secure an enemy scalp, over which purification rituals could be performed in order to dissipate adverse influences. They were, however, subject to fewer restrictions than raids and were frequently led by the family suffering loss. Both men and women took part and, although the number of women fighters was limited to direct kin, they have been credited with being bolder and showing a greater willingness to take risk.

Avenging parties were larger than those assembled for raiding, often containing as many as forty participants. In an often repeated tale of a revenge battle between the Navajo and Hopi, the Tasavuh (Navajo) assembled a large force in the valley below the Hopi villages. The Hopi, whose own name Hopitú means 'People of Peace', had driven their sheep into the village, posted guards around the perimeter to protect the women and children, and issued bows, arrows, clubs and two or three stout buckskins to serve as armor to each of the warriors, who established a line between the avenging Navajo and the village.

'Obeying the chief's order, they did not draw their bows but waited for the Tasavuh to shoot the first arrow and so take the blood of battle upon themselves'; but the Navajo waited, explaining years later that their shamans had a vision of two tall men dressed in white who marched back and forth in front of the Hopis to protect them. This stalemate continued until noon, when 'a strange thing happened. A woman with a spear burst out of the ranks of the Tasavuh, calling them cowards and men with faint hearts and demanding that they follow her. Two Tasavuh warriors, carrying

Above: *There is some confusion over this photo of Ya-Va-Ki-Shi, since his name is Yavapai but he is described as being an Apache scout. The Yavapai did not make owl feather caps, and the one shown here is Western Apache, so it is probable that Ya-Va-Ki-Shi was working as a scout in one of the Apache detachments.*

Right: *The Navajo adopted the use of precious metals for bridles from their first contacts with the Spanish, from whom they obtained horses and silver through trade. It was not until the 1850s, however, that they learned silver-working techniques from the Mexicans and began to incorporate symbols that derived directly from their own mythology. The Sun String Bridle shown here was made about 1870 and was felt to draw the power of the life-giving Sun into the pony.*

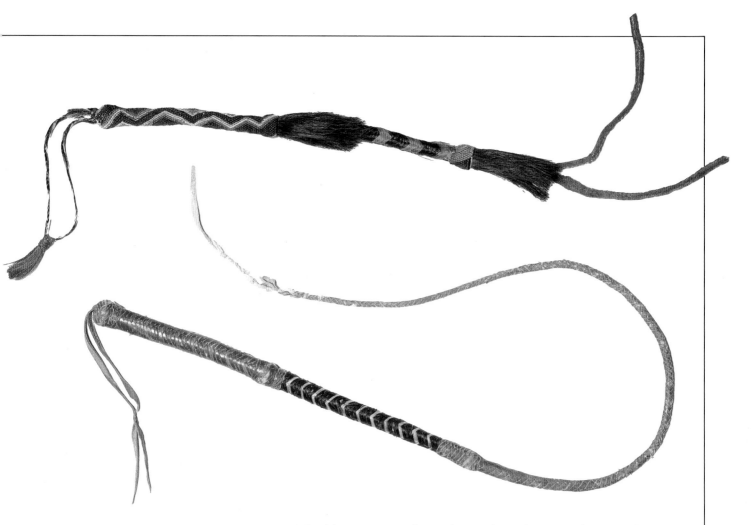

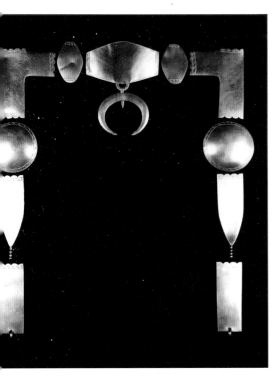

Above: *Closely associated with the adoption of an equestrian lifestyle by the Navajo was the development of a related complex of horse trappings and riding gear. The Sun String Bridle shown below is an example of this, as are the fine examples of riding quirts here.*

shields to protect her, advanced to the Hopi line ... whereupon a Hopi threw his throwing-stick with a wide, rolling motion. The stick flipped over the shield of one of the warriors, struck the man on the head, and killed him. The battle then began.'

It was a terrible fight that lasted until sundown, and in which a young Hopi warrior named Chiya killed many of his enemies, leaping from behind rocks to kill one Tasavuh after another. The Tasavuh were driven back with heavy losses on both sides and the Hopi village was saved; but Chiya, at the sight of the innumerable dead and wounded and of the horrible mutilations that had taken place, 'had bad dreams night after night and had to be given ceremonial help before he was finally cured of them'.[11]

The Hopi in this battle with the Tasavuh were one of the Pueblo tribes. The Pueblo Indians lived in adobe villages scattered throughout Arizona and New Mexico, many of them situated along the Rio Grande Valley and the neighboring vicinity, and although each of these villages was a politically and economically independent unit, they traded regularly among each other and can be grouped by language. Speakers of various Tanoan dialects, which represents the largest language group of the area, include San Juan, Santa Clara, San Ildefonso, Pojoaque, Nambe, and Tesuque (speakers of the Tewa dialect), Isleta, Picuris, Sandia and Taos (speakers of Tiwa), and Jemez (speakers of Towa). Speaking a separate language known as Keresan were

Acoma, Cochiti, Santo Domingo, San Felipe, Santa Ana, Laguna and Zia. The Hopi were speakers of a Shoshonean dialect, very distant relatives of the Tanoan group, and the Zuni spoke an independent language unrelated to either Tanoan or Keresan.

All the Pueblo tribes shared the Hopi ideal of peace, and although far from being meek and submissive were essentially non-aggressive, striking back when forced to do so but without any tradition of unprovoked warfare or raids for depredation. Warriors were here the guardians of the villages, often forming a distinct ceremonial group, and any acts of violence came under the ritual control of the War Priests who, in many respects, are personifications of characters equivalent to the Apache Twins, Monster Slayer and Child-of-the-waters. Among the Keresan-speaking Pueblos, for example, the War Priests are Masawi and Uyuyewi, which are also the names of the mythical Twin War Gods.

The War Priests, however, clearly have a defensive rather than offensive role and function in many aspects of Pueblo life that are only indirectly related to war. Thus at the Pueblos of San Felipe and Cochiti it is their duty to guard the medicine societies during ceremonies, to supervise the tending of the Cacique's (Chief Priest) fields, to control all activities relating to communal rabbit hunts, and to censure and punish any member of the community who breaches the customs and etiquette of the village. They also seek out and punish the instigators of instances of witchcraft. In this manner they are the guardians of Pueblo life and custom, because it is their duty to discover and prevent anything that might upset daily routine or ceremony.

In war, of course, the War Priests were dominant, although this has to be understood from the view that the Cacique was the repository of power, including that for war and the hunt, but it was through the War Priests that this was exercised. Power itself came to the Cacique from the Kachinas, the messengers of the spirits who had originally lived among the people and who now appear as costumed dancers in many Pueblo ceremonies, with the Chakwena Kachinas specifically controling the forces that might be used in war. At Zuni the Chakwena songs are war songs, and a Chakwena Woman Kachina features in myth as a warrior; at Hopi, however, the Chakwena has no song but merely utters "hu-hu", indicating he is short of breath since he was shot with enemy arrows when he rushed out to defend the village after the Spider clan introduced evil into the world through a misuse of their power. Also associated with this battle at Hopi is Héhewúti, or He'e'e, the Warrior Kachina Maiden.

Above: *The pride of the Navajo warrior was expressed most succinctly through his blanket, which was also a reflection of the power of the women in the family. Woven by women but worn only by men, the blanket, when worn, was considered to become animated by the forces inherent in the canyons and landscapes of the Southwest. Although weaving was a skill the Navajo learned from the Pueblo tribes, the patterns and meanings incorporated in their blankets derive from an Athapascan view of the world which has its origin in the far north.*

Right: *This pointed Navajo cap was said to have already been old when it was collected by Jesse Walter Fewkes in 1895. Unlike some of the Apache feather decorated caps, this example has been dyed with red ochre, has painted seams, and is decorated with bird talons and red dyed horsehair in addition to feathers. It is of a type that the Navajo claimed could only be worn by warriors.*

She is a frightening figure. 'On her black mask are painted two great yellow eyes with black pupils, a rectangular mouth edged with red and showing her bared teeth. From it protrudes her long red tongue. Her hair is done up in a whorl on one side and hangs full length on the other side.'[12] She looks untidy, and carries a bow and a quiver full of arrows. He´e´e's appearance is a reminder of the terrible day that war was introduced. When the village was attacked at dawn, He´e´e had only recently risen and her mother was still dressing her hair, which is why this is done up in a whorl on one side but is long on the other (the traditional 'butterfly' hairstyle of a Hopi maiden has a whorl over both ears). Throwing on her clothes but with no time to dress properly, and grabbing a bow and quiver of arrows, she rushed out in a unsuccessful attempt to defend the village. Because of this her song is said to echo the cries of the people in distress.

It was at this time that the Kachinas separated from the people. Realizing the situation was hopeless and that the Spider clan would overrun the village and destroy the inhabitants, the Kachinas advised the Bear, Corn, and Parrot clans

Above: *Photographed in Keams Canyon on the Navajo Reservation in 1892, this man is described as a war captain. Note the similarity in shape between his cap and that shown below, and the typical Apache/Navajo lance.*

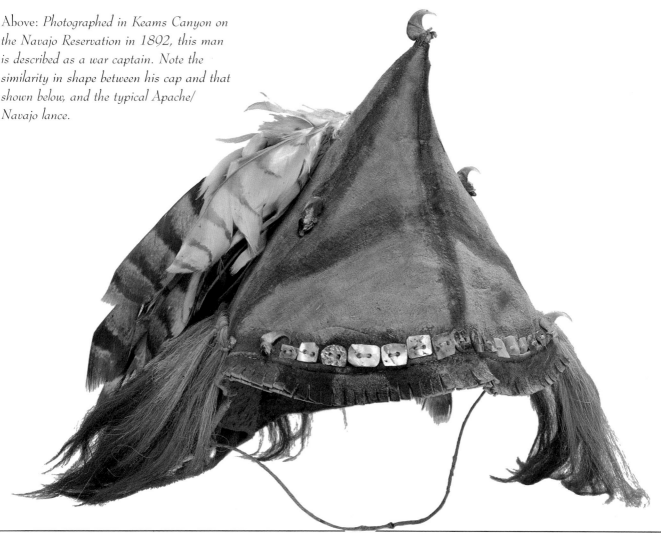

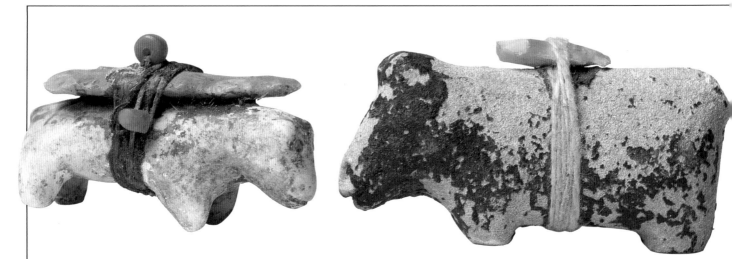

to dig a tunnel through which they could escape, telling them that they would stay in the village to defend it until the clans reached safety, but would then retreat to the high mountains from which they could be recalled when need arose. They instructed the Coyote clan to follow last. Coyote, although he was indestructible, was a Trickster who thought only of his own needs and who might therefore disrupt the escape of the other clans if he felt there was any advantage to be gained for himself.

It may be, however, that Coyote followed last because of his reputation as a warrior. Mischief-maker he may have been, but at times he was also known as First Warrior and there were few, even among the Kachinas, who were able to openly challenge his power or defy his cunning, even though they might deride him for his foolishness and unbearable vanity. When Coyote was defeated in any endeavor, it was usually because his own pride prevented him seeing danger and taking steps to avoid it. At other times he is referred to as First-to-get-angry, due to his unpredictable character and tendency to take umbrage at any slight; but it is also a fact

Above: *The Zuni believed animal powers could be propitiated through likenesses that were kept as fetishes. Some of these came to have tribal significance through their link with animals that protected the tribe, and those which occurred in natural shapes resembling the animal, or which required little change to make the form evident were most revered. Feathers or arrow heads attached to the fetish were felt to empower it.*

Below: *Acoma Pueblo is popularly known as Sky-City due to its location on top of a 400 foot mesa near Albuquerque. With the advent of nomadic raiders in the Southwest many of the Pueblo tribes relocated to sites such as this, or reinforced the township with strong adobe town walls that could be easily defended. This photograph was taken inside the Pueblo in about 1885.*

that anger, because it disrupts the normal pattern of life, is an essential component of war power. This aspect of Coyote is reinforced at the Hopi village of Walpi, where an image of Masawa (equivalent to the Keresan war god Masawi) is kept in the Coyote clan house and has an associated ceremony that is conducted by the Coyote clan chief and is connected with war traits.

Coyote is an appropriate character to have warrior power, since his contrary nature and the almost totally negative light in which he is seen reflects the Pueblo view of warfare. We find none of the positive aspects of war that were indulged in by the Apache, and it is considered wholly as an evil that has to be borne reluctantly but which is nevertheless unavoidable; even though the Pueblos did not fight among themselves to any great extent, with the exception only of some family feuding that the War Priests generally kept in check, there were aggressive tribes such as the Apache and Navajo, the Ute and the Comanche who regarded the townships as a source of rich plunder. It is, in fact, a widely believed local tradition that the once populous Pueblo of Pecos was abandoned after a shattering raid by the Comanche because Pecos was harboring a fugitive war party of Jicarilla Apache.

Warrior Societies provided active defence against raiding by these tribes. At San Felipe this was the Opi, whose members 'wear a bear claw necklace, have a bear bone whistle suspended from the neck, a katsanyi apron, or kilt [a grey buckskin kilt with a black horned toad painted on the front]; the body is painted black, they have stcamum on the face under the eyes [a black sparkling granulated substance]; the hair hangs down the back; there is some waboctca [fine white eagle down] on the top of the head; in the right hand each carries an arrow, in the left a bow.'[13] At Hopi the corresponding society is known as the Kaletaka, whose members attend every sacred ceremony carrying whips of yucca with which they drive back anyone who is uninitiated in the rite and therefore forbidden to see its performance, and at Acoma and Santo Domingo this role is fulfilled by the Flint Society. Among the Zuni they were the Priests of the Bow.

Members of these societies were warriors who had killed an enemy in battle and taken the scalp, but this needs to be

Above: *The characteristic high-sided moccasins of the Pueblo tribes provided a firm footing and, worn with a type of gaiter, effective protection against rattlesnakes with which the area abounds. Everyday pairs were often undecorated white leather, but for dance performances in which the benefits of the spirits that brought rain or which protected the village were sought elaborate colored insets and quillwork might be applied. The Zuni moccasins shown here were made in 1915.*

thought of in terms of Pueblo theology. The dead of both the enemy and of the community were believed to be potent Rainmakers – essential to these farmers living in a semi-arid environment – and the scalp, if treated properly, harnessed these powers and brought them to the people's aid; thus the scalps would be brought back and entrusted to the care of the War Priests.

At Zuni, 'the scalp throughout the long and elaborate ceremonial of the war dance is the symbol of the man who has been killed. The purpose of the ceremony is both to signalize the initiation of the new member of the war society and to convert the scalp into one of the Zuni rain-making supernaturals. It must be honored by the dance and must be adopted into the pueblo by the usual adoption rites. So the scalp is washed in clear water by the aunts of the slayer and adopted into the tribe [transforming] the valueless enemy into a sacred fetish of the people.'[14]

Being in the proximity of a scalp was, nevertheless, considered a grave risk, to the extent that at the Hopi village of Walpi they could not be brought into the village precincts but were deposited in a crevice, or shrine, in the boulders of a rock terrace to the southwest. Another shrine placed to the west of the Hopi village of Oraibi suggests this was formerly a widespread practice, although more recently the power of the scalps was contained within the 'scalp-house', an irregular conical mound of earth and stone slabs on the edge of the village in which the scalp, having been placed in a pottery jar and ritually 'fed' with pollen, was placed together with carved fetishes of the war gods.

Similar fetishes placed in the six war shrines surrounding and protecting Zuni Pueblo are connected with Masawa, thereby bringing the power of the War God directly to bear in the protection of the trails and paths leading to the village. They were also carried by warriors at all times. It is said that 'the [flint] arrow-point, when placed on the back of the fetich, is emblematic of the Knife of War, and is supposed, through the power of Sáwanikia or the "magic medicine of war" to protect the wearer from the enemy from behind or from other unexpected quarters. When placed "under the feet" or belly, it is, through the same power, considered capable of effacing the tracks of the wearer, so that his trail may not be followed by the enemy.'[15]

Inspired by such powerful and dangerous fetishes as these, the Warrior Societies were ready to take the lead in defence of the village, to guard its perimeter if enemies were reported nearby, and to ensure that men were protected in the fields by day, that women and children were secure in the houses at

Below: *The Hopi always felt more secure after the arrival of the Heheya marked the return of the Kachinas to the villages after their annual sojourn in the mountains. In the background of this photograph, taken in 1870, is Poli Kachin Mana, the Butterfly Maiden, whose white cloak of deerskin is symbolic of purity and virginity.*

Right: *This Heheya mask was worn by a dancer who initiated the Powamu, or bean-planting season. Most Kachinas were concerned with growth and fertility and thought of as Rain-Bringers, not as warriors, yet their presence in the village when workers in fields were vulnerable was felt to offer supernatural protection.*

night. They also undertook their role as the guardians of the villages from any other adverse influences stemming from outside or within the community.

Additional security was provided by the construction and location of the village. External pressures about AD1100 had forced the ancestors of the historic Pueblo tribes to abandon their earlier scattered encampments and coalesce into larger and easily defended communities, or townships. The now-abandoned Pueblos of Mesa Verde, for instance, are in natural caves located on the canyon walls where access was only possible via rope ladders dangling over precipitious, near vertical cliff faces. Other villages, such as Pueblo Bonito in Chaco Canyon, are three or four storys high and surrounded by solid exterior walls in which there are no windows, doors, or other openings. Entrance to Pueblo Bonito was by wooden ladders over the tops of the walls and across the roofs of the buildings.

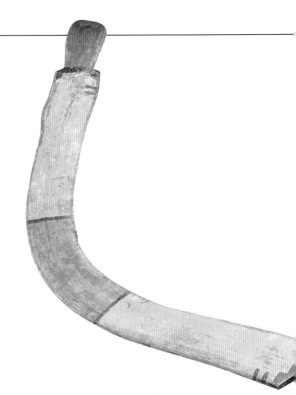

Why the people should have left their previous dwellings to move into the caves or what urged them to construct formidable fortresses remains a mystery and is probably due to a combination of factors; prominent among these is almost certainly a threat from roving bands of nomadic raiders and hunters, even though there is no archeological evidence to support an argument that large-scale warfare was taking place.

Their occupation of these fortified towns was, however, short-lived, since by AD1300 the populations were moving out again and establishing settlements close to their fields on level country; but with the arrival in the area of the ancestral Apache and Navajo, and possibly increased raiding from other tribes in the vicinity, many of them again moved their villages, this time to defensive locations on the mesa tops. Perhaps the most stunning of these is Acoma Pueblo, known as Sky City from its magnificent location several hundred feet above the plain on the top of Corn Mesa.

The perceived threat to village security was apparently so strong that simply locating at naturally protected sites was insufficient, and the architectural design of many of the Pueblos shows they were clearly intended to resist any attempts at storming them that the nomadic raiders may have considered. Part of an ancient protective wall remains standing at Acoma Pueblo, while at Taos, which is a valley rather than mesa town, the old town wall still completely encloses the village and shuts it off from outside intrusion. Taos tradition maintains that this wall was sentinelled by the Warrior Society as 'guardians against invasion'.[16]

Not all the neighbors of the Pueblos harbored aggressive instincts. Trade was brisk and friendly relations maintained with the Pima and Papago, who were highly successful agriculturalists and cotton growers living in villages on the Gila and Salt rivers which they had occupied for as long as the eldest members of the tribes could remember, and whose grandfathers had recalled living in these same places in their childhood. They shared Pueblo ideals of peace but when besieged by the Apache or the Yuma they fought back hard, 'like beasts of prey, like raptorial birds' according to their ceremonial war songs; yet their general attitude to bloodshed is summed up by the ritual phrasing with which these songs always close: 'You may think this over, my relatives. The taking of life brings serious thoughts of the waste.'[17]

This sense of waste meant that among the Pima and Papago warfare was limited to retaliatory raiding instigated by the family who had suffered damage, or by a group of several unrelated warriors if the loss were felt as a tribal one. At

Below: *Sip-ikne, the All-Color or Warrior Kachina, was a powerful protective deity of Zuni Pueblo. His warrior character is indicated by the yucca leaf whip and bow and arrows carried by the dancer who impersonated him. The colors are those of the six directions.*

Left: *The throwing stick was an inoffensive weapon that was widely used by the Pueblo tribes for hunting rabbits rather than for aggressive purposes. That it could be used for defence is, however, indicated in the story of the fight between the Hopi and the Tasavuh (pp. 132–3). This wooden example is painted red and black and was collected at Zuni Pueblo in 1915.*

Below: *This photograph was taken from the rooftops of Zuni Pueblo and provides a clear view of the flat-topped mesa of Taaiyalone, or Corn Mountain, in the background. In 1632, under increasing pressure from the Spanish, the inhabitants of Zuni fled for temporary refuge to the top of Corn Mountain.*

such times they designated certain men to act as scalp-takers, others to recite formal speeches which appealed to the spirits for assistance, and called on the shamans to utilize the powers they obtained in dreams to guarantee success. In many ways this was an essential aspect of defence, since their settled villages of pole and brush houses strung along the river banks were highly susceptible to surprise attacks and raids. They posted guards if there was any suspicion of danger, but the first line of defence was to ensure their neighbors knew beyond doubt they would strike back in force if they were molested.

Even though they had no functional war chiefs and no means whereby acts of courage or daring by the warriors could be publicly recognized and encouraged, they were nevertheless capable of fielding large numbers of fighters when the occasion demanded and fully able to inflict punishing damage on anyone who dared interfere with the tranquility of their lives. Both Pima and Apache traditions state that when these two tribes fought it was always the Pima who emerged as the victorious party, reinforcing the fact that

when the Pima were forced to act in this manner they did so regretfully but determinedly. The scalps taken in their battles, consisting of only four hairs from the head of the deceased, were purified and used in rain-making rites similar to those of the Pueblo tribes; but sorrow accompanied any killings, and the shedding of blood was avoided if possible.

Someone who had killed an enemy and the person appointed to take the hairs that represented a scalp were considered to be contaminated and regarded as dangerous influences until released from the stigma of having undertaken aggressive actions. On their return to the village they were separated from other people, obliged to wear their hair in a peculiar knotted fashion through which a scratching stick was inserted, since touching one's own body would spread the contamination, and were generally avoided by the general populace. Only after a sixteen-day curing rite, marked by periods of thirsting and fasting and during which they stayed in seclusion, were the slayer and the scalp-taker considered free from evil influences that could result in insanity if not ritually cleansed.

Ruth Benedict described a slightly different treatment in the case of someone who had taken a scalp '... they made of it a terrible danger crisis. The slayer was in supernatural danger, and was purified for twenty days, sitting in a small round

Above: The black and white striped Ka-Hopi Kachina, or Koshare, offered relief from everyday worry by presenting a burlesque of normal activity. In a contrast to Hopi ideals of restraint the Ka-Hopi were gluttons and free from restraint, running around the plaza during sacred ceremonies begging food and making ridiculous imitations of the dances that were taking place. As invisible spirits of the deceased they were highly respected and believed to possess power that influenced the growth of crops and magically protected the Pueblo from enemies.

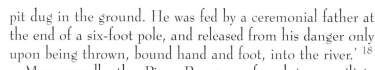

Above: A mask of Koyemsi, the Mud Head, who, like the Ka-Hopi, is also a clown. The Koyemsi perform in the periods between dances while the Kachinas are resting, entering the plaza across the roofs of the buildings and encountering many mock problems in the course of their journey. For them everything is insurmountable without numerous false tries and loud discussions in shrill voices. The horseplay of the Koyemsi is not without sacred significance, since it is they who protect the Pueblo while the Kachinas rest.

pit dug in the ground. He was fed by a ceremonial father at the end of a six-foot pole, and released from his danger only upon being thrown, bound hand and foot, into the river.'[18]

More usually the Pima–Papago preferred to conciliate their enemies rather than antagonize them. An example of this was when the Maricopas, speakers of a Yuman language and formerly hostile to the Pima, incurred the displeasure of the more powerful Yuma tribe in the early 1800s. Under pressure from the Yuma, who had allied with the Cocopa, the Maricopa fled to the Gila River, where they asked the Pima for protection with a request that their former disagreements be forgotten and that they join together to fight their mutual enemies. The Pima deliberated on this matter for several days. Such an alliance was clearly to their advantage, but they were worried that the Maricopa, whose aggressive character they were well acquainted with, would flout the Pima principles of restraint.

Eventually they agreed to let the Maricopa settle in their territories, 'but it was made a sine qua non that the newcomers must forever renounce their warlike propensities – for, said the Pimos, we do not wish to incur the vengeance of the Tontos, the Chimehuevis, the Apaches, and others, by making useless raids against them; they have nothing to lose, and we have, and you must confine yourselves solely to revenging any warlike incursions made either upon us or upon yourselves. You are free to worship after your own manner, and govern yourselves according to your own laws; but you must be ready at all times to furnish a proportionate number of warriors to protect the general weal.'[19]

This generosity on the part of the Pimas was readily accepted by the Maricopa, as it was by numerous other groups who, though previously hostile, joined the Maricopa under Pima and Papago protection. By the end of the 1800s their territory was home not only to the Maricopa, but also the Halchidhoma, Kohvana, Halyikawamai, and Kaveltcadom or Cocomaricopa, all of them refugees from the Yuma. It is likely these refugees introduced some changes in Pima and Papago warfare, since in spite of their obvious reluctance to act in anything other than a defensive manner they developed some specialized warriors, skilled in the use of either the bow or club, who formed fraternities in which membership was clearly based on fighting ability.

Even so, these fraternities never acted in concert and appear to have functioned more as social organizations than as military ones, since they did not have appointed officers

Above and above right: *Zuni Pueblo was ritually protected by small shrines outside the town on the pathways leading into it. To propitiate the spirits and ensure their help, offerings were left at the shrines accompanied by pahos, or prayer sticks, such as those shown here.*

Left: *He´e´e, the Warrior Kachina Maiden, is a familiar figure at both Zuni and Hopi Pueblos, where she is believed to have rushed out half-dressed to save the town when it was besieged. Her name reflects the cry of distress she uttered at the apparently impossibly task she faced to prevent the destruction of the Pueblo.*

Right: *In alternate years at the Hopi Pueblos, the Snake Priests perform the Snake Dance in which dancers circle the plaza carrying live snakes in their mouths. Hopi priests claim the snakes, by association with Lightning, bring rain to the village and secure the help of this war god.*

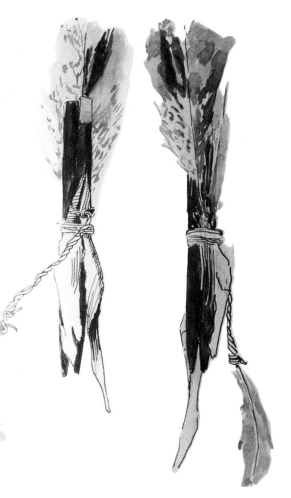

or ranked positions, and offered no incentives to aspiring warriors. That they were influenced by Maricopan ideals is readily apparent. All the Yuman-speaking tribes of the Lower Colorado in Arizona and California separated their fighting members into club-men or bow-men, who were inspired to develop skills in the use of these weapons after receiving sanction to do so in dreams. Such men placed themselves under the tutelage of older warriors with proven proficiency in the use of these weapons.

Here, too, we find the same use of formal speeches on the warpath, the appointment of specialized scalp-takers, a belief that a scalp is maleficent, and lengthy purification rites that were incumbent on both the slayer and the scalper. But contrary to the Pima–Papago belief that war should only be resorted to for retaliatory or deterrent purposes – they would terminate a fight and return to their villages to undergo purification from the shedding of blood as soon as deaths occurred – among the Yuma and Maricopa it was 'a nationalized sport: national in that large numbers were involved; a sport in the sense of displaying both a formalized procedure and a willingness to stay in the fight to the finish'.[20]

There is little evidence to show that the Yuma were an especially aggressive people, and it has even been suggested that warlike tendencies developed only because of a need to defend their unprotected flank from incursions by bands of raiders from the east. According to Kroeber the Yuma were 'exposed to harrassment from the nomadic Apaches beyond the river [and had] long since become tough defenders of their land ... they did not look for trouble, but if they wanted to travel or to hunt, they did not hesitate to leave the river and to risk a fair certainty of confrontation of an enemy'.[21]

This does not, however, explain their tendency to war in other directions, since the Pima and Papago represented no threat unless antagonized into taking retaliatory action; neither does it provide adequate reason for their desire to press home an advantage gained in battle. It is also apparent that the Yuman-speaking sub-tribes were decimated through warring among themselves and with the Yuma, to the extent that many tribal identities became lost as the groups fled to the Pima country seeking refuge.

Furthermore, winter was considered by the Yuma to be 'the time of the war trail', when, with their close and equally nationalistic and warlike allies, the Mohave, they went out as a large body of warriors under the leadership of men carrying feathered spears, or 'war standards', who were under no-flight obligations; after the Pima–Maricopa alliance, however, they regularly sent large forces out at other times of the year. Many of these were directed to the Gila Bend desert in the hope of cutting off small detachments of the Pima–Maricopa who visited this area to collect the fruits of the petajaya, a large cactus species.

Yuma warfare was clearly instigated by reasons beyond the protection of their village sites. Men gained status from warlike achievements, particularly in the use of the club since this was a hand-to-hand weapon that demanded close conflict – for which they developed a unique form of club which was used in a short upward stabbing motion – and prominent warriors would regularly challenge opponents to single combat where their skills as fighters could be established before witnesses. These men became war leaders who were chosen as the bravest and fiercest fighters, men who would not flinch from rushing single-handedly against their opponents, thereby setting an example for others to follow.

Left: *The Pima were ancient inhabitants of the Southwest whose Hohokam ancestors had established peaceful relationships with the Pueblo groups. Although non-aggressive, the Pima had to contend with warlike nomadic neighbors and fought fiercely when needed. These war clubs are of mesquite wood.*

Above: *This Pima cap, which is described as a war headdress made from the feathers of raptorial birds, was collected in 1885. The Pima were not predatory raiders, as the description of the cap suggests, but refer to themselves in song and myth as being able to strike as swiftly and effectively as the raptors if occasion demanded it. Pima defence rested on the fact that their neighbors knew they would retaliate in this manner if need arose.*

Left: *These unidentified Yuma men were photographed about 1870 and show the characteristic striped body paint employed by this tribe. In common with other groups of the Southwest, such as the Pima and Mohave, their main weapon was the club which was used in a thrusting motion. The long bow shown here was a weak weapon which, in combination with untipped arrows, was effective only against small game and birds.*

Shamans, who accompanied war parties as seers and clairvoyants, predicted their success in these endeavors, but the fighter's skill was his own. Yuma warriors had no recourse to spirit helpers or guardians and did not consider themselves to be supernaturally protected in battle. We have to conclude that war for the Yumans meant a great deal more than mere protection and that it provided individual benefits that were readily sought, benefits that it was worth fighting to achieve.

Speakers of the Yuman language extended across the narrow neck of land from the Lower Colorado on to the California coast, where it was spoken by tribes living in the region of San Diego, one of the Spanish missions established between here and San Francisco (also a mission) between 1769 and 1823. The aggressive traits of the Yuma, Mohave and Maricopa do not, however, seem to have penetrated deeply in the California area, possibly because there was little danger to the Californian groups, since war in the Lower Colorado area was focused more on threats to their security that came from the nomadic raiding tribes to the east, and from which the Yuma acted as a buffer between California and the Southwest.

Arguments have been put forward that some of the mission tribes, although they offered no resistance to the military forces of Spain, Mexico or the United States, had 'ofttimes distinguished themselves in warfare with other tribes].[22] One of the weapons the Gabrieleno (who were the Indians of the mission of San Gabriel) devised when they did

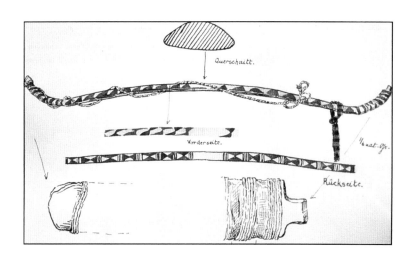

engage in combat was the war club, which ranged from a heavy stick to a shorter form with a definitely marked cylindrical end.'[23]

Most reports, however, emphazise the total lack of any aggression among the southern and central California tribes. Typical of these is the comment that 'there were few armed revolts (against the Spanish); but none of any consequence – these people were hopelessly simple when it came to making war'[24] and that there was a 'wholly negative value put upon war by the Californians ... there were no special weapons as such and when an altercation became a fight, rocks, stones, the hunting bow and the ever-handy digging stick were used.'[25]

Whichever of these two extremes we care to believe, it is nevertheless clear that warfare in any true sense of the word was lacking throughout much of the Californian area and that California tribes had little inclination for fighting with each other. When fights did break out, as happened occasionally, they were usually the consequence of inter-family feuding, but 'here was to be found none of the accouterments or behavior of gallantry, bloodshed, and bravery. No horses, no buffalo, no counting coup on a fallen enemy. No war whoops. No war bonnets. No shields. No armor. No victory orations, no boasting speeches by triumphant braves.'[26]

Indeed, there was no system at all whereby any aggressive act could be sanctioned, and no status or privilege to be gained by going to war. These mild and inoffensive tribes had few reasons to fight: they lived in a land of plenty, where the gathering of natural plant foods provided a surplus without need for any agriculture or farming, and each community had well-defined territories that were respected by their neighbors. Competition for resources was absent as were any incentives to encourage raiding, since the material possessions of each group were similar, and, for the most part, each

Above: *This photograph, from 1870 to 1880, depicts a Cocopa warrior. The Cocopa, who were linguistically related to and shared many of the customs of the Yuman-speaking Mohave, were nevertheless bitter enemies of most of the Yuman tribes, with whom they argued over territorial rights. The facepaint shown here has probably been added to the negative after the photograph was taken, a popular trick used by photographers at this period to make their subjects appear more exotic.*

family group was content to stay where it was and not intrude into the country of its neighbors.

Wiunu, a Mono Indian woman of central California, for example, was famed for her wanderlust because she had never lived for longer than five years in any one village during her long lifetime (she was ninety-five years old when she told her life story in 1915), yet she never actually crossed the borders of Mono territory and completed all her wandering within an area of only sixty-eight square miles.

Among the southern and central tribes a killing was universally regarded in the same light as murder and was punished accordingly. This might be by banishment from the tribe, although this extreme required the approval of all members of the community, since it was in effect a death sentence. Any stranger, in this country where people did not venture far from their homes, was viewed as a potential trouble-maker and would be unlikely to find acceptance among people whose language he did not speak. More usually, an indemnity payment was decided on by the village head men, respected people of considerable age and wisdom who were pledged to remain impartial even though a close relative or kinsman may have been injured or killed, and who were chosen because they had never displayed signs of anger or quick temper.

Above: *The Yuman groups developed a specialized weapon for hand-to-hand fighting which is known by the popular name of a 'potato-masher club'. This was used in an upwards movement to break the jaw of an opponent, and was wielded by a special group of warriors known as 'club-men'. That other tribes of the region adopted this is apparent from the Pima clubs shown on the preceding pages.*

Right: *Yuman-speaking peoples were represented in southern California by the Diegueno, who are named after the Spanish Mission of San Diego. The four warriors in this photograph, which was taken in the 1880s, wear traditional feather headdresses and black and white body paint. The women in the foreground wear shawls and skirts, introduced by Europeans for reasons of modesty. Traditional women's dress was a short apron.*

CALIFORNIA, BASIN AND THE NORTHWEST COAST

CHAPTER FIVE

Left: *Warfare in California centered on feuding and was largely concerned with maintaining positions of wealth and influence. Alice Spott, a Hupa woman, is shown here wearing a shell decorated costume that could only have been afforded by the wealthiest members of the tribe.*

Above: *This abalone necklace is labeled Northwest Coast but is probably Californian, and would have been worn by a woman of high status. Abalone was collected off the Californian coast, but the beads are of a type introduced by early European traders.*

Below: *This shell string shown was collected by Captain Vancouver in Santa Barbara between 1790 and 1795. It is of a type known as kaia which was used as currency in northern California and sewn into clothing or worn as a necklace by the women.*

THE TRANQUILITY OF southern and central California is disrupted and fragmented further north, where the peaceful life of the Californian Indians was punctuated with increasing frequency by a tendency to allow slights and offences to develop into inter-family feuding that could result in bloodshed. The Pomo Indians, living on the coast north of present-day San Francisco, and the nearby Maidu and Miwok tribes of the forested regions of the Coast Mountains, viewed warfare negatively, considering it as a regrettable incident that marred the normal tenor of life and as something to be resolved as rapidly as possible. But they nevertheless felt that a death required satisfaction through the execution or banishment of the offender and payment of indemnity in dentalia shell-string or red woodpecker-scalp 'money'.

Head men of these villages professed to achieve parity in arranging settlements, but the choice between execution or banishment was generally dependent on the respective status, persuasive powers, and wealth of the parties involved. A wealthy family was in a better position to pay highly and could thereby avoid additional deaths, whereas the poorer family often had no recourse than to submit to the execution of the offender, which was carried out by members of kin to prevent it being viewed as further cause for conflict.

Killing was, however, regarded as an extreme. Even the celebratory dance marking the cessation of hostilities was viewed as a demonstration of thanks that an unpleasant interlude had been brought to a conclusion, rather than a rejoicing at the successful defeat of an opponent. Fighting, when it occurred, usually involved only local groups, although a hostile response might be directed against another tribe who were considered to have carried insult to the point where

aggression could be justified. In such instances a war party would be organized, but it is clear this was done reluctantly.

A general aversion to war is reflected in the Pomo feather sash, or 'war belt'. These are stunningly beautiful. Woven from thousands of brilliant irridescent red and yellow woodpecker feathers whose colors gleam and shimmer in the Californian sun, they are worn across the body over the right shoulder and passing under the left arm, where the flash of color (according to a Pomo Indian belt-maker who described their former function in the early 1900s) is said to have 'the power to overcome, to dazzle and frighten an enemy into submission; thus preventing the shedding of blood'. Even so, the Pomo felt revenge needed to be exacted, and if peaceful overtures and 'fright displays' did not bring satisfaction they would resort to force, which, though undesirable, was then considered necessary to ensure justice.

A desire to achieve retribution through imposing penalties was expressed more fully by the Tolowa, Karok, Shasta, Yurok and Hupa, living on the northern coasts of California and inland in glades and clearings in the redwood and pine forests of the coastal slopes of the Coast Range Mountains and the Sierra Nevada. Though speaking varied languages, these groups shared a volatile temperament and any minor insult might be taken as an affront that demanded settlement. Aggression could readily escalate into situations in which members of the extended family, distant relatives and even tribal affiliations determined who took sides against whom. Anyone who held a grudge against one of the disputing parties might join the conflict, and serious fighting could result.

Justifiable causes for a hostile response could relate to the exploitation of tangible rights as well as to cases in which a killing had occurred, and instances of poaching by entering another group's territories and using their resources would almost certainly lead to a fight. More frequently, tempers flared at accusations of witchcraft. Shamans were thought capable of striking opponents dead by sending poisoned arrows over the hills against them, and although this was mostly conducted on their own behalf and in secret they could sometimes be persuaded to use these powers by a family suffering loss. Deaths from natural causes might also attract accusations of witchcraft and lead to reprisal killings.

Among the Karok 'the poison arrow, called ip-pesh-re-hap-po, was not shot into a person at all, but after a certain ceremony was put in a "bad place" where it was left over night. This appeared to endow it with magic power.'[1] Use of these arrows was not, however, limited solely to the practice

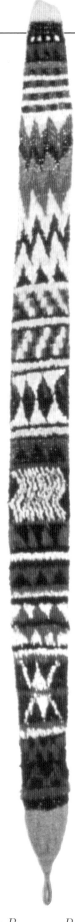

Above: *Charles Benson, a Pomo Indian, made this feather belt between 1875 and 1900 in an attempt to keep the art of featherwork alive. Such belts were said to dazzle and frighten an enemy into submission by their brilliant coloring.*

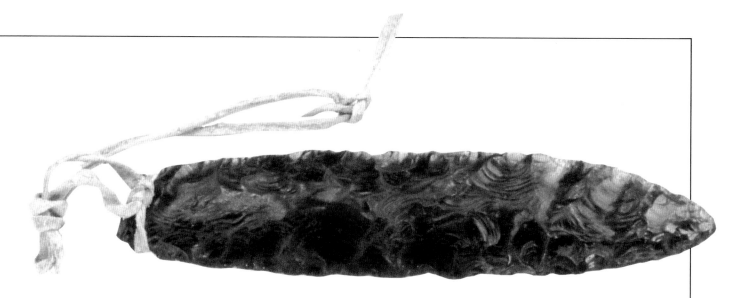

Above: *Maidu shamans called on super-natural power for curing and in avenging perceived insults. This obsidian blade, or 'magic arrow', was instrumental in such activities. Worn around the shaman's neck, it could be 'sent out' to counter danger.*

Below: *These feather darts were part of Pomo costume in annual rituals, but relate to the 'magic arrows' of the shamans in that they were imbued with power that could be used for collective good. These were collected by Captain Vancouver before 1800.*

of witchcraft, and at Tolowa settlement dances 'one side sometimes shoots a poisoned arrow over the ranks of the other to cause them to fight among themselves.'[2] That uncertainty was felt about the intentions of an opponent during settlement dances is further indicated by the Yurok habit in which participants faced away from each other, since it was felt the mere sight of their erstwhile enemies could overwhelm them with 'bad memories' and cause fresh fighting.

War was a logical extension of feuding, made more bitter when no ties of kinship were involved that could help to pacify tempers. In such cases, due to the absence of relatives who would intercede, efforts to resolve conflicts were made by peace envoys. Usually unremarkable men, except among the Shasta where they had to be chiefs, they acted as spokesmen for their respective groups and traveled back and forth between the warring parties to determine settlement payments. Their own lives were in jeopardy, since journeying into enemy territory was not without risk; but, again excepting the Shasta, they were well paid for these services. Some men, who had sold themselves into debt slavery, used this as a means of raising finance for purchasing their freedom and regaining status, although certain tribes, among whom the Wiyot appear regularly in early reports, refused compensation because revenge was preferred. Their refusal was a declaration of their determination to continue the war.

In the extreme north of California and in Oregon war was more frequently inter-tribal and could involve populations quite distant from each other. The Klamath, Modoc and Pit River Indians fought with the Paiute of the Great Basin, with the Salish and Chinook tribes who lived in Washington and traded between the Northwest Coast and California, and with the Cayuse of the Plateau. The Great Basin, Columbia and Plateau tribes formed links between the tribes of California, the Northwest Coast and the Plains, regularly trading and raiding into adjacent areas and sharing many culture traits: the tribes of California and the Great Basin, for instance, shared a belief in a race of powerful, though very small, hairy men who would kill Indians by shooting them with invisible arrows. This has a clear parallel with the magic arrows of Karok and Tolowa shamans.

Much of the raiding, although supported by ideological considerations, was for material gain. Thus the sinew-backed composite bows of the Shoshone tribes, who are known in the sign language as Snakes, had a practical value as trade items, since they were more powerful than the bows of the other regions, but were also sought because of the magical power they could be seen to possess. Wrapped in rattlesnake skins and with arrows dipped in rattlesnake poison, said to be so deadly as to cause instant death just by breaking the skin, these bows were felt capable of defeating their enemies just by pointing them in their direction.

This desire to gain advantages over opponents is clear from Klamath warfare, of which it is said it 'is not mere retaliation, murder for murder, but is engendered by patriotic motive and tangible benefits ... raids are exchanged with the Shasta several days' journey down the Klamath River, the Upland Takelma on the Rogue River, and the Northern Paiute of the desert to the east. [They] fight the Kalapuya and take horses from the Warm Springs Indians. Since horses were obtained by them, raids may be expected of the Ya´mökni two hundred or more miles away; northerners generically, but in this connection the Sahaptins of the Columbia and the Cayuse seem meant.'[3]

Klamath shamans predicted the outcome of the battle before the warriors departed on a raid, determining who would kill an enemy and who might be likely to suffer injury. It is unclear whether these predictions had any material effect on who went to war; some reports suggest an omen of death or injury would prevent someone from going, whereas others indicate he would be too brave to turn back. It is nevertheless obvious that a prediction of success gave the warriors confidence and courage, and shamans accompanied the war parties as seers and to assist in caring for any wounded.

Women also went into battle. There is little evidence to suggest they took part in heavy fighting, but it is clear their role extended beyond that of giving ritual encouragement and that they were active participants. They urged the warriors forward with songs and shouting, and 'armed with short spears by preference, they help to catch women and children and to slay the aged as they run to hide.'[4] These short spears of the women were rarely used by men. They preferred the

Above: *This painted wooden wand was used by a Diegueno shaman to throw 'pains' into an opponent, and was also employed in curing. Set into the handle is a stone projectile point dating back to 1500 BC. North American Indians regularly used such 'found objects' in shamanistic performances or attached them to objects used for shamanic purposes. The antiquity of the point linked its user with the ancient ones and with the power of the ancestors.*

Right: *Lieutenant P. H. Ray collected this beautiful quiver and arrows from the Natano band of the Hupa Indians in 1885, noting that they were then 'very old'. Note the owners' markings on the foreshafts of the arrows, which identified them both by tribe and individual. The quiver is made from the complete skin of a small mammal.*

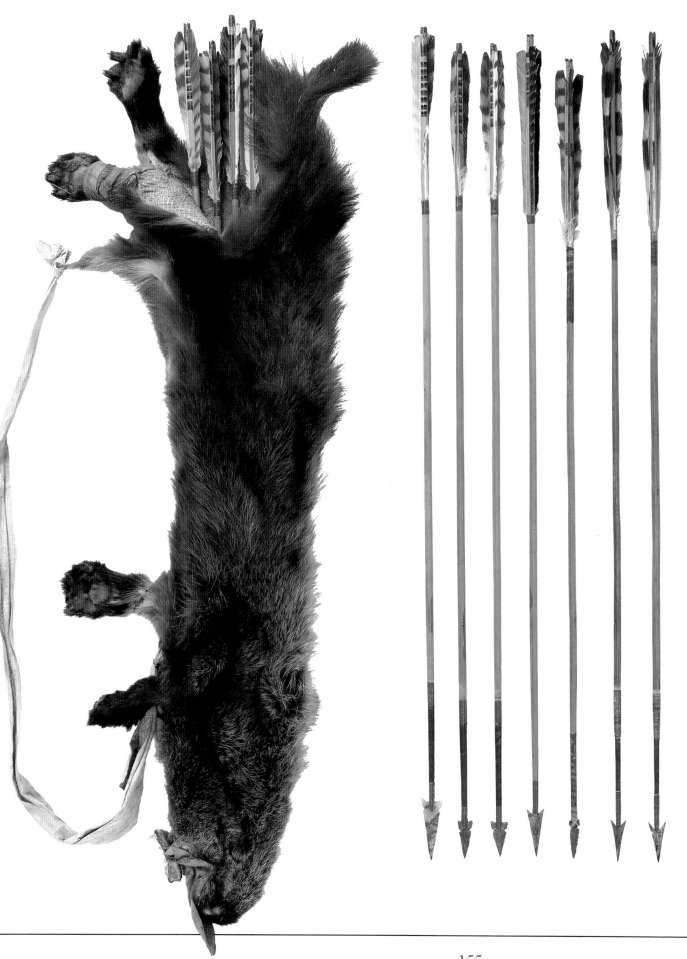

club for close-contact surprise attacks, but resorted to bows and arrows in distance fighting when resistance had been met. The war leader – a rich man who avoided the initial affray – carried several quivers of arrows, one under each arm and a third across his back, while the fighting men arrayed themselves in armor of elk hide or wooden slats.

Klamath and Modoc armour, known as ska-lam (wood slat) or bow-we (elk hide), protected the upper body and covered the lower half of the face. This would repel arrows and was an effective form of defence until European muskets were introduced. Similar armor was worn by other tribes, both in this region and further south, and is referred to in Hupa traditions of being raided by 'Yuke' bear-men; presumably referring to the coastal Yuki Indians. 'Some of these tattooed Yuke used to imitate bears. They would put on the skin of a grizzly bear, first lining the hide with bark and shaping it like the body of a bear. They would get into this skin and act and walk like a bear. In the hand they would carry a spike made of the antler of a deer, with which to kill the

Left: *Although John Daggett clearly asked this Karok warrior to pose for him when he took this photograph in 1898, it nevertheless reveals a number of interesting details about this warlike northern Californian tribe. Note the rod armor, which the Karok adopted from the Northwest Coast; the animal skin quiver held under this right arm, which is similar to that shown on the previous page; and the method of holding a reserve arrow between the teeth. Such a warrior would have been a wealthy man and regarded as a war captain who did not engage in the initial hand-to-hand fighting but waited in reserve, ready to employ his long range weapons if the initial onslaught failed to overwhelm the enemy.*

Left: *Livingstone Stone was in charge of a salmon-hatching establishment on the McCloud River between 1872 and 1875, where he made friends with the Wintu Indians and obtained a number of artifacts from them. Among these was this head ornament made from red wool and decorated with feathers, a woodpecker scalp and the rattles from two rattlesnakes.*

Indians they attacked. The Hoopah Indians learned this and learned how to tell real bears from these human enemy bears.'[5]

This practice was followed, at least in part, by the Wintun neighbors of the Yuki, who also claimed to be 'strong on bears' and had a distinctive armor of bearskin which was lined with the skin of a deer. Wintun armors 'while not absolutely arrow-proof, deadened the force of the arrow and were thus a protection. They were worn so as to cover the left shoulder and pass under the right arm, giving freedom of the right arm for fighting. The Wintoon always carried a dagger of elk antler or shinbone in their back hair, to be prepared for close-up fighting.'[6]

In spite of the Wintun comment on close-up fighting, much of it was actually conducted from cover and at a distance if the initial raid failed to overwhelm the enemy. Under such circumstances casualties were inevitably light and the battles were often inconclusive, leading to later retaliatory raids which tended to perpetuate the feud. When killings did

Right: *Heavy skin robes were used as protective armor by the tribes of northern California and of the Northwest Coast. The Karok war captain shown at the left wears a skin cloak beneath his armor which is part of a tradition of such clothing that extended throughout the area. The elkskin cloak, or war robe, shown in this photograph was collected among the Tlingit Indians by J. J. McClean in 1884.*

Above: *Northwest Coast culture was maritime and conflicts often occurred at sea when trade or war canoes of opposing tribes met off shore. This photograph shows Swinomish warriors launching a dug-out canoe which has been made from the trunk of a red cedar. Such canoes were as much as fifty feet long and had curved projections at bow and stern to ensure stability in the rough seas of the area.*

Left: *The Coast Salish had only one masked dance at which the distinctive Swaie Swaie mask was used. Swaie Swaie was regarded as the supernatural ancestor of the Coast Salish and was believed to have descended from the heavens to make his abode at the bottom of a deep lake in Salish territory. When confronted by the Kwakiutl tribes, the Coast Salish gave permission for them to make masks representing Swaie Swaie to avoid a disastrous war.*

occur, war trophies, including scalps, were taken from the bravest of the enemy fighters.

In a reprisal raid against the Upper Takelma by the Klamath, instigated by the fact the Takelma had previously killed some Klamath warriors and taken their scalps, hands, and feet as trophies, among the enemies killed by the Klamath was Töktö´kli, the Takelma war leader. After Lele´ks, a legendary Klamath chief, lanced his opponent through the throat they brought Töktö´kli's hands and heart back to the village, where Lele´ks sponsored a huge victory dance. This was a five day celebration of vengeance achieved through the defeat of their enemies, and when a woman danced with Töktö´kli's heart in her teeth, some female captives were made to sing in praise of the man who had killed him.

Even though the Klamath went north to engage the Takelma, a marked feature of warfare in northern California and Oregon was regular slave raiding against the more peaceful southerly tribes. The Klamath and neighbouring groups kept few slaves themselves, and these were generally their own kin who had chosen debt-slavery in preference to living as debtors, but captured women and children from other tribes could be taken to The Dalles, an inter-tribal trade market on the Columbia River, in the autumn and exchanged for goods unavailable further south. Because of their rarity these goods constituted a form of wealth, and one of the indicators of chieftainship related to the possession of trade goods and the ability to acquire them through the exchange of slaves. Some aggressive individuals gained both wealth and a position of authority through their activities as the leaders of war parties. Spier goes so far as to say that '[Klamath] chiefs become such largely by the prestige of successful leadership in battle.'[7]

Trade at The Dalles was controlled by the Chinook, who acted as middlemen between the southern tribes, those of the Northwest Coast, and interior groups from the Plateau. It may be that they suspended hostilities with certain of their neighbors for the period of autumn trading, since when Lewis and Clark crossed the Rockies and entered Chinook territory their 'Nez Percé [Plateau] guides now proved very reluctant to go any farther. They did not, they said, speak the language of the people below the falls, who were quite likely to attack the party. Even if the white men were not killed, they, as traditional enemies, certainly would not escape.'[8]

Lewis and Clark nevertheless found the Chinook generous open, and friendly. One of their important chiefs, whom

Right: *This whale bone spatula club was collected among the Clayoquot by Victor Justice Evans. The handle is wrapped with red cedar bark, which suggests the club served a ceremonial function and was used in rites that determined the status of a local leader.*

Below: *The painted house front shown here was photographed before 1899 at the Nimkish village on Alert Bay, Vancouver Island. The painting shows a Thunderbird carrying off a Whale, a popular motif for this period and relating to clan affiliation of the various divisions of the Kwakiutl. Vertical planking suggests that the house was already old when this photograph was taken, since horizontal boarding had already been in vogue for some years prior to 1900.*

they met on 29 October 1805, wore 'a fine coat of scarlet and blue cloth and a sword given him by European visitors who had come from the sea' as evidence of his good relations with white people. They were, however, 'taken aback when this same chief told his wife to produce his medicine bag. This proved to be decorated with fourteen forefingers which he had hung there as trophies of enemies killed in battle.'[9]

More usually Chinook contacts with other tribes were amicable, and during the trade fairs they hosted visitors from a vast area. Tsimshian and Tlingit traders maneuvered sixty foot long dug-out canoes through 1,000 miles of dangerous coastal waters to bring furs, porcupine quills and valuable eulachon oil from southern Alaska. Plateau tribes crossed the mountains, bringing in buffalo robes obtained in hunting and trading on the Plains farther east to exchange with the Salish-speaking groups of the interior and with Californian tribes for products of the southern coast. Dried salmon was traded back up the rivers to the inland tribes, and all the groups eagerly sought dentalia shells harvested off-

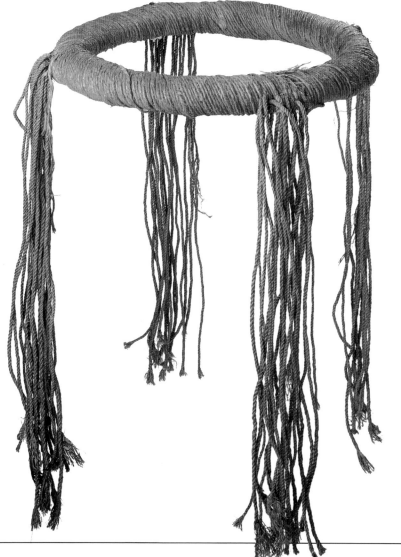

Right: *This Hamatsa neck ring of red cedar bark was collected by Franz Boas about 1895. The Hamatsas, or Cannibal Dancers, were elected from the most prominent families and represented their clan at potlatches where status was acclaimed and family privileges validated. Rivalry between these families was the major cause of conflict on the Northwest Coast.*

shore of Vancouver Island by the Nootka and traded into The Dalles via the Chinook-speaking Wishram and Wasco.

But it was the exchange of slaves that was central to the success of The Dalles, and they formed a valuable commodity from northern California throughout the coastal regions of British Columbia and Alaska, to the Aleutian Islands. Although generally treated no more harshly than the poorer members of the community, carrying out some of the heavier burdens but otherwise sharing equally in the pleasures and hardships of other members of the household, slaves had no status. They were considered as the property of their owners, a form of wealth that could be bartered, exchanged, occasionally ransomed, or, at times, even killed in demonstrations of property rights and ownership.

In close contact with the Chinook, and sharing many of their culture traits, the Coast Salish tribes living north of the Chinook in Washington, southern British Columbia and on the landward coast of Vancouver Island, actively participated in slave raiding and in The Dalles trade, but aggressive warfare does not seem to have played a major part in their life. They did, however, have to contend with other groups of the region, in particular the Kwakiutl, who considered both the Coast and Interior Salish as the principle targets from which

Above: *Kwakiutl dancers photographed in the early nineteenth century by Edward Curtis display many of the masks associated with status and privilege that would be demonstrated during potlatches. In the foreground is the mythical Raven, with his long pointed beak, and the Thunderbird, with a short curved beak. Background figures include representations of the Mountain Goat and the Grizzly Bear, as well as a figure wearing a mask that may be intended to portray an Underwater Monster. The carved posts in the rear are roof support poles bearing crests of the family owning the house.*

Above: *The Kwakiutl forehead mask shown here was made before 1882 and depicts Hoxhok, the helper of Baxbakualanuxsiwae. Hoxhok traveled the world searching for people as food for his master, and anyone he found he killed by driving his long pointed beak through their eyes. His ferocious aspect is indicated by the carved wooden skulls, said to represent slaves who had been killed at potlatches where this mask was featured.*

they would obtain slaves to supply tribes living further to the north.

Their relation with neighboring groups is summed up in the statement that the '[Coast Salish] Squamish would sometimes wage war with their northern neighbors the Stlatlumh (or Lillooet) They had also to defend themselves from marauding bands of Chilcotins, but their most dreaded enemies were the Ukeltaws, a band of the Kwakiutl tribe ... the very name of this band was a terror to the other tribes, and the mothers would frighten their children into silence and quiet by saying the Ukeltaws were coming for them.' [10]

Salish–Kwakiutl conflict, and the Salish desire to achieve peaceful solutions wherever possible, is reflected in a legendary tale of the Comox, a Coast Salish group living on both sides of the Strait of Georgia. The Tsowatenok Kwakiutl wished to acquire the powerful Swaie-Swaie mask and dance, which represented the legendary ancestor who came down from the sky into a lake in Salish territory and from whom all the people of the numerous Coast Salish sub-groups were believed to have descended.

This was the only masked dance of the Coast Salish tribes, and ownership of the mask was an exclusive privilege belonging to the chiefs' families. It was through them that the right to use the mask could be handed down, and since the Comox were reluctant to allow this to pass out of their control they resisted the Kwakiutl entreaties. Eventually the Tsowatenok threatened to send war parties and begin a disastrous war, averted only by the Comox inviting them to a huge feast when they transferred the right to make the mask -- which can still be traced in many different forms among the Kwakiutl – but retained the original character.

The principal reason for conflict between the Salish and Kwakiutl was their close proximity to each other, since Wakashan-speaking southern Kwakiutl groups lived on the northern shores of Vancouver Island and in numerous settlements along the southern British Columbia coast. The Coast Salish also faced some hostility from the Nootka (Nuu-chah-nulth) on the western coasts of Vancouver Island, who were distant linguistic relatives of the Kwakiutl and shared their propensity for slave-raiding, and from the

Above: *After the introduction of European goods, Kwakiutl potlatches featured Hudson's Bay blankets as a standard item of currency. This photograph, taken about 1900, shows piles of blankets waiting to be distributed at a chief's potlatch where his rank could be validated and the claims of rival chiefs were challenged.*

Below: *The arrival of visiting chiefs at a potlatch was a grandiose affair, with the clan of the visitors made evident by a costumed figure dancing in the prow of their canoe. This still is taken from a film made by Edward Curtis and depicts an Eagle dancer.*

Below: In excessive demonstrations of wealth intended to undermine the status of a rival, Northwest Coast tribes used 'coppers' which might have a value of several thousand Hudson's Bay blankets. Coppers were rare items, since their manufacture was dependent on the trade of native copper into the area or, later, on the acquisition of metal from Europeans.' They increased in value each time they were used, the Kwakiutl doubling their worth on each occasion. The painting on this example depicts the Bear.

Nootkan's relatives, the Makah, whose villages were on the Olympic Peninsula in Washington.

On the coast, in central British Columbia, an uneasy and frequently broken peace existed between the Salish-speaking Bella Coola and the Wakashan-speaking Bella Bella, or northern Kwakiutl;, although relations among the groups living to the north of them seem to have been a little more relaxed. There was a regular pattern of trading, interspersed with violent exchanges, between the Haida, Tsimshian and Tlingit, living, respectively, off-shore on the Queen Charlotte Islands, with the Kaigani Haida on the Prince of Wales Archipelago, along the northern British Columbia coast and inland on the Nass and Skeena rivers, and in southern coastal Alaska as far north as Yakutat Bay.

This narrow coastal strip extending from Washington into Alaska is, for reasons of convenience, generally referred to as the Northwest Coast, though this implies an homogenous area and ignores the variations between the tribes, and the fact that Northwest Coast influence extended south into northern California and north to the Yupik Eskimo speaking Chugach of Prince William Sound and even to the Unalaska of the Aleutian Islands.

Most of the coast is, however, characterized by countless small islands that are the peaks of a submerged Ice Age mountain chain, and by deep fjords and narrow channels with frequent fast eddies and whirlpools. Stands of temperate rain forest cedar and spruce rise almost vertically from the banks of these islands, disappearing into low mists caused by the high precipitation of the coast. Sheltered coves and inlets provide narrow beach heads above which the massive gabled plank houses of the coast tribes were erected. These can only be approached from the sea, and one comes upon them suddenly and unexpectedly, since they are hidden from view by the rugged coastline until passing a point of land reveals the village's location.

European travelers were astonished at the impact a first view of these villages presented. The houses of the central and southern regions, some of them 200 feet long and 50 feet wide, often had their entire fronts painted with totemic crest symbols of the Killer Whale, Bear, Wolf, or Eagle; the red, black, and white of Kwakiutl paintings contrasting sharply with the impenetrable dense green of the rainforest that provided a backdrop to them. Intricately carved posts

supported the roof beams of the buildings, while among the Bella Coola rows of 'welcoming figures', often of the Bear Mother, their empty palms facing the sea to show they carried no weapons, lined the top of the beach on which were lying carved and painted 60 foot long war and trade canoes. After the introduction of metal tools, house posts were often elaborated into magnificent totem poles carved with family crests and depictions of ancestral supernatural contacts.

These supernatural beings have their origin in a land that is breathtakingly beautiful, but is also mysterious and frequently enveloped in deep mists when sea, land and sky form a continuous chain, blurring and blending detail and forming a 'half-world' peopled with powerful and ferocious creatures. It takes little imagination to hear the voice of Tsonoqa, the Cannibal Giantess of the Kwakiutl, in the sound of the wind rushing through trees that are hidden from view. Earthly counterparts of the spirit forces are diminutive in comparison.

Wren, the smallest of the supernaturals, made his bow from an entire cedar and used arrows that even Black Bear was unable to lift; but his power was insignificant compared with that of Baxbakualanuxsiwae, the Cannibal-at-the-north-end-of-the-world:, the one to whom everyone looks up, and before whom everyone trembles. He travels to the very edge of the world, consuming humans whom Hoxhok kills by driving his sharp beak through their eyes and devouring their brains, and whose bodies are brought to him by Qominoqa, the Female Cannibal, whose own body is covered with blood from the corpses she collects.

Humans could not normally hope to compete in a world full of such terrors, but in the days when animals and people

Above: *The Wolf featured prominently in the art and ritual of the Nootkan tribes, whose major ceremony was an initiation known as the Nutlam in which ancestral Wolves taught the initiates the secrets of the supernaturals. The Nutlam is an old form of dance and parallels the shamanistic and dancing societies of other tribes, such as the Kwakiutl. The Wolf mask shown here was collected by Judge James G. Swan between 1861 and 1884 among the Clayoquet subtribe living on Vancouver Island. The form of these masks, which were an important aspect of Nutlam ceremonies, is highly characteristic of the Nootka.*

Above: *Also collected by Judge James G. Swan, the bow, quiver and arrows shown here are from the Makah sub-tribe living at Neah Bay in the Olympic Peninsula. The quiver is carved from a block of wood and terminates in the head of a Wolf.*

Below: *This magnificent yew club was collected by Captain James Cook in Nootka Sound in the 1770s. It depicts a Wolf carrying a human head in its jaws, with other human heads carved on the back and at the end of the club handle. This may depict the episode during the Nutlam when the Wolves seized and carried away the initiates to be instructed by the shamans. Such an interpretation is reinforced by the fact that the head on the back of the club reclines, a stylistic feature that characterizes many Northwest Coast carvings of shamans.*

spoke the same language, the ancestors of the clans communicated with these mighty beings and acquired some of their power. Killer Whale, Raven, and Wolf, among others, told the ancients this could be handed on within family lineages and inherited by future generations. Baxbakualanuxsiwae and the spirits of the Dluwulaxa (Those-who-descend-from-the-heavens) did not pass their strength directly to these families, but instead initiated secret societies through which their powers could be acquired by initiates in the ceremonies. The Kwakiutl Hamatsa, or Cannibal Dancer, is lured into the sacred winter ceremonial house by Kinqalalala, a counterpart of Qominoqa, who dances naked and carryies a corpse in her arms to entice him; the Grizzly Bear Spirit Dancer is possessed of the power, not of an ordinary grizzly, but of that of Nane, the Grizzly Bear Spirit, who guards the north end of the world and delights in killing people.

Both the family crests and the insignia of the secret societies were an important means whereby these potent supernatural forces could be controlled and utilized, and as such their inheritance within the family and society lineages was carefully and jealously protected. All aspects of the clan

totems and society memberships, including masks, names, songs, and dances, were held as either inherited rights (family totems) or acquired privileges (society memberships) which could be exercised only by those whose positions had been validated before witnesses through extensive gift giving.

This resulted in a stratified society in which the resources of a family group were used to elevate certain individuals to high positions of rank and status. Household heads, who are often referred to as 'chiefs', and their eldest sons and daughters held these rights on behalf of the group and exercised immense power over other members of the community. Everybody contributed in these attempts to maintain a household and clan position above those of neighboring families, and rivalry between the different household heads was endemic, resulting in fierce competition to maintain the power of the family's rights and privileges or to undermine or acquire those held by others.

All the tribes of the Northwest Coast placed an emphasis on the status of the leading members of the group, but it was taken to an extreme by the Kwakiutl, who viewed any status raising event involving important members of households as a kind of 'war' with their neighbors. Even marriages were referred to by a word that translates as war, and since these were outside the clan group the wedding guests arrived in war canoes displaying the crests through which their rank was recognised. This was a deliberate attempt to overawe their hosts with the wealth and privilege they possessed, and in a dramatic approach to the host village's beach costumed figures representing the totem spirit of the clan danced in the prows of the canoes to the accompaniment of a rhythm beaten out by the warriors manning the oars. According to

Left: *A uniquely shaped club, known as a 'slave-killer', was used by tribes of the central and northern Northwest Coast, although there is little evidence that these clubs had the specific function of despatching slaves. This 1885 example is from the Tlingit.*

Below left: *After the introduction of iron-bladed tools, elaborately carved house posts depicting crests were developed into totem poles. The Haida village of Skidegate, on the Queen Charlotte Islands, is shown in this nineteenth-century photograph.*

Below: *This Eagle clan hat shows the Tlingit preference for keeping design elements to the upper half and off-setting this against a decorative weave on the lower part. Hats of this type were important indications of clan among the northern tribes.*

Helen Codere, 'the general conclusion is that the binding force in Kwakiutl history was their limitless pursuit of a kind of social prestige which required continual proving to be established or maintained against rivals, and that [this came] from a time when success in warfare and head hunting was significant.'[11]

The connection between war and status tends to be confirmed in Kwakiutl speeches. A warrior who had actually killed many men in war and on head hunting forays related past events during a ceremony held in Fort Rupert in 1895 to validate a position of high rank by declaring 'When I was young, I have seen streams of blood shed in war.',[12] and at the same ceremony 'each man carries as many hemlock wreaths as he has killed enemies during war expeditions. They also carry bows and arrows. Then they step up to the middle of the house and throw one wreath after the other into the fire, calling the name of the enemy whom it represents. As soon as a wreath is thrown into the fire they call 'yë', and all repeat this cry. At the same time they shoot arrows into the fire. This ceremony is called yï'lxoa, which

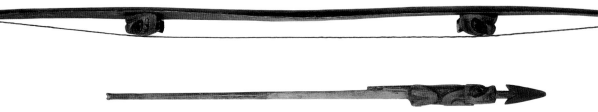

means placing the head of an enemy on a pole. The fire is called xuse´la which means fighting place.'[13]

The extremes of Kwakiutl rivalry stem from the fact that the heads of several families could lay claim to equal prominence, but by killing a rival chief or a member of the aristocracy, the victor inherited all the privileges associated with that person's name, thereby reducing the standing of his opponent's family group while increasing that of his own. At the same time the death of a prominent member of one of these families, even if by natural causes or accident, was considered to be a cause of disgrace and shame and a serious affront to the family name, the grief of which required 'killing to wipe one's eyes'[14] Compensation could only be made by the death of a person of equivalent status from one of the rival groups. War parties therefore set out with a specific purpose: to cause equal or greater loss to a rival.

Who this was exacted against was often irrelevant, and revenge raids might be made on a group that was wholly innocent of any involvement in the affair, especially if the guilty party was prepared for an attack and had made preparations to resist it. These were not strictly reprisal raids, in that the intention was never to exact punishment but was to wipe out shame and regain status. In cases where a murder had been committed and the murderer's identity was known he could even escape punishment if his rank was lower than that of the person he had killed, since the death of a chief's son, for instance, of one household would be revenged by the equivalent killing of a chief's son from the murderer's clan. The murderer might, however, be executed by his own kin for having caused the loss of a prominent family member.

The pattern of Kwakiutl warfare is apparent in a series of well-documented battles recorded by Franz Boas. In about 1840, a famine in the country of the Bella Coola forced them to move to Knight Inlet where the Kwakiutl permitted them to fish but made fun of them and raped some of their women. That autumn, the Bella Coola and their allies sought vengeance. Leaving their war canoes out of sight behind a headland, the revenge party traveled overland on foot to the unsuspecting village, where the war leader stationed men at the rear of the houses to prevent any escape.

Above: *Judge James G. Swan obtained this chief's bow and arrow from the Haida at Skidegate in 1883, commenting that it was the property of 'Captain Skedans'. This bow was not a practical weapon, but was carried during dances to commemorate an event from the family history which was considered to be one of their inherited privileges through which status could be displayed.*

Above: *The Haida used portrait masks during dances to demonstrate family and ancestral privileges. Abstract painted elements on the mask indicate facepaint showing the clan of the person whom the mask represents. The mask shown here dates from the mid-nineteenth century and would originally have had fur glued to the leather strips on the upper lip and chin to represent a moustache and beard.*

At a signal the war party, armed with knives and clubs, burst into the houses and killed all the sleeping men before they had time to realize they were under attack. In retaliation for the earlier rapes they stripped the clothing from the dead warriors' wives and daughters and subjected them to shameful insults.

Five years later the Kwakiutl responded to this by attacking a different Bella Coola village. The houses here, however, were well protected by high stockades surmounted with thorns and the attack was repulsed by the vigilant inhabitants, who had taken the precaution of sleeping on the roofs of the buildings to avoid being surprised in a dawn attack. Two Kwakiutl villages, which had been uninvolved in the dispute, were less fortunate when the Bella Coola struck back. All the men of these two villages were killed and a number of women and children carried off into slavery. Not satisfied with this, a large Bella Coola war fleet sailed against yet

Right: In addition to using face- and bodypaint to symbolize their clan crests, the Haida often employed tattooing prior to 1900, sometimes using a combination of both paint and tattoo. Johnnie Kit Elswa was photographed at his home in Skidegate in 1886. He has the crest of the Bear tattooed on his chest, while a Dogfish is tattooed at each wrist. Both the Bear and Dogfish were important Haida crests and referred to mythological events in the family history when an ancestor had an encounter with one of these supernatural beings. As a token of the power he acquired by this, he was given the right to use symbols of the animal and to pass these on as a privileged right to his heirs.

another innocent Kwakiutl village; this time only seven men and five women escaped.

Among the people killed in this last battle were visitors from several Kwakiutl communities, and as news of the Bella Coola successes spread, warriors from these different towns began to gather at Fort Rupert. When all had assembled the head warrior at Fort Rupert rose and made a speech: 'Fathers, uncles, brothers, children! Thank you for coming. Now let us go and look for our exterminated tribe, which was eaten by the Bella Coola. Let us make them vomit our tribe. Therefore I called you to make war against the Bella Coola. Nobody we meet hereafter shall live.'

Chief Potlatch, one of the household heads of the Ma'maleqala (a Kwakiutl sub-tribe), rose to reply: 'You are good, you are great, Kwakiutl! What is it you are saying? Do you say we intend to go to war? ... Thank you, friend! Thank you, Kwakiutl. Look at the tears on my face which I wept for the [Gua´ts'enox – the destroyed village], for our lost names. Now take care, warriors! else we may not get any heads. Let us start in the morning. I shall be your guide, for my ancestor was the killer whale. Therefore I am not afraid of anything.'

Fifty war canoes manned by warriors from the various tribes are said to have left Fort Rupert the next morning under the command of Chief Potlatch, sailing in the direction of the Bella Coola country. The men had rubbed their bodies with hemlock branches to give them strength, and blown into inflated kelp neck rings which they gave to the women of their families. If one of these should burst, it was an indicator the warrior was killed and his 'breath of life' contained in the ring had been extinguished; if it slowly deflated, he was wounded.

Scouts were sent ahead in four canoes, and when the main war party rounded a point of land they saw the canoes of the scouts lying side by side with six canoes from one of the Bella Bella villages (a Kwakiutl sub-tribe, but uninvolved in the dispute since they lived on the mainland to the north of the Bella Coola). The Bella Bella told them that the Bella Coola had news of the impending attack and had fortified their villages. Meanwhile, Chief Potlatch came alongside and asked who among the Bella Bella were chiefs. Chief-in-the-World replied they were all chiefs, that they were preparing a great feast and in order to honor the guests they went as chiefs to take the invitations instead of sending messengers.

Above: *When Judge James G. Swan collected this wooden clan helmet in 1876, he recorded only that it was a 'chief's crest with top plume'. It is probably Haida and demonstrates the addition of rings to the top of a crest helmet each time a chief sponsored a successful potlatch. These potlatch rings served as an immediate and highly visible statement of the wealth and status of the chief's lineage group.*

Above: *The introduction of trade goods created new forms, and woven cloth largely replaced mountain goat and dog hair for making blankets. This gave rise to the distinctive 'button blanket' shown here in which a clan figure of the Bear Mother and her cubs has been outlined in mother-of-pearl buttons, although some early button blankets used abalone shell for the outlining. The Bear Mother was important throughout the coastal region, and is often shown as a symbol of peace and friendship when she is usually depicted, as here, with her hands raised and turned palm outwards to show that she carries no weapons and is therefore not a threat. This blanket was made by the Tsimshian about 1900.*

At this news, Having-Badness, Chief Potlatch's head warrior, killed the steersman of one of the Bella Bella canoes, and although the chiefs opened the boxes containing sacred red cedar bark and blew on their whistles in an attempt to place ceremonial restrictions on the warriors and prevent a fight against such impossible odds, the Kwakiutl ignored this convention and before long all the chiefs except one were dead. Exultant at this great victory, through which they acquired the rights and privileges of the chiefs, the Kwakiutl returned to their own villages, satisfied that revenge had been achieved even though not a single Bella Coola had been killed.[15]

Many of the slain Bella Bella chiefs had relatives in Fort Rupert and at other Kwakiutl villages and for years afterwards Chief Potlatch, who was blamed for causing the slaughter, lived in fear of his life. He was unable to return to Fort Rupert, where Wrong-Around-the-World, Potlatch-Dancer, and Stones-on-Fire were powerful chiefs of part Bella Bella descent who had vowed vengeance. The affair was eventually forgotten and the vow to kill Chief Potlatch was dropped. Boas' informants were unaware of how this came about, although it is likely that he made his peace by a distribution of property to the aggrieved families.

Such property distributions, or potlatches – from the Chinook word patshatl meaning give-away – were known all along the coast and had an influence that spread into Alaska as far as the Athapascan-speaking Tanaina of the Kenai Peninsula and the speakers of Yupik Eskimo. In Kwakiutl culture they acquired a highly competitive character and began to supersede warfare after the middle 1800s, following rapid increases in wealth through the introduction of trade goods, which also coincided with a proliferation of masked dances through which ancestral links can be traced, and an elaboration of the masks themselves. Many of them have intricate attachments and concealed strings by which, for example, a somber face can suddenly be opened to reveal a brilliantly painted Sun. Seen in the half-light of feast fires, these were spectacular representations of inherited power.

Potlatching had, of course, been of importance prior to this date, as is reflected in the names of some of the chiefs in the war against the Bella Coola, but speeches recorded from Kwakiutl competitive potlatches make it clear they came to have prominence over actual fighting and were viewed, not only as a form of intense rivalry, but as a replacement for war. The Kwakiutl, referring to the period of extensive trade contacts, say: 'The time of fighting has passed. The fool dancer represents the warriors, but we do not fight now with weapons; we fight with property.'[16]

The principle governing the potlatch is that at any change in a person's life guests are invited as witnesses to a feast where they are given gifts. These occur on the giving of a name at one year old, of a new name at puberty, and of a potlatch name (a name that entitles its owner to exercise family privileges), as well as at such events as marriages, births, and in mourning ceremonies. The value of the gift is dependent on the nature of the change and the status it confers, as well as the status of the recipient. Thus, the son of a wealthy chief gives proportionately greater gifts to higher ranking members of the community than would a poor family, who might distribute only token gifts among immediate members of kin.

Acquisition of a potlatch name, which implies very high status since this privilege could only be conferred on the eldest son of a chief, required a large distribution of gifts which were borrowed from other household and clan members and had to be repaid after a year at one hundred per cent

Above: *This procession of Haida potlatch dancers was photographed at Klinwan circa 1900, and shows a variety of crest blankets. The leading figure, who is beating a tambourine drum with a rattle held in his left hand, wears a tailored coat which has been decorated in the traditional style of the button blanket using pieces of abalone. A similar application of abalone, this time to a blanket, can be seen on the figure who is third from the right. Behind him is a man wearing an older style painted blanket. The central figures each wear a highly distinctive type of paneled blanket known as a 'Chilkat blanket'. These are named after one of the Tlingit sub-tribes who were the main producers of these, and from whom the Haida would have obtained them in trade.*

Right: *The northern tribes (Haida, Tsimshian and Tlingit) used frontlets, or forehead masks, to depict high status and can be seen worn by the central figures in the photograph above. The example shown here is a very early example, collected by the first Russian travelers in Alaska during the mid-1700s. It is probably Tlingit and is made from a piece of carved and painted wood which has been decorated with abalone shell inserts, fur, trade cloth, feathers and sea lion whiskers. The crest figure depicted is the Beaver, shown in a characteristic pose holding a stick and readily identified by the upturned cross-hatched tail and prominent incisor teeth.*

interest. These also had to be repaid by the guests who received them, again with interest, and could not be refused without a consequent loss of face as indicative of the fact they did not possess sufficient property of their own by which the repayment could be made.

The interest bearing element of gift giving enabled the potlatch to replace warfare, since, by inviting a rival and lavishly bestowing gifts upon him, he was placed under an obligation to return double the amount later; failure to do so led to a shameful loss of status. A refusal to attend or to repay was, of course, inconceivable since it would be understood as an admission of defeat. He could, however, attempt to better his opponent by returning the gift and repaying more than necessary, in which case the recipient of these was required to

Left: *This Chilkat house with crests on display prior to a potlatch illustrates the richness of Northwest Coast interiors. The panel behind the man wearing a Beaver coat acted as a partition to separate living areas from a room at the rear where the family's ceremonial paraphernalia was stored. Note, too, the carved roof support posts.*

Below: *During his visit to the Northwest Coast between 1776 and 1779, Captain James Cook collected this mountain goat wool cloak from the Tlingit. Geometric patterns are very rare on later cloaks and blankets, which have stylized crest figures. Increased competitiveness possibly led to the more frequent display of crests on clothing.*

return double this amount simply to remain even.

Under the impetus of trade with Europeans in sea otter furs, the competitive element in potlatching escalated to the extent that the manufacture of goods was unable to keep up with the demand. Trade blankets, which had a fixed price, became a standard of currency, replacing many of the earlier items of Native manufacture. Even articles produced locally were described in terms of how many trade blankets they were worth; thus 'coppers' – riveted plaques, or shields, of native copper traded into the area from Alaska, used only for potlatching, and prized for their rarity - came to acquire substantial blanket values which increased each time they were used. In 1893 the copper 'All-others-are-ashamed-to-look-at' was held by the Fort Rupert Kwakiutl and was worth 7,500 blankets, although reports from other villages suggest that many coppers had values in excess of 10,000 blankets.

An invitation to a rival was issued as a challenge to war. "This I throw into your face, you whom I always tried to vanquish; whom I have maltreated; who does not dare to stand erect when I am eating; the chief whom even every weak man tries to vanquish ... Now my feast! Go to him, the poor one who wants to be fed from the son of the chief whose own name is 'Full of Smoke' and 'Greatest Smoke' [this refers to the great smoke of a grease feast, caused by burning valuable eulachon oil in a demonstration that he possesses so much wealth he can afford to waste it]'.[17]

The challenged chief responded by denigrating the achievements of his opponent. 'I thought another one was causing the smoky weather. I am the only one on earth –

Below: *Chilkat blankets, woven from a mixture of goat wool and dog hair, were highly valued trade items among the northern tribes, and were covered with stylized panel designs in which it is virtually impossible to identify any particular animal species. These designs were often copied from standardized pattern boards which had the main forms painted on them. The use of such patterns meant that the blankets could be traded more widely, since they were not linked with the specific crests of individual families.*

the only one in the world who makes thick smoke rise from the beginning of the year to the end, for the invited tribes. What will my rival say again – that "spider woman"; what will he pretend to do next? The words of that "spider woman" do not go a straight way. Will he not brag that he is going to break coppers [destroy them instead of presenting them as a gift. This was the ultimate insult, because it required no return and indicated both contempt and disdain by implying the rival had insufficient property to be able to respond. His opponent could, of course, destroy a copper of greater worth to avoid being shamed].'[18]

The manner in which these contests might lead to open enmity and war is shown in the famous tale of Fast Runner and Throw Away, two chiefs from the same Kwakiutl village. These chiefs were great friends, but when Throw Away invited the clan of Fast Runner to a feast, Fast Runner felt that the canoes containing the food were dirty (food was served in

massive quantity as a demonstration of wealth) and lay down with his black bear blanket pulled over his face as a sign of his displeasure. Throw Away poured scorn on his erstwhile friend, accusing him of behaving in a manner only worthy of a wealthy man', thereby implying that he wasn't entitled to do so.

Fast Runner immediately sent for the copper 'Sea-monster' which he thrust into the fireplace 'to put out the fire of his rival', whereupon Throw Away did the same with the copper 'Looked-at-askance' to 'keep the fire burning'. Fast Runner had another copper, 'Crane', which was brought into the house and used 'to smother the fire'. Throw Away, lacking a second copper and unable to match this demonstration, was defeated in the first round of the challenge.

On the following day, Fast Runner returned the feast, but in the meantime Throw Away had pledged enough property to obtain the copper 'Day-face'. He refused the food that was offered and then used 'Day-face' to 'put out' the feast fire. Not to be outdone, Fast Runner put on the Dance of the Fools in which war dancers carried heavy lances on which were suspended carved wooden skulls representing the enemies they had slain. The ownership of such a prestigious dance was another demonstration of his wealth, and he showed this further by ordering four precious canoes to be destroyed and their pieces thrown on the fire. The fire

Right: *Tlingit warriors preferred close range shock weapons which could be used to advantage in surprise attack at dawn. This two-bladed iron dagger, collected at the Tlingit village of Sitka, was highly efficient in such encounters and was carried in a sheath worn around the neck. The long slender blade penetrated easily between the ribs of an opponent, while the shorter blade was effective in an upwards thrusting movement beneath the jaw.*

Left: *According to Tsimshian mythology, numerous flying frogs came out of a lake two years after the disappearance of a clan ancestress, and soon after this she was seen floating on a raft made from a painted house front with her knees, breasts, eyebrows and the backs of her hands covered in frogs. Because of this the Frog was adopted as a clan emblem. The headpiece shown here came from the village of Kitwancool in the nineteenth century and has attached copper plates for the eyes, eyebrows, lips, underside of the wings and tail. Frogs were greatly feared because they were believed to possess power that could be used by a shaman against an enemy.*

blazed, scorching the rafters of the house, singeing Throw Away's blanket and blistering his legs, yet he remained sitting calmly and unconcerned, and when the fire died down ate from the feast as though nothing had happened and the demonstrations he had witnessed were so miserly they did not demand his attention.

The contest continued that winter when both sponsored initiations of their children into rival secret societies. Throw Away initiated a son and daughter, but Fast Runner two sons and two daughters. In addition, Fast Runner had a slave killed and scalped and presented the scalp to his rival; he then sponsored performances by the Fool Dancers, the Grizzly Bear Society and the Cannibal Dancers, and, finally, had two more slaves burned. These slaves impersonated his own daughters, who had been initiated as war dancers and were therefore immune from harm by fire, and after four days in seclusion the daughters were brought forth miraculously raised from the dead. Throw Away was unable to match this great show of power, privilege and wealth. In deep shame and in thorough disgrace he and all his warriors set out on a suicidal attack against the Nootka from which only one man returned.[19]

Few other tribes of the Northwest Coast took the competitive element of the potlatch to the same extreme as the Kwakiutl. The Nootka, in fact, claimed to have no competi-

Right: This particularly fine mask dates to between 1800 and 1850 and shows the typical pentagonal shape of Tshimshian portrait carvings. That it may represent a warrior is suggested by the human hair attached to the top of the mask and the red shapes on the cheeks. It may be, however, that this is intended to portray a shaman uttering his call through cupped hands which have been painted red to place him in communion with the supernatural beings.

tion potlatch and said 'you couldn't quarrel in a potlatch. That would give a bad name to your child, and be a disgrace to your whole family.'[20] Among them the major initiation and means of acquiring rank was through the Nutlam – a name which translates as The Shamans, but which is more generally referred to as the Wolf Dance. Persons of high status performed the ceremony several times during their lives, on each occasion receiving a different hereditary name and crest.

In the Nutlam, an initiate is 'captured' by the wolves in a re-enactment of the origin story in which an ancestor entered the House of the Wolves and was taught the songs, dances and displays of these supernatural animals, thereafter passing these on as hereditary rights. In contrast to the frightening performances of Kwakiutl Cannibal dances, the Nutlam was marked by levity. Wolf impersonators were

Above: *Various forms of protective body armor were developed among the tribes from northern California along the coast and up to the Aleutian Islands. This rod and slat armor is from the Tlingit and was collected in the 1880s. The main body part is of hardwood slats, with rods inserted under the arm sections to provide greater flexibility, the whole bound together with twisted sinew and strips of rawhide. The central panel not covered with threads would have born a painted crest figure.*

Right: *Tomás de Suria traveled with Alejandro Malspina's expedition to the Northwest Coast in 1791, where he sketched this Tlingit warrior wearing hardwood slat body armor and a visored helmet. The helmet is carved into the form of an animal crest and has human hair attachments on it. Note the horizontal position in which the bow is held. This was a method of using the weapon employed by several of the northern tribes.*

Below: *Rod armor was more flexible than the heavier wood slat type, but offered less physical protection. That shown here was collected at the Tlingit village of Hutsnuwu in 1882. Also shown is a wooden collar of a type that served to protect the neck and lower part of the face by fitting between top of the armor and the war helmet. This collar dates from 1874 and came from Sitka.*

insulted when they swept in from the sea to abduct the initiates rather than being treated with the respect due to a supernatural, and a 'search' made to find their lair and recover the captives was conducted using ludicrous traps and other devices. One man, claiming to be an expert wolf-catcher, might set out carrying an over-sized halibut hook, while another felt a bird-snare to be a more appropriate weapon. Upsetting canoe loads of these experts was a game into which everyone entered, as was attempting to trick people into using the word 'wolf', tabooed during the ceremony, when the transgressor was stripped of all his or her clothing.

Yet despite this apparent disrespect it was understood that the Wolves were powerful beings who had the ability to kill with ease if they chose to do so, and occasionally an initiate, who for some reason had displeased them, might be thrown on the beach with blood streaming from his nose and mouth.

Behind the humor, and disguised by it, lay a real fear of the Wolves' power. Alice Ernst, who made a detailed study of the Nutlam, believes 'it was once a warrior ceremony, having as its aim the fostering of bravery and those qualities that make for bodily and mental endurance.'[21]

The Wolves were certainly considered to be far stronger than other supernatural beings. Even the Ya'ai spirits, who bestowed skills in shamanism, ensured success in deep-sea whaling and guaranteed wealth in ritual displays and songs, but who would slay without mercy anyone they met who was ceremonially unclean, possessed lesser power; as did the short-tempered and antagonistic mountain lion that walked backwards and killed men with its long lance-like tail, and the souls of trees that were only ever seen as shadows presaging death.

Malignant war spirits lived on land rather than in water, and the Nootka, who were thoroughly maritime, felt that the creatures of the sea were more benign and would more readily confer their benefits. But even here enormous sharks capable of swallowing entire canoes dwelt in deep pools at the bases of cliffs, and wide detours would be made through dangerous channels to prevent a confrontation. War leaders demonstrated their immunity to harm by deliberately seeking such dangerous spots in which to bathe. Their ability to successfully defy the giant shark lent a confidence and ferocity to hostile undertakings they led, and when Throw Away chose the Nootka for his suicidal expedition he did so knowing he could expect no quarter from warriors who were respected and feared along much of the coast for their aggressive slave raiding and their willingness to take risks.

The invincible power of the war leaders was given specific recognition during the Nutlam, when groups of dancers who were organized into societies based on age and experience imitated the actions of the spirits that inspired their members. Thus 'there might be seven such groups, three of men, three of women, and one of war leaders [who gave dances] related to the property rights of the chiefs ... In one chief's house dancers would mimic the cormorant by imitating the motion of its wingbeat and throwing flour behind them to represent the cormorant's droppings. In another village dancers would imitate the black bear or land otter' ,[22] both of which were associated with warrior power.

Similar privilege dances owned by chiefs were performed by the Haida, Tsimshian and Tlingit living further north; among the Haida, however, much of this power was actually expressed by the shamans, who often held status as village leaders. The equation between chief and shaman was such

Right: *Although the catalog entry for this describes it as a 'leather dancing shirt', it is in fact an example of heavy hide armor. Usually made from elkskin, hide armor was worn either on its own or beneath wood slat or rod armor such as those shown on the preceding pages. This example is decorated with cut fringes, paint, sharks' teeth and Chinese coins. Chinese coins were traded along the Northwest Coast and obtained as part of the Northwest Coast–China–Europe trade. This lucrative network saw European traders obtaining sea otter pelts on the coast in exchange for coins, other metal items and some trade cloth and beads. These were sold at a vast profit in China, where tea and silks were purchased and sold at high profit in Europe. The trade led to a decline in war as coastal tribes used their newly acquired goods in competition potlatches.*

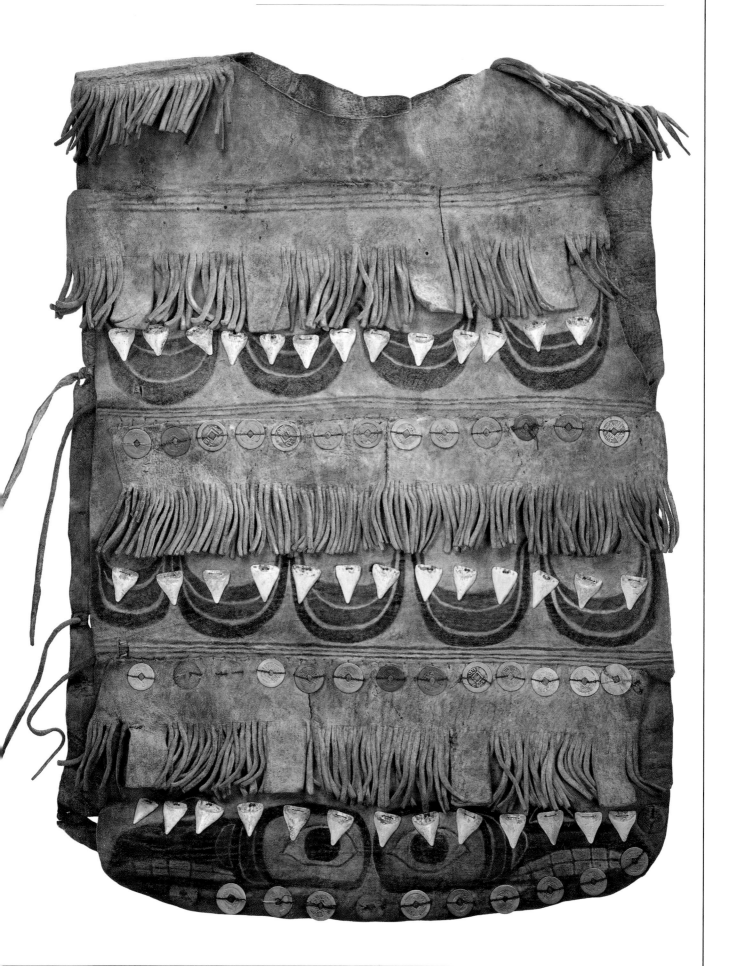

that declarations of challenge and war, normally made by the chiefs and war leaders in other groups, were here a shamanic responsibility. Yet in spite of the fact that Haida shamans introduced direct elements of supernatural practice into these performances, they were ultimately linked with demonstrations of wealth. There was no emphasis on grand, and crushing, displays of excess, but there was, nevertheless, a sense that wealth should ultimately be shown in such abundance as to render a rival incapable of surpassing it.

Among the Haida and Tlingit the status of the individual and clan was gradually established by holding a series of successful potlatches. Each added to the prestige that had previously been acquired; thus the worth of a clan was judged according to what was given at its last potlatch added to its previous prestige value. The Haida extended this concept to include ancestral privileges, which were brought into the performance through wearing portrait masks bearing clan crest markings that formed an historical record of the rights established by family groups. The majority of the masks depicted women, matriarchs of the clans through whom the rights to perform particular dances and ceremonies were handed down. Because these abstract crest markings referred to privileges owned by individuals who could be identified and traced back in a lineal sequence to original contacts with the mythical beings, they could, theoretically, refer to events occurring at the 'beginning of time'.

Frontlets, or forehead masks, depicting the clan crests were used throughout the area to denote chieftainship, although their use among the Tsimshian seems to have been more important than it was with other groups.

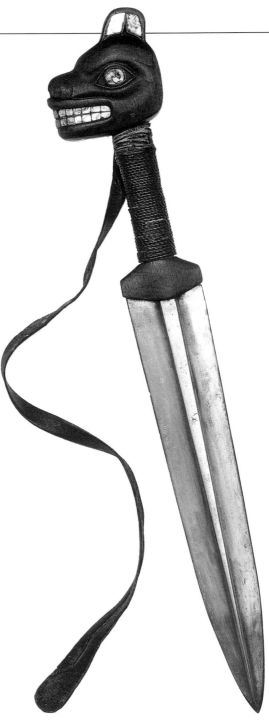

Above: *This double-edged steel-bladed Tlingit dagger has a wooden hilt which is inlaid with haliotis shell and carved in the form of the Bear. In use, the middle finger was placed in the slit at the end of the strap, and the rest wrapped around the wrist to prevent dropping the weapon.*

Left: *Wosnessenski collected this wooden war helmet with a hair fringe in the 1840s and describes it as being that of the 'Evil Spirit'. While it is unlikely this description is accurate, it is clear that the helmet was intended to present a frightening visage. Helmets were worn above the warriors' heads to increase stature.*

Below: *The Bear is featured again on this frontlet, which is made from a piece of hide and worn tied around the forehead. A very early wooden war helmet covered with seal fur, which is now in the Leningrad collections, has an identical form and coloration, suggesting a development from early helmets used in actual warfare to later frontlets that served to demonstrate status in competitive potlatching.*

The Tsimshian also stressed greater ideals of equality and parity in their potlatching, reflected in the fact that chiefs frequently worked co-operatively. This is, perhaps, because major Tsimshian potlatches were actually mortuary ceremonies during which rights were passed on to heirs, but in which the opposing clans had specific duties that it was customary for them to carry out. The carving of a memorial totem pole, for example, was the responsibility of an opposite clan rather than that of direct relatives.

Much of the relatively peaceful interaction existing between the Tsimshian clans resulted from a dependency on trade, which was a major part of their economy. Tsimshian trading canoes regularly plied the dangerous waters of the

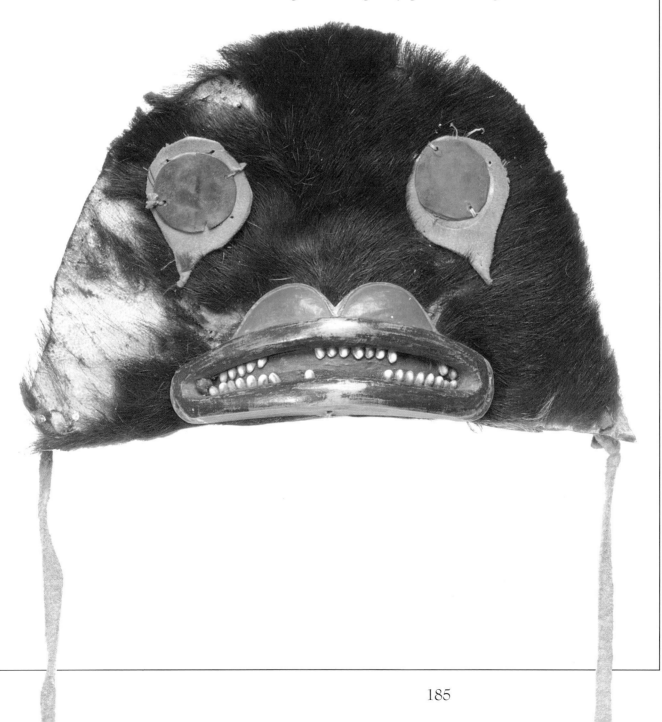

coast, visiting tribes hundreds of miles from their own villages on the Nass and Skeena rivers. They even equated a number of their clans with those of the Haida and Tlingit, based on the similarity of crests. A member of the Wolf clan of the Tlingit would, for instance, find refuge and shelter even during periods of war at a Tsimshian Wolf clan house, recognizing them as 'relatives', although he spoke a different language, through the crests associated with the building and house poles.

Crest markings were also applied by these northern tribes to hats surmounted by hollow basketry rings which served as indicators of potlatch sponsorships, since a new ring was added each time a potlatch was given. During dances, which have been described as 'wild, frenetic, and frenzied', vigorous head movements scattered bird down from inside these rings over the audience. This was symbolic of supernatural goodwill and believed to ensure success and prosperity, as well as being an obvious statement of the family's wealth and ability for gift-giving adequate to maintain a whole series of performances. The great value of the crest hats is clear from their names: Slaves-halfway-around-the-room, Slaves-all-around-the-room, A-stack-of-blankets, and Two-coppers-facing-one-another are typical examples. These names changed each time a potlatch was held, and were added to the permanent name by which the hat was known. Thus the names associated with a single hat were on their own sufficient as a record of sponsorship and wealth.

The rivalry and competition between clans implicit in crest hat names is evident in the Tlingit distinction between two kinds of warfare – feuding between the Tlingit-speaking groups and that fought at an inter-tribal level with speakers of other languages – since it was only in feuding among themselves that privileges could be acquired. Foreign wars were wars of survival, intended to deter or repulse intruders and, perhaps more importantly, to ensure that trade routes into the interior were secure since much of Tlingit wealth stemmed from trading goods from the inland tribes to those of the Northwest Coast.

Above: *These painted paddles were collected in Alaska in 1876 and are probably Tlingit. War parties beat time on the gunwales of their canoes while confronting each other, and some tribes sharpened the ends of the paddles so they would serve a secondary purpose as a weapon.*

Below: *This shaman's mask was collected in 1890 by Tschudnowski on Admiralty Island, Alaska, in Tlingit territory. It is of painted wood, with hair, fur and copper additions. Tlingit shamans featured prominently in warfare, often training the warriors and engaging in supernatural contests with shamans protecting other villages.*

Right: *Carved prow ornaments were mounted on the large sea-going Tlingit war canoes as imposing emblems of the power of the clan. This carving, which is described as being that of the 'Owl-Man', was one of the crests used at Klukwan, the largest Chilkat village. It has been painted, inlaid with abalone shell and trimmed with the fur of the brown bear. The human–animal character of the supernatural beings that guarded and protected warriors is readily apparent in the carving of the head. The grimace on the face is one of determination and shows bared teeth that indicate his warlike intent.*

Tlingit warfare, to an extent unrivalled even by the Haida, was controlled by the shamans. They predicted war by going alone into the forests where they sought signs of whom the war would be fought against and what the outcome would be, and where they renewed their own existing spirit powers and sought additional ones if their quest revealed the presence of a powerful shaman among their intended victims. It was the shaman who recruited the crews to manage the war canoes and who selected the warriors – men who had been trained from birth as fighters through a strict regime of whipping, bathing in ice rivers in winter and prolonged fasts, all intended to toughen the body for the rigors of war. These men were feared even by the people of their own villages, since they walked around scowling and finding fault with everything, knocking down anyone who displeased them.

This fighting elite went into training under the shaman's direction, which could last for several months and was in weapons skills, further toughening of their bodies, and in acquiring the aid and assistance of spirit protectors, rather than in tactics. The Tlingit, in common with all the tribes of the coast, chose to make surprise dawn raids and to kill

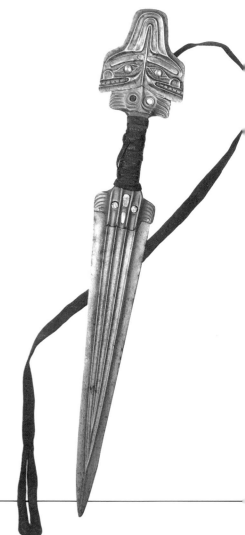

quickly before the occupants of the houses realized what was happening. The shaman also set ceremonial restrictions that women relatives of warriors were under to ensure the successful outcome of a fight while the war canoes were away from the village, and it was he who directed and guided the canoes when the party set out.

A Tlingit war party was impressive. Each fighter wore a heavy elkskin tunic beneath an armored breastplate of wood slats or rods, painted with the crest figures by which he was inspired, and above a collar or visor which covered his face towered a massive wooden helmet carved and painted to represent a war animal or bird, or a human face depicting a shamanic spirit. Such figures step straight from the mists of mythical time and are endowed with supernatural strength They are no longer human, transformed instead into seven foot giants whose terrifying visages are intended to strike fear into the hearts of their opponents. These masked warriors invoked the power of the shamans who guided and protected them, and their helmets may relate to the northern use of decoy hats to lure their victims to the hunters' weapons.

Bows and lances were carried into battle, but the preferred arms of the Tlingit were for hand-to-hand fighting. Their characteristic war daggers, admired today for the beauty of the wolf and bear figures on their carved hilts and the ele-

Above: This magnificent elkskin armor from the Tlingit village of Sitka was collected by the Russian Geographical Society and presented to the Ethnological Society at Leningrad during the Moscow Ethnographic Exhibition in 1867. The armor dates from an earlier period and is a superb example of Tlingit skill in painting on skin. The central motif is a stylized face, but note the manner in which the two flaps on either side of the face have been adapted to represent either wings or fins.

gance of their tapered double-edged blades, were highly effective and deadly weapons capable of passing easily between the ribs of an enemy or severing the jugular vein. A dawn raid, when the half-light and stillness of morning was broken suddenly by a ferocious onrush of these armored figures yelling their spirit cries, left the surprised defenders of a household with little chance of survival.

If, however, the attacking party was discovered and lost the advantage of surprise, instead of following the Kwakiutl practice of seeking an easier target the war fleet was brought up to a distance off-shore, close enough for a voice to carry, while the entire population of the village rushed down to gather on the beach. The oarsmen, using war paddles with sharpened tips, beat time on the gunwales of the canoes while the warriors sang the songs given them by the spirits, until,

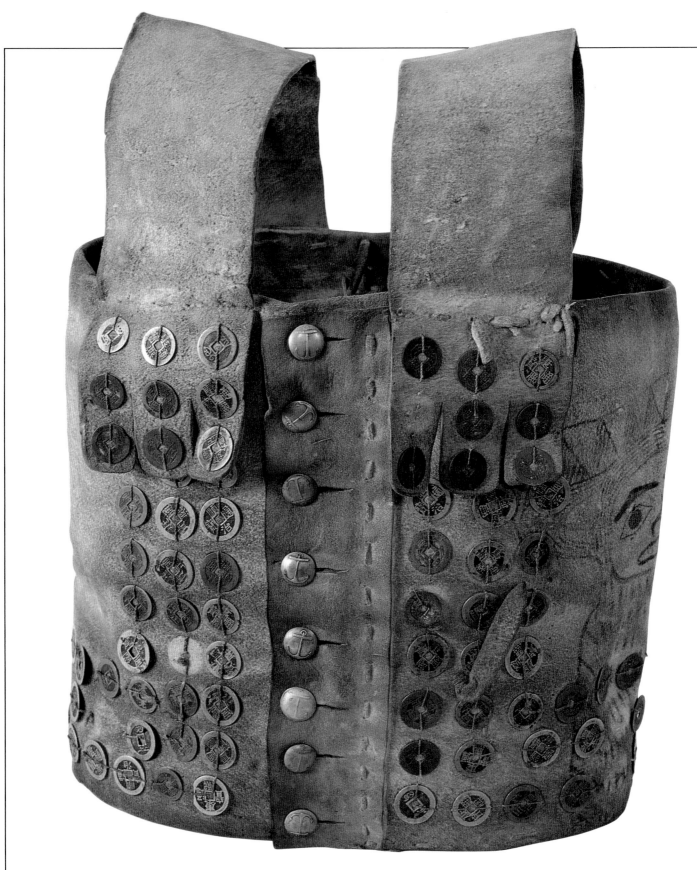

after some time, a dishevelled figure stood up in the prow of the leading canoe.

Although wearing neither armor nor helmet, this figure was no less impressive than the warriors. His hair, which had never been cut, hung in twisted and matted ropes which were said to have an independent life of their own and, without bidding, would begin to curl and curve like snakes. Around his neck were long bone pendants and deformed and twisted roots strung on sinew, while his painted cloak marked with

Above: The shape of this elkskin armor resembles that of wood slat examples, rather than being cut as a shirt. It may have been worn with an undergarment to provide protection for arms and neck. Of interest is the use of Chinese coins and buttons. All Northwest Coast tribes coveted metal and many individual sailors supplemented their meager pay by selling their coat buttons.

Above: *The Yupik-speaking Chugach Eskimo were at the crossroads of Northwest Coast, interior Athapascan and Eskimo groups and display a bewildering variety of cross-cultural influences. The man shown here wears a hat which is suggestive of Northwest Coast clan hats, but also wears a hooded gut parka typical of the Eskimo. Because the Chugach hunted and raided in Tlingit territory there was frequent conflict between these groups.*

Right: *This Seal war helmet from the early Russian collections shows the massive quality of Tlingit carving, which was later to be expressed in a more delicate manner through frontlets. The seal was a major cause of conflict between the Tlingit and the Chugach Eskimo and Aleut, since they all hunted seal in the same areas and felt the others were intruding on territories to which they had exclusive claims.*

symbols of the octopus, grizzly, or otter indicated that he was possessed of shamanic power.

The warriors and the people gathered on the beach fell silent as the shaman began to sing, summoning up his power. 'Whu! Bear! Whu Whu. So you say. Whu, whu, whu! You come. You Grizzly Bear. You come.'[23] Slowly his voice grew stronger as the spirits responded and then, with wild gesticulations and many curses, transported by his fury and anger into something that was no longer of this earth, he began to harangue the people on the beach, telling what spirits assisted him and how they would eat the hearts of the villagers, peck out their eyes, and tear out their tongues. Of how the serpent would twist their necks so they faced backwards, transform their women and children to stone, and leave their bones scattered over the beaches. The shaman's monologue ended abruptly and he sat down.

At this sign, an equally unkempt figure stood up on the beach to screech back at the men in the boats what his spirits would do to them if they dared approach any closer. On completion of his torrent of curses, the shaman in the boat then repeated his performance, adding in additional spirits he could call to his aid. This exchange might continue for several hours, and many Tlingit 'wars' came to a sudden end when the aggressors were convinced they needed greater spiritual help since the village was too well protected by its own shaman. Screaming curses at his rival and telling him he would return after contacting stronger and yet more powerful spirit help, he directed the canoes away from the beach and the war party returned home defeated.

In fighting a foreign war, although the spirit help of the shaman was still considered invaluable to success, the Tlingit relied more directly on surprise in attack or on the fortification of their villages for defence. Some of their villages have been described not only as palisaded, but with tunnels leading from one house to the next to enable escape, with false partitioning and disguised doorways to stop an enemy posting guards who could prevent flight, and even with bear deadfalls scattered liberally over the local terrain to act as a minefield.

Since there was no possibility of acquiring rights or privileges through the defeat of such an enemy, there was no honor to be gained in killing a non-Tlingit. Neither could they be subject to the usual peace ceremonies, in which fighting was concluded by the ceremonial capture of equally ranked members of the opposing parties. These 'captives' lived with their captors for a period of a year, during which they were under ritual constraints and when they and the various names, dances and songs they owned were adopted into the rival's household so that peace could be concluded. For a non-Tlingit, however, this was impossible, since they did not recognize ranking positions of other groups and had no mechanism for assimilating them. Thus wars with foreigners could never be ritually concluded and, accordingly, continued perpetually.

Some of these threats came from the Yupik Eskimo-speaking Chugach of southwestern Alaska and from the Aleut, with whom they shared a number of culture influences. Ideals of status privileges, the importance of shamans and demonstrations of wealth were all mutual customs, as was raiding, which often provided cause for conflict. The Tlingit refer to both the Aleut and Chugach as traditional enemies, distinguishing them from clan rivals, and say the 'Chugach raiders were especially hated because of their sneak attacks and because they raided anybody they saw, without warning and without valid provocation.'[24]

It is clear the Tlingit distrusted the Chugach and Aleut. Language differences undoubtedly contributed to this, and it was frequently implied that their women made poor slaves because they refused to learn the Tlingit language and were always looking for ways to escape or betray their captors. That they came into frequent conflict was unavoidable. They utilized the same resources, and Chugach and Aleut sealing kayaks were seen regularly in coastal waters near Tlingit villages, which the Tlingit interpreted as a violation of the territorial rights they had to these areas. Kodiak Island, which functioned as a trade center for the north, also brought these groups into close proximity with each other.

According to Russian reports, inter-tribal warfare in the area declined after the middle of the nineteenth century. Alexander Baranow, in 1792, and Admiral Lütke, as late as 1828, were confronted by war parties of armored Tlingit warriors. With a decrease in actual conflict war helmets gradually became objects of ceremonial significance, and Wosseneski, in a routine report of 1840, refers to them as

Above: *A Chugach Eskimo woman from Kenai Peninsula is shown here wearing a fur cape typical of interior tribes but displaying shell inserts in her lip that are characteristic of the Eskimo and Northwest Coast. Raiding for women was a common cause of conflict, but the Tlingit claimed that Chugach women made poor slaves because they refused to learn their language and were always looking for an opportunity to betray their captors.*

Right: *The Aleut, occupying the chain of small islands stretching from America toward Siberia, were close linguistic relatives of the Eskimo. Decimated by their early contact with Russian adventurers, there are few examples of Aleut artifacts in modern collections. This walrus ivory armor is one of only three examples and, remarkably, is virtually complete. It follows in the tradition of wood slat armors from the Northwest Coast, but in the absence of timber so far north relies on the use of other materials. It was collected by Kuprianoff, the Russian Governor of Alaska between 1836 and 1840, and passed from his family into the collection of the Grand Duke of Oldenburg.*

'forehead masks' used in ritual dances, implying a change from a war function in battle to a status use as chief's frontlets. It is apparent that the acquisition of wealth through the fur trade, as on the rest of the coast, led to a shift from fighting to potlatch rivalry, and that there was a massive increase in masks and carvings necessary for the increasingly competitive and provocative displays of family privileges and ancestral rights.

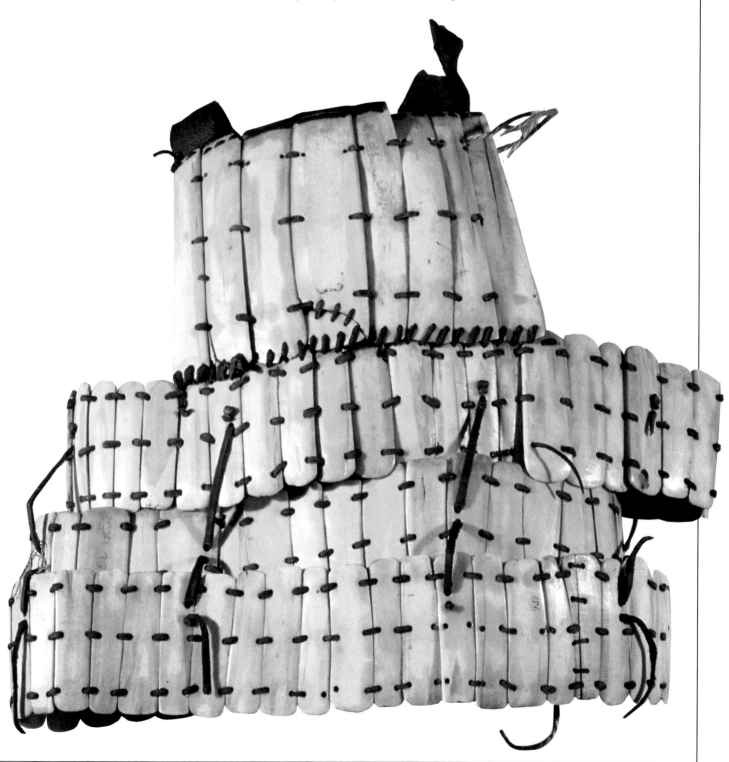

194

THE ARCTIC
AND SUBARCTIC

CHAPTER SIX

Left: These Icy Cape Eskimo men were photographed in Alaska about 1880. Status was important among the Western Eskimo groups and wooden or ivory labrets, or lip plugs, were worn by men who had achieved recognition of their prominent standing in the community.

Above: *This rare Aleut wooden shield with painted designs was collected on Kagamil Island by Dr Ales Hrdlicka in the 1930s, but is from the prehistoric period. Aleut culture was similar to that of the Western Eskimo.*

THE FAR NORTH is an almost unimaginably vast area, comprising half the total land mass of the North American continent; but it was always very sparsely populated. Only the northwestern regions in Alaska and the Yukon River Valley had an occupation of any appreciable size, and even this was never large, consisting of Athapascan (Dene) tribes in the interior, of which the principal groups were the Ingalik, Kutchin and Tanaina, with Yupik-speaking Eskimo on the western coast along Bering Strait and Inuit-speaking Eskimo on the north Alaskan coast.

Although subject to extremely harsh climatic conditions, the Alaska and Yukon region supported a surprisingly large number of game animals and plant resources, resulting in a similar lifestyle among the various groups in spite of their language differences. All have some traditions in common, determined by the environment but also derived in part from inland trade contacts with the Northwest Coast people, and shown particularly in the status of the 'rich man' as a village leader and in displays and give-aways of property to establish social position; the Tanaina even employed the word 'potlatch' to refer to the give-away. The interior groups depended to a high degree on salmon fishing and caribou hunting during the seasonal migrations, which was supplemented with other fish, water fowl, and by gathering herbs, rootsand berries; the coastal Eskimo, however, utilized the resources of the sea and engaged in sea mammal hunting from kayaks in summer, and winter hunting on the ice.

Territorial limits throughout this area were clearly defined. The stability of resources resulted in the establishment of scattered and small, but nevertheless permanent, communities close to the salmon-bearing rivers or on known caribou paths, or on isthmuses and narrow points of land from which sealing kayaks and the larger umiaks could be readily launched. This dispersal of the population, coupled with the uncomprising nature of the lands in which they lived, result-

ed in social extremes whereby a rare visit from distant relatives was greeted by an almost complete cessation of other activities, when the people indulged in feasting, storytellingand exchanges of news. Anyone they did not know was regarded with deep suspicion.

The immediate reaction on seeing strangers approaching was to view them as a potential threat. Travel into these cold and inhospitable northern regions was usually either by invitation or with hostile intent, and they believed that a moving object, if studied carefully enough, would reveal details that identified both it and its purpose. Careful scrutiny of an approaching party was therefore made to identify clothing decoration that was familiar or whether women and children traveled with the group, indicating a friendly approach; but 'if the strangers were all men [the women and children] ran and tried to hide ... the men of the settlement armed themselves and formed a line in front of the village'[1] ready to repulse any attack.

Sometimes these meetings resulted in a cautious exchange of courtesies, since both Native traditions and reports from the occasional European travelers in the area suggest that friendly overtures might mask an intention to catch the other group off-guard and unawares; but often they led to conflict, when opposing lines of warriors engaged in fire fights from a distance using bows and arrows. These tended, however, to be threatening displays and shows of warrior power that caused little harm to either party, resulting in woundings but only rarely in serious injuries.

Among the Eskimo, battles might be initiated and decided by shamans without any physical contact occurring at all. In this region of occasionally scarce resources, the caprices of the weather and of animals were felt to be controlled by some metaphysical force. Shamans drew on this power, and inspired by the spirits of the sea – which were under the authority of the Underwater Goddess, Sedna, who periodically lost patience with the failings of humans and withdrew the sea mammals or caused men to fight among

Above: *The Athapascan-speaking Ingalik shared many cultural traits with the Yupik-speaking Eskimo and often traded with them, although it is also clear that conflicts did occur. This bone Ingalik knife is decorated with typical Eskimo designs and may, therefore, be an item that had been exchanged either through trade or by capture.*

Below: *This Bear mask was collected at the Ingalik village of Shageluk on a tributary of the lower Yukon River. Unlike other Athapascan groups, the Ingalik had a rich tradition of masked dances which they shared with their Yupik Eskimo neighbors and from whom there appears to have been a cross-cultural influence. The mask depicted here was collected by the Rev. John W. Chapman, missionary at the Ingalik's principal village of Anvik, prior to 1905.*

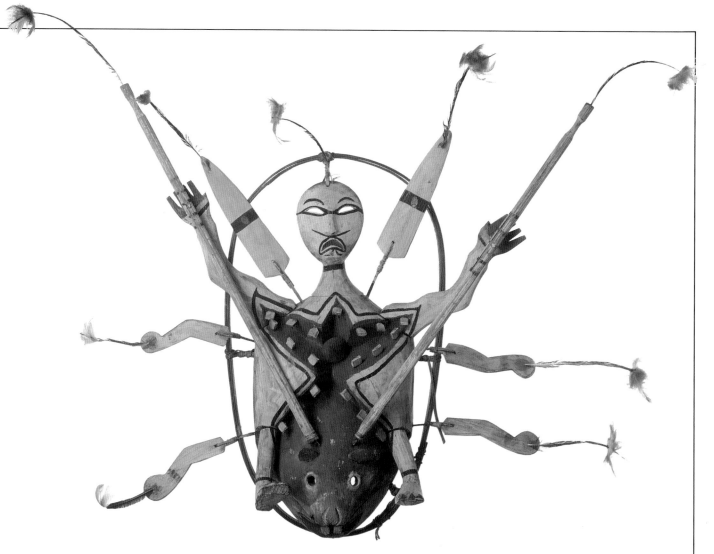

Above: *A shaman's spirit astride an animal that appears to be a Beaver is shown on this spectacular Eskimo mask from the lower Kuskokwim River. It is inscribed 'September 1881', and is of painted wood, with feather, willow, gut fiber and twine decorations and attachments. The shaman is shown in the characteristic X-ray style of the Yupik Eskimo that denotes a spirit figure rather than a representation of an actual person. The Beaver is the shaman's helper. Shamans were felt to be able to send their spirits on out-of-body journeys when, with the assistance of their animal helper, they would locate game or determine the direction from which danger threatened. Much 'warfare' was carried out at this spiritual level between shamans of opposing groups, who tested their powers against one another.*

themselves – they sent their souls on out-of-body journeys beneath the waves where they fought for supremacy. The outcome of such a conflict was often indecisive and might become apparent only after several years, when the debilitating effect on the defeated shaman began to show in increasing lethargy, loss of appetite, inability to sleep and a general weakening of his powers.

Battles in which a war party came upon an unsuspecting village during the night while the occupants were sleeping proved more immediately deadly. Kutchin warriors recall carrying containers of oil with them to pour over the driftwood and sod houses of their main enemies, the Eskimo, with the intention of setting fire to the buildings and burning the inhabitants alive, claiming this was because the Eskimo would do the same to them. They also tell of fixing sharp bone spikes to the undersides of their snowshoes to enable them to detect anyone hiding under the snow, and boasting that many of the tools and weapons in daily use had been captured from Eskimo villages.

Much of the tenor of these comments suggests bragging, which is also apparent in references they contain to the effect that the Eskimo always started the wars but the Kutchin always won them! When fighting did occur it may have been brutal, yet the population was too thinly scattered for opportunity to have arisen with any regular frequency, and the size of the communities meant that warfare was limited to small-scale raiding and never carried out as pitched battles involving considerable numbers of participants.

But it is impossible to overlook the fact that warriors might show no compassion and give little quarter to their enemies. Reports of the Eskimo torturing their victims, dismembering their bodies, and of head-taking, are recorded too frequently to be ignored, although they appear never to have scalped their foes. Athapascan treatment of both Eskimo and other Dene groups, since fighting was usually inspired by revenge, might be no more lenient: tales exist of them breaking an opponent's bones to render him helpless and then leaving him on the ice without killing him, or of stripping him of all his clothing and suspending him from the branch of a tree where he was left to freeze to death.

Attitudes to warfare did, however, vary among the Athapascan tribes of this area. Most name the Eskimo as their 'traditional enemy', the Tanaina taking this to the extent that animal skins and hides were regularly hidden because they were relatively scarce in the coastal regions and

Below: *The brown, yellow and white quillwork on this quiver suggests that it originates from the Kenai Peninsula and should be attributed to the Tanaina. It is an early and unique example which was placed in the Museum collections in Berlin prior to 1850.*

Above: This Tanaina caribou antler club was collected by Kuprianoff between 1836 and 1840. It is large and heavy, and would originally have had an inset obsidian blade.

Below: The Bear was a symbol of physical and spiritual power to the Athapascans of the Subarctic, and was often sought as an aid in dangerous undertakings. This small nineteenth-century charm is made from a bear's tooth and is decorated with fine quillwork.

a desire to acquire them might provide reason for an Eskimo raid. But the Ingalik - whose culture and use of masks is more similar to that of the Eskimo than any other of the Athapascan groups – deny they fought with the Eskimo, and say their only 'wars' were retaliations carried out if they felt they had been shamed. Certainly the Ingalik were traditionally peaceful, more given to trading than fighting, and inclined to rely on the resolution of disputes through contests between shamans.

They would burn or throw away a bow that had been used in war or a lance which had taken someone's life, yet war must have played some significant role in Ingalik belief, since they also possessed moose or caribou bone clubs and slate knives which had a primary function as offensive weapons. These were considered to be family heirlooms, and instead of being destroyed they formed part of the inheritance a boy received from his father or uncle. When such importance is given to clearly aggressive objects, it is hard to ascribe a totally negative attitude toward the importance of war skills or the existence of some level of recognition of fighting ability. This is further suggested by a war custom in which a warrior, on defeating an enemy who had fought with particular courage and bravery, might eat the eye of his opponent in order to gain some of his strength.

It may be that the destruction of the lance and bow after warfare was because these, unlike the club and knife, were hunting weapons, bows being in general use whereas the lance was reserved specifically for killing bears. The animals were believed to give their lives willingly to enable the people to survive, and would be resurrected if the proper ritual observances were performed; thus contamination with human blood could easily be thought of as noxious to the animal spirits, whose role was a supportive one, thereby rendering weapons ineffective in the chase whose power had been 'abused' through war.

This concern for placating the spirits is also apparent in another curious Ingalik war custom. Before entering a fight, the warriors changed out of their everyday clothing, bathed and perfumed themselves, dressed their hair, and then put on clothes that had not previously been worn. In this way, should they be killed, they would enter the spirit world appropriately dressed and in a manner the spirits would find pleasing.

In contrast to the Ingalik, the Kutchin have been described as 'fighters, that at least among the Northern Athapaskan tribes they have been regarded as enemies to respect, superior on the whole to surrounding groups'.[2] They told Osgood they had four reasons for going to war: to capture Eskimo possessions; to acquire prestige; the capture of women; and revenge. Of these, revenge seems to have been paramount 'and the bitterness of this feeling is perhaps the greatest cause of all.'[3]

Prior to setting off on a raid, the Kutchin held a council at which the views of the rich men and the warriors were presented. These might be quite acrimonious, leading to argument and heated discussion between those in favor and those against. Village leaders, who were likely to err on the side of caution rather than risk a confrontation that could prove disastrous, relied on their persuasive powers to win over the warriors, but they had no authority whereby they could forbid hot-headed young men from continuing a feud with an enemy. Other older people encouraged them to fight. An old man might recite the brave deeds he had performed as a youth, and sometimes women made speeches in which they recalled being caught by the enemy and told of how they had been mistreated, urging the young men to do the same to any women they captured.

Once consent for the raid had been reached, the council elected a war leader; usually younger than the village leader, this was someone renowned for his bravery and courage in difficult situations and who could be relied upon to remain calm in the excitement of battle. The young men painted their faces black 'so the enemy will not recognize us if we meet them again at a later date', rather than using their usual facepaints through which both personal and tribal identity were known, and consulted the shamans for auspicious signs. The shamans sometimes killed a ptarmigan and made each member of the war party eat a little of the raw meat; anyone who vomited on this would remain in camp, since it was a certain sign that bad luck awaited him.

Reports suggest that the warriors, on their way to the enemy camp, demonstrated their aggressiveness by killing

Above: *This Loucheux, or eastern Kutchin, Indian was drawn by W. G. R. Hind in the 1840s. The skin gun case in which his rifle is carried was an essential requirement in the Subarctic, since low temperatures would cause any moving parts of such weapons to freeze and render them ineffective.*

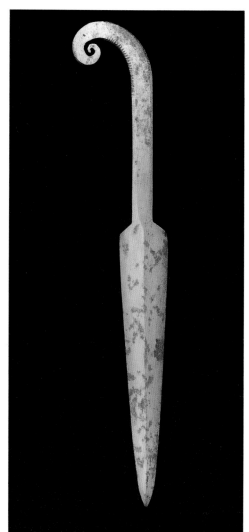

any animal that crossed their path. It is said this was done to prevent the animals carrying news of the war party to their opponents, although it is also suggested they would prove their bravery by killing a bear with lances. This may have been intended as proof that the weapons had the power to overcome these human-like adversaries and would, therefore, prove equally effective against real humans when the fight took place, since the bear was feared as a potent supernatural force and often considered as a 'relative' to man. It is also possible that the blood of the bear was thought to transfer some of the animal's supernatural power to the lance, thereby rendering it more deadly, an inverse effect to that of the

Above: *Steel knives, traded into the area, quickly became popular items to supplement the other weapons a warrior carried with him and for general all-purpose use. The form of the knife shown here is similar to that depicted by Hind in the belt of the Loucheux warrior shown in his pencil sketch at the left.*

Right: *A Kutchin shirt from the Yukon River, circa 1860, showing decoration similar to that in Hind's drawing. Such shirts were made from caribou hide and decorated with cut fringes, porcupine quillwork, beads and paint. Although the traditional seaming lines at the side of the shirt are depicted in red ochre, it has been enlarged at some time with gussets sewn at the sides.*

Left: *This Loucheux shirt or tunic, from before 1860, is decorated with beads, cut fringes and dentalia shells. Such richly ornamented clothing indicates its owner was a wealthy individual by Kutchin standards and enjoyed high status, possibly as the leader of a local community.*

Above: *Alexander Murray, in his **Journal of the Yukon, 1847–48**, described this Han Kutchin man as being a prominent leader of his people. Note the striking similarity between the status shirt he is wearing compared with that shown in the photograph.*

Ingalik where human blood contaminated the lance and made it ineffective for use against a bear.

Kutchin belief credited power not only to blood, but also to the fat of an animal or human. Animal fat was fed to the fire as an offering at meals, and the Fire Spirit was appeased in a similar manner. Thus, 'when the fire made a hissing noise [the spirit's voice] they threw in some fat, and asked to be able to kill some animal'.[4] Human fat was thought to be equally effective in warding off the convulsions said to beset a novice warrior after killing his first enemy. To prevent these, the dead man's stomach was cut open and the novice ate a small piece of the raw fat, thereby ensuring freedom from 'war sickness' and bringing good luck in the future. This human fat was considered so powerful, that ritual consumption after his first killing was sufficient to protect the warrior for the rest of his life.

Eating human fat also helped stop a warrior turning into a wild man, or Na-in, by acting as an antidote to 'bad medicine'. The origin of the Na-in, who travel invisibly during the summer months and steal people for their chief, is said to be the result of 'magic' which 'caused much strife and bloodfeud inside and between the tribes. Some men would finally reach the unenviable state of having a bloodfeud with every person in their own tribe and being connected with intertribal quarrels also. With every man's hand against them, they become like hunted beasts, living in holes under the banks of rivers, not daring to light fires, killing anyone they could.'[5] In addition to their power to kill, the Na-in were responsible for many of the dangers and frustrations facing the community; thus if a hunter failed to get within range of his quarry it was felt a Na-in had scared the animal away, and if a branch of a tree fell on a building it was because a Na-in had thrown it.

Much of the power of the Na-in was credited to their extensive use of shamanism, and the shamans of the people were accordingly expected to use their abilities to try to counteract this, although they were also often under suspicion of acting in collusion with the Na-in and directing 'magic' against someone who had displeased them. This negative power could, however, be used positively by the community through sending it against their enemies; the Han Kutchin actually believed that all war and feuding was initiated by shamans who sent their power out to kill at vast distances.

A belief in the ability of shamans to kill at a distance was not confined to the northwestern areas, but

Above: *Although this steel knife is inscribed 'Esquimeaux' on the back, it is nevertheless a classic example of the typical volute-handled knives used by the Northern Athapascans. It dates from 1866.*

Right: *This has been cataloged as 'an ornamented leather pouch for suspension around the neck' but a knife sheath such as would have been worn around the neck by Northern Athapascan groups.*

was widely held throughout the Arctic and Subarctic. In many ways it helped the scattered tribal groups come to terms with the hostile environment in which they lived, and where any slight misfortune might bring disaster. If migratory animals were late or the fish runs were delayed, entire communities might starve, and a hunter who broke a leg even a short distance from camp was likely to freeze to death before he could be rescued. Under such circumstances it was believed that a series of accidents or deaths were caused by power being worked against the community, and since shamans interacted with these forces it was logical to assume they were in some part responsible for directing them.

In the area considered so far, a belief in shamanic feuding might result in retaliatory raids when the death of an important member of the community occurred; elsewhere the populations were even more widely separated – with a density that has been estimated as only one person per 100 square miles – and although a belief in the powers of the shamans was just as strongly held, raiding was generally prevented simply by the fact that different groups so rarely had contact with one another. This meant there were no local village groups against whom aggression could be directed, resulting in few formalized procedures for the conduct of war or the organization of war parties.

That the people of the central and eastern areas were far less warlike than those of Alaska and the Yukon was noted by Lord Lonsdale in a letter sent from the Arctic to Lady Lonsdale in the late 1880s. He wrote 'It seems a very remarkable fact that the Esqimeaux of the East & up to the Coppermine River are so charming obliging and friendly, small stout men, & that the McKenzie River Esquimeaux are over 6 feet high, savage, & as tretcherous as its possible to Imagine. Every one I meet warn me of the danger But I cannot & will not believe that if properly delt with, that they varie from their Eastern brethren to such a considerable degree.'[6]

They did, however, vary from their western relatives in a number of important respects. The central and eastern Inuit, living on the innumerable islands of the Arctic Ocean and Baffin Bay, and on much of the shoreline of Hudson's Bay, viewed warfare in a decidedly negative light. Feuding within a village was common and might last for years, pitting one family against another in a struggle to settle personal scores, but this rarely led to bloodshed and was not carried beyond the immediate group to involve distant families. Infrequent contacts with other Inuit communities were usually cooperative ones, to the extent that caches of frozen meat were

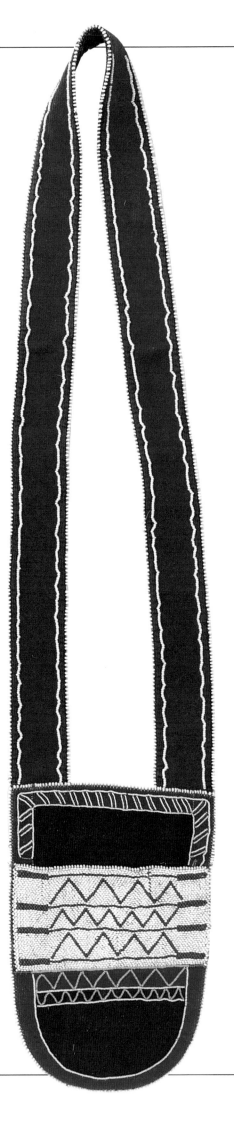

clearly marked so that during periods of shortages any travelers in the area had access to them.

It may, in fact, be that the unpredictable Arctic environments forced a policy of non-violence, since cooperation was essential to survival, and the needs of the group always took precedence over those of the individual. Deaths were treated as an inevitable consequence of living under difficult conditions, and because no single person held a dominant position there was little impetus for insult feuds to concern anyone other than those directly involved. The belief that a shaman, or angakok, could use power for evil-doing was seen in a similar light, as a result of individual animosities and jealousies between rival shamans but only of interest to the group if it disrupted other activities. When arguments of any kind did become disruptive they might be resolved peacefully; thus among the Baffin Land Eskimo 'grudges were settled by the opponents meeting by appointment and singing sarcastic songs at each other. The one who creates the most laughter is regarded as the victor.'[7]

The non-aggressive ideal of the Inuit was general throughout much of the central and eastern Subarctic. Athapascan-speaking groups extended across the continent from their linguistic relatives in Alaska and the Yukon to the western shores of Hudson's Bay, and south into British Columbia and Alberta. Although referring to themselves by derivatives of the word Dene, meaning The People, for purposes of classification and convenience 'tribal' names have been given by which they are now better known. The main groups are the Carrier, Sekani and Tahltan in interior British Columbia; the Beaver and Slavey in Alberta, with Slavey areas extending further to the north; and, from west to east, the

Above: Warfare was conducted by men but involved women, since their abduction was often the intent. Awls might be employed by the women in defence. This one, though not Subarctic, shows a generalized form in which the point is made from an old file blade.

Left: The small caribou skin pouch shown here is decorated with blue and red flannel and beads and was made by the Tahltan on the Stikine River in British Columbia. Though described as being worn on ceremonial occasions, it is of a type that was often used for carrying shot.

Right: Rocks feature prominently in Athapascan myth and, in the barren northern habitats, were important landmarks or served as fortresses. Shown here is Franklin's Big Stone Hill, a landmark for the Dog-Rib Indians.

Mountain, Hare, Dogrib, Yellowknife and Chipewyan of the North West Territories.

Chipewyan lands bordered on those occupied by the Algonkian-speaking Cree. Scattered in small hunting bands throughout much of Alberta, Saskatchewan, Manitoba, Ontario and Quebec, but with relatively large and settled communities in the James Bay area, the Cree were the dominant force in the eastern Subarctic. The region was also occupied by other Algonkian-speakers: northern Ojibwa in Ontario; the Montagnais-Naskapi in northern Quebec and Labrador; and the Beothuk in Newfoundland.

All the groups of the Subarctic lived as highly nomadic, small, extended family bands, without any tribal structure and no recognized chiefs. The shamans, however, had tremendous influence. By using their skills either as a means of direct intervention, or indirectly by empowering sacred objects that would guarantee individual successes, they were responsible for both the physical and spiritual survival of the camp. In war, other than shamanic feuding, they were expected to locate the enemy, to foresee the outcome, and to travel with the war party for the purpose of singing songs before an engagement that were intended to put the enemy to sleep. 'War', of course, refers to rare events, usually revenge raids, since the groups were so scattered. The fact that it was so infrequent is reflected in the fact that one old blind man was a recognized war leader because during his lifetime he had killed two men during a fight.

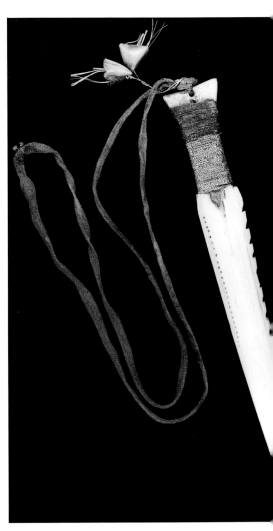

Below: *The Naskapi, living in areas where weather conditions could be extremely severe, relied on the power of charms, dreams, songs and even of good thoughts, to ensure their survival. These good thoughts, or wish dreams, were incised and painted on clothing using stylized symbols that related to various forces in nature, to the animals, or to trees and plants. Through them the spirit power inherent in them was encouraged to return goodness to the hunter or warrior by protecting him and ensuring his survival through signs advising him when danger threatened.*

Another war leader, a very old man, was clearly considered as such because of his possession of shamanic powers. 'He had a cap with eagle feathers on it and pelican's skin under his throat. He did not kill people himself for that would spoil his medicine. He would come close to the camp and sing. That would blind the enemy.'[8] The use of 'medicine' or 'magic' to overcome an enemy occurs very regularly in tales of the Athapascans and Algonkians. A typical Athapascan tale, from the Beaver, is about a young hunter who left his wife and child alone in their caribou skin tipi while he went searching for food.

In his absence the child saw the face of a man peering over the tipi entrance reflected in a bowl of water. His mother looked to see what was attracting the child's curiosity, but said nothing and carried on with the rawhide lacing she was putting on a pair of snowshoes. On telling her husband about the stranger when he returned, he urged her to finish the snowshoes before nightfall and then to take the child and go to her parent's tipi, which was nearby; he intended to wait

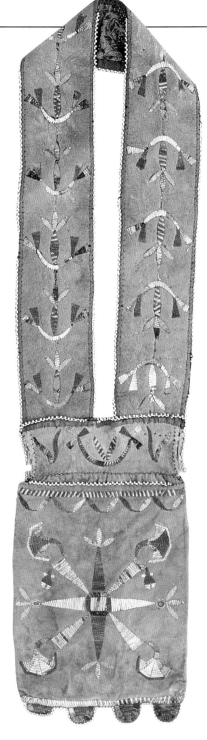

for the enemy. That night he built a large fire in the tipi, giving the impression it was occupied, and waited close by hidden in the trees. He soon heard a shaman's sleep song, which his own power enabled him to resist, and shortly afterwards several men rushed out of the forest, shouting loudly, shooting arrows into the tipi, and stabbing through the skin cover with long lances.

When they realized the lodge was empty, the young hunter leaped from cover and began to run. His large snowshoes, the ones he had asked his wife to complete that day, carried him swiftly over the surface of the snow, whereas his pursuers were having difficulty keeping up. 'Making use of his medicine, he called for a south wind. It came and the party pursuing him began to sweat and drop off their clothes. When he had led them a long way from their clothes he called for a north wind. It came, and the sweating enemy turned to go back for their abandoned clothing. On their way back they huddled around fires trying to keep warm. The man now turned on them and speared them, half frozen by their fires and killed them all.'9

These tales give superhuman strength to a culture hero, who is able to use his power in defeating the natural elements as readily as he uses them against human opponents. A magic song might be sung to attract moose, or a hunter carrying a male and a female arrow would track down and unerringly employ them to kill a bull and cow caribou. These were not the exclusive property of men. In one tale, where the entire village was starving, a woman sang a song for caribou, and although she only had a sewing awl, by tying this to a long stick she was able to kill so many from the vast herd which responded to her singing that the dried meat was sufficient to last through the winter.

The close correlation between tales of war and hunting, and the fact the same magic is effective in both, suggest these should be considered as tales of survival rather than be read too literally as descriptions of actual warfare and war practice. Indeed, the regularity with which war is mentioned seems to imply they refer to battles against difficult odds and not necessarily to fights with other people. Warfare was never as frequent as a cursory reading of the stories would indicate, but it was not unusual for entire hunting bands to perish during the bitter winters, and their failure to rendezvous with other families in spring for cooperative hunting and fishing might well be ascribed to enemy action.

The Chipewyan, however, specifically name the Cree in all their stories of war. As the most easterly of the Athapascan-speaking groups they were in close, and presumably hostile,

Above: *Athapascan lore suggests the Cree were regarded as a more formidable enemy by those tribes living near them. This pouch, for carrying shot, is probably Cree.*

Left: *The Cree had been heavily influenced by Plains culture and by the introduction of European trade goods when Paul Kane painted this portrait in 1847. They acted as middlemen in the fur trade between the Hudson's Bay Company and Athapascan tribes living too far west to travel easily to the trading posts, often forcing the less well-armed Athapascans to part with their rich furs at a fraction of their value.*

contact with the Cree, who appear to have made regular incursions into their country. Sir Alexander Mackenzie, following two remarkable journeys of discovery through the Subarctic in 1789 and 1793, noted in his 'General History of the Fur Trade &c' that 'as for the Kniſtenaux [Cree], there is no queſtion of their having been, and continuing to be, invaders of this country, from the Eaſtward. Formerly, they ſtruck terror into all the other tribes whom they met.'[10] That the Cree were the aggressors in also reflected when Mackenzie, commenting on the Chipewyan, says 'In their quarrels with each other, they very rarely proceed to a greater degree of violence than is occaſioned by blows, wreſtling, and pulling of the hair, while their abuſive language conſiſts in applying the name of the moſt offenſive animal to the object of their diſpleaſure, and adding the term ugly, and chiay, or ſtill-born.'[11]

Chipewyan tales have the same ethos and point to the Cree as intruders. In one of these 'a band of Chipewyan were staying by a lake. While the men were hunting, some Cree stole two of the Chipewyan women, who were sisters. Returning, the Chipewyan wanted to go after the Cree, but there were too few of them. So they stayed where they were, and continued to hunt deer.'[12] This tale is often linked with that of Marten-Axe, a wonderful medicine man and brother to the stolen women, who set out alone determined to revenge their abduction.

Marten-Axe was said 'to know all languages', and when he found the war party was easily able to convince them that he, too, was Cree and that the Chipewyans had killed all his friends. The Cree, believing this story, permitted him to travel with them to the top of a high mountain where they intended to camp overnight. Waiting until they were asleep, Marten-Axe unwound a long rope he had wrapped around his body, and with this tied all the legs of the sleeping warriors to the same rock. Then he rolled the rock down the mountain, killing them all.

The higher level of aggression among the Cree stems from their formation of larger settlements, which gave them the ability to organize war parties in which greater numbers were involved; the harsh interior conditions, however limited these excursions to the summer months when sufficient resources were available to maintain them. Since this was also the time of year when Chipewyan families worked cooperatively it is quite possible that confrontations of some size could have taken place, although probably never numbering more than about thirty warriors on either side. Most war parties, however, consisted of ten or fewer men.

Above: *The decoration on this knife sheath from the Vancouver collection in the British Museum suggests that it is from one of the more southerly of the Northern Athapascan groups, possibly the Sarsi.*

Right: *Chula, the great Sarsi chief who was known to the Blackfoot as Bull head, was a reluctant signer of Treaty Number 7 at Blackfoot Crossing in 1877. This treaty assigned reservation lands to the Blackfoot and Sarsi, but the Sarsi quarreled with the Blackfoot, and when Chula was asked where the Sarsi wished to live he asked each warrior to place a stone at the place. This pile of stones reflects the significance of the rock in Athapascan thought and it is said it can still be seen on the Sarsi reservation.*

Throughout the eastern Subarctic, Algonkian warfare followed a very similar pattern of small and infrequent raids guided by shamans or, at least, under some form of shamanic protection, as has already been described for the Athapascans. Generally, the harsher the conditions the more infrequently raiders set out with hostile intent; thus among the caribou-hunting Montagnais-Naskapi of Labrador, where temperatures remain below zero all year, warfare was virtually unknown. Even in summer, conditions here are so severe that the formation of large groups or communal gatherings is impossible except for a short summer rendezvous on the coast, while winter is known as 'the time of starvation'.

The absence of warfare is explained simply by the fact that time and energy were expended continually on obtaining adequate supplies and provisions, and hunters resorted to many 'magic' procedures to ensure their efforts would be rewarded. Caribou skin hunting coats, painted with stylized representations of spirit power, kept the hunter in constant contact with these supernatural helpers, some of the coats bearing designs on the inside so that the hunter is literally 'wrapped in power'. Wish power was also used, in which by concentrating all his thought on the successful completion of an objective the hunter was believed to will game animals to his traps or to bring them close enough for him to effectively deploy his weapons.

Yet avoidance of starvation, even for the most successful hunter, was often a question of luck, and each spring brought news of families that had perished during the previous win-

Above: *This Dog-Rib lodge, photographed in the summer of 1910, is erected on a bare windswept rock, the favorite camp site for the Northern Athapascans. Note, however, the horizontal stripe painted on the skin cover. This characteristic division is a distinctive Athapascan trait and can be seen today on Sarsi tipis, even though they adopted a fully equestrian Plains lifestyle after moving south and allying with the Blackfoot.*

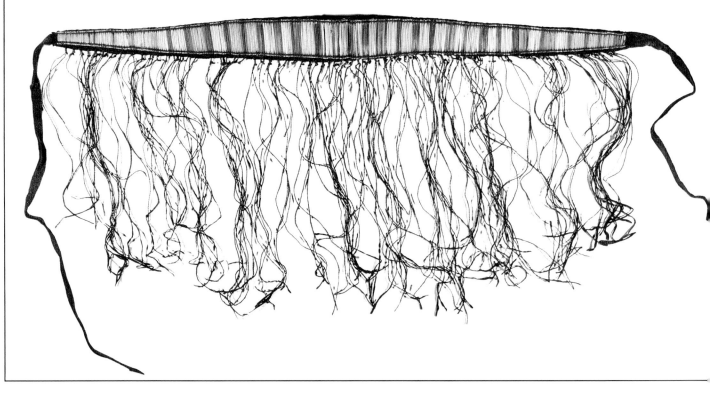

Above: This knife and sheath date from the 1840s and are decorated with dyed bird quills. The hilt is part of a bear's jaw. It was collected by the Duke of Württemberg and is labeled 'scalping knife, Blackfoot Indians', but the reference to the Bear and the patterning of the quillwork suggests it may be of Northern Athapascan origin.

Left: Details of the decoration on this burden strap are remarkably similar to that on the knife sheath shown above. Such straps are typical of the Dog-Rib and Slavey, Athapascan-speaking tribes living to the north of the Blackfoot and sharing the same cultural traditions as the Blackfoot's allies, the Sarsi.

ter. Reports of cannibalism being resorted to in cases of extreme famine were common, and there is no doubt the Montagnais-Naskapi firmly believed in it as a possibility; since their traditions say that someone who has eaten human flesh becomes a wi'tigo, and that this was thought to affect the spirit, making it so strong that only a shaman's power could cause him harm.

To what extent cannibalism was actually practiced is, however, a matter of dispute. One report mentions a woman who 'had eaten no less than fourteen of her friends and relatives during one winter'[13] whereas another says 'at present there is not a single authentic instance of anthropophagy within the area among the Indians themselves, although one actual case within the last twenty years is on documentary record where whites were guilty of it and an Indian the victim.'[14]

Regardless of the frequency, or indeed the existence, of cannibalism among the Montagnais-Naskapi, their life was simply an extreme instance of the continual struggle for survival which faced all the people living in the Arctic and Subarctic. For some of the southern Cree and Ojibwa, summer movements on to the northern Great Plains gave access to buffalo, eventually leading them to virtually abandon their Subarctic homelands and adopt the customs and lifestyles of the Plains tribes. The Athapascan-speaking Sarsi made a similar move to southern Alberta from the dense forests of the northwestern regions, adapting to a fully nomadic equestrian buffalo-hunting culture, and later allying themselves with the Blackfoot where they became the defenders of the Blackfoot's northern borders although retaining their own language and beliefs. Thus the Sarsi, brought Dene traditions and ideals with them that they continue to express.

WARRIOR SOCIETIES AND GAMES

CHAPTER SEVEN

Left: Pitätapiú, an Assiniboine warrior, holds a bow-lance indicative of Warrior Society membership in his right hand in this painting by Karl Bodmer. Bodmer met him at Fort Union in 1833, when this portrait was made and when Prince Maximilian commented that Pitätapiú's rawhide shield had an attached amulet to ensure success in horse raids, that he had a wooden riding quirt hanging from a fur loop around his right wrist, and that the bow-lance he carried was decorated with soft cured bear entrails. Although Prince Maximilian felt that the bow-lance was carried only 'for show', it is clear that Pitätapiú was a prominent member of one of the Assiniboine military societies.

Aᴛᴛᴇʀ ᴛʜᴇɪʀ ᴍɪɢʀᴀᴛɪᴏɴ from the north and the alliance they made with the Blackfoot, the Sarsi, who refer to themselves as the Tsu T'ina, 'many people', adopted a number of highly characteristic Plains traits or modified the emphasis in existing patterns of Subarctic belief to accommodate the different demands made on them by a grasslands environment and a nomadic buffalo hunting culture. One of the most important of these adaptations was the formation of Warrior Societies. Tsu T'ina societies show obvious Blackfoot influence, in that most of them are said to have originated with the Blackfoot, and the purchase of memberships is a Blackfoot practice; the Sarsi, however, claim that membership was not decided according to age as among the Blackfoot, and that the Mosquitoes, to which many of the young warriors of the tribe belonged, originated among themselves and passed from them to the Blackfoot tribes.

Although fully age-graded systems are known only for the Blackfoot, Arapaho, Gros Ventre, Mandan and Hidatsa, some aspects of grading are, however, suggested for the Sarsi; since the Mosquitoes were considered least important and less dignified than the Dogs, Police, Preventers and Dawö, and most men successively joined the Societies in this order: the Dawö consisting almost entirely of older warriors who were no longer active fighters. To what extent any of the Sarsi societies were directly involved in warfare is debatable,

Right: These pictographic tipis were photographed by Fiske at Fort Yates and show the characteristic style of the Siouan-speaking groups in making records of war honors. The foreground tipi is that owned by Old Bull, and has richly decorated smoke flaps as well as a 'medicine tail' fastened to the top of one of the poles.

215

but war symbolism nevertheless plays a part in much of their ritual practice. Thus among the Preventers, the transfer of the office of leader was marked by remaking the bow and four arrows that were emblems of his rank, and this could only be done by someone who had killed an enemy. Similarly, the end of a society performance was followed by the recounting of war honors and a distribution of property, which was common practice on the return of a successful war party.

In most details the Sarsi organization follows a generalized Plains pattern in which warriors joined fraternities of men at various stages of their careers, and whose ceremonies were largely those of proclaiming the war honors of their members during the summer tribal encampments; they also acted in the capacity of controling the camp under the authority of the chiefs and of regulating the communal buffalo hunts (though the Sarsi say their societies did not function in this capacity). According to Sarsi traditions one of the collective responsibilities of the young warriors was to dance over the tall prairie grasses to level them prior to the

Left: *This painted carving of a mounted figure carrying a lance was used by a Piegan (Blackfoot confederacy) warrior during council meetings as a symbol of his heroic accomplishments. It is set on a pointed stick so that it could be thrust into the ground in front of the warrior's place in the council, and depicts him riding down an enemy. It dates from about 1880.*

Right: *The war medicine shown here, from the 1870s, was collected among the Blood (Blackfoot confederacy). It is made from painted wood, with a horsehair 'scalp' attached to the bridle, dyed wool mane and a horsetail. The two red arrows are tipped with leather points. It was worn on the warrior's back during battle to give him the power of his magic horse.*

Left: *Karl Bodmer met this Piegan warrior at Fort Mackenzie, just north of Great Falls, Montana, in 1833. Of interest here are the striped leggings, showing him to be a prominent warrior, and the valuable cougar skin thrown across the back of his horse as a saddle blanket. This skin appears to have been sewn to red cloth which is cut to match its shape. Note, too, that he is armed with a rifle but also carries a combined bow and arrow quiver slung across his shoulders.*

performance of the Sun Dance; crossing the area with movements that echoed those of the grass in the wind, they made the ground safe and ensured that warrior power protected the people.

In the age-graded systems such as that of the Blackfoot, it was customary for all the members to relinquish membership at the same time. Thus, a young man having joined the Pigeons at about fifteen or sixteen years of age would transfer to the Mosquitoes in his twenties by selling out his membership in the Pigeons to a younger man and purchasing Mosquito regalia from someone who, in turn, was selling out of the Mosquitoes and buying in to the Braves. The principle of purchase was, in fact, a form of exchange in which horses, blankets, guns and other property were given to the retiring member in return for the right to belong to the society.

The Blackfoot define successive membership in the series as being, first, of boys and young men who were unmarried and beginning to gain war honors (Pigeons), then of young married men who were constantly on the war path (Mosquitoes), proven warriors (Braves), older warriors about forty years of age (Crazy Dogs), and finally of old men (known by different names – such as Tails, Kit-Foxes, or Horns – in the various Blackfoot sub-divisions). In addition, there appear to have been at least two other societies: the Catchers, which was associated with the medicine pipes and had responsibility for settling disputes in the camp; and the

Bulls, which was limited in number and imposed a No-Flight obligation on its members.

Of these the Horns, which included the wives of its male members, were viewed with considerable fear by many people. It is said that 'the members of the horn society are regarded as very powerful men and women. It is very dangerous even to talk about them and one must not tell what is done in the society; ill luck will surely befall him if he does. The ceremonies are secret. The power of members is so great that to wish anyone ill or dead is all that is needed to bring the realization.'[1] In fact, so strong was this dread of the Horns that even in very recent times a Blackfoot appearing in court would take the oath by saying 'I will speak the truth by the horns.'

The leader of the Horns was a prominent man who had responsibility for deciding when and where the tribal summer circle camp would be set up, while every member was believed to hold the power of life and death over outsiders. That the Horns had influence in both war and hunting is likely. The Piegan members of the confederacy state that the Kit-Foxes, which in virtually every respect is identical to the Horns of the Blood, had the ability to command the weather to conceal a war party when 'if they were at war in summer and wanted a storm to come up, they would take some dirt and water and rub it on the kit-fox skin, and this would cause a rain-storm to come up. In winter, snow and dirt would be rubbed on the skin and this would bring up a snow-storm.'[2]

The secret aspects of the transfer ceremony among the Horns, when the 'father' sold out to the incoming member, or 'son', by passing on his male potency via the son's wife in a ritual that symbolized the mating of buffalo, was, however, clearly intended to ensure the security of the tribe through encouraging the increase of the herds. Potency was passed on in a similar manner by the Kit-Foxes, and the relationship between the two societies is further emphasized by the singing of Kit-Fox songs during the rites of the Horns.

Membership of any Warrior Society, whether age-graded or not, imposed obligations to act in a manner that reflected favorably upon the group and which exemplified the qualities by which they were inspired. Among the Oglala Sioux, the Tokala, or Kit-Foxes, elected members who were 'supposed to be as active and wily on the warpath as this little animal is known in his native state. It is said that the kit-fox has great skill in finding things, as for example, marrow bones buried in the earth; hence, the members of the tokala organization regarded themselves as foxes and all their enemies as marrow bones.'[3]

Left: *This feather decorated coup stick was used during battle to count coup upon an enemy. It was collected among the Crow in Montana, and has an iron head with a shaft wrapped with red stroud trade cloth.*

Right: (top) *A battle scene between Pawnees and Kiowas. The Pawnee war party is on foot, having expected to ride captured horses home, and wear less elaborate costume than the mounted Kiowas. The two figures in the center show a Kiowa novice, indicated by his lack of war costume and the water bag on his lance, counting coup on a fallen Pawnee. The standing Kiowa holds a Society lance. (center) Osage dance. Although labeled 'Kiowas, Pawnees, and Osages participating' this must be inaccurate, since there was no cooperation between these groups. The warriors carry decorated weapons, wear war shirts, and have hair styles and headdresses associated with the Osage. The two figures at right are singers, and are beating drums. (below) Pitched battle. It is difficult to identify which are Kiowa and which Cheyenne in this drawing. The central figure appears to have been struck a blow by the warrior wielding a captured cavalry sword, while the left-hand figure has fired a bullet which has gone wide of its mark and is indicated by the tadpole-like shape at upper right.*

Left: *Little Wolf (left) and Dull Knife were prominent leaders of the Cheyenne in their attempts to stop encroachment on their lands in the 1870s. Their village of over 200 lodges on the Powder River was destroyed by troops under General Ranald Mackenzie in November 1876. Not content with merely routing the Indians, Mackenzie ordered all the lodges and the entire supply of winter meat and provisions to be destroyed, leaving the starving tribe, including the women, children and elderly, to fend for themselves without supplies.*

The Tokala defined its rules of membership as 'bravery, generosity, chivalry, morality, and fraternity for fellow-members ... they taught that one should be brave before friends and foes alike and undergo hardship and punishment with fortitude; that one should give to the needy, whoever they may be, excepting an enemy, of everything one possessed; that one should search for the poor, weak, or friendless and give such all the aid one could. They taught that a tokala should not steal except from the enemy; should not lie, except to the enemy; and should set an example by complying with the recognised rules of the hunt and camp. If a fellow-tokala were in trouble of any kind he should help him to the best of his ability and if a tokala died or was killed and left a widow he should keep her from want.' [4]

Strict adherence to these codes of conduct was demanded, and any breach was met with a ceremony of public humiliation at which membership was withdrawn, leaving the unfortunate victim few chances of being offered a position within a different society. In these cultures, where recognition of individual achievement was so crucial and in which warrior power and political influence were both wielded through occupying positions of increasing prestige and honor, loss of membership usually drove the individual to an almost suicidal pledge in which he might set out alone to find the enemy and bring back scalps that would restore his status or see him die in the attempt.

In many respects, joining a society created a bond between its members similar to that of the Hunka, since each was bound to the other in a brotherhood in which individual concerns were for the well-being and protection of all the members and their relatives. This is indicated in the red stripe facepaint of the Hunka. Red is said to be the most powerful and sacred color, so powerful in fact that it is the color given to fire; and if one wears red without an entitlement to do so then Tatanka, the Buffalo, will inform all men, women, and animals to withdraw their protection and guidance. Yet in spite of its awesome power and the responsibilities associated

Below: *Sitting Bull was a shaman of the Hunkpapa Sioux and is remembered for the shattering defeat inflicted by his and Crazy Horse's warriors against the troops mustered under General Crook in 1876. During this campaign Sitting Bull had a vision of white men falling into the Indian camps, an event that was followed by Custer's abortive attack in which his entire command was killed.*

Left: *During the wars for the southern Plains the Dog Soldiers of the Cheyenne formed a fighting elite that was both respected and feared. This long feathered lance was an emblem of the Society and signified their willingness to fight to the last.*

Right: *The mounted Kiowa in this ledger pad drawing has struck a double coup by knocking the Ute warrior from his horse and making off with the pony as a prize. That the Ute has not been killed is suggested by the fact that no blood issues from his mouth, a stylization that generally indicated a mortal wound.*

Below: *One of the leading warriors in Sitting Bull's camp at the time of the Custer attack was Gall. Major Reno had been sent to attack the camp, which was stretched in a line along the Little Bighorn River, from the other end and catch the Indians in a pincers movement. Gall led the warriors who repulsed Reno's assault and prevented any help reaching Custer's besieged troopers.*

with it, red, by itself, is unable to motivate things: it indicates only the possibility, or potential, to achieve something great and sacred.

The realization of this potential depends on other forces that will motivate red, forces that have the power to set things in movement and which will have the authority to do so without dispute. This is achieved within the Warrior Societies when the chiefs elect leaders to select the Akicita, or 'police', who will control the summer camps and communal buffalo hunts. The black stripe insignia of the Akicita imparts an authority to set things in motion and to exercise control to which even the chiefs, elders and shamans are subject. Thus the Hunka and Akicita stand in a mutually dependent opposition to each other: the red stripe indicates the possession of power, whereas the black stripe gives authority to use it.

The Akicita were also charged with functions that might be operable only in a battle or in situations where disagreement could arise. Most derive from a vision of a shaman in which a war party is formed to test the validity of his power; thus it is plain that the Oglala conception of Warrior Societies is closely linked with the formation of war parties and the performance of brave deeds against an enemy. The Hunka, by contrast, were pledged to maintaining peaceful relationships and overlooking differences of opinion to ensure stability. In this way, Oglala Warrior Societies incorporated the principles of both the Hunka and the Akicita.

Intense rivalry could, however, develop between Warrior Societies in attempts to gain status and position above one another through the acquisition of war honors and by an

increased recognition of its bravest members; age-grading tended to preclude this among some tribes, since the same group of society 'brothers' moved collectively and progressively from a lower ranking group to the one above it. Elsewhere rivalry probably reached its most extreme among the Foxes and Lumpwoods of the Crow, who took this to the extent of mutual wife-raiding during the summer encampments when a Fox would attempt to abduct the wife of a Lumpwood and vice versa. Sometimes this was arranged with the woman in advance, and, in theory, the abductor and abductee must have had a previously intimate relationship. Wife-raiding therefore provided an outlet whereby a woman could escape from an unsatisfactory husband and become wife to her lover without initiating a feud; since on these occasions the husband was forbidden to show anger or to make any attempt to prevent the abduction.

Yet it is clear the Foxes and Lumpwoods often carried this

Above: *The painted buffalo robe of Péhriska-Rúhpa (Two Ravens), who is shown at the right, depicts the war exploits of this Hidatsa warrior. The figures are divided into two rows, showing six battle scenes, in which Péhriska-Rúhpa can be recognized by his yellow and black painted pony or by the four painted circles on his shield. Although Hidatsa, Péhriska-Rúhpa lived permanently in the Mandan village and was a friend of Mato-Tope (Four Bears) the Mandan second-chief. Prince Maximilian was given this robe during his residence in this village in 1834.*

Above: *This deer dewclaw rattle, decorated with a feather at its tip and mounted on a slender wooden stick, was part of the regalia of the Dog Dancers. The portrait of Péhriska-Rúhpa, right, clearly shows a similar rattle that he carries in his right hand.*

Right: *Péhriska-Rúhpa was painted in the Mandan village by Karl Bodmer in March 1834 wearing the regalia of an Hidatsa Dog Dancer. This consisted of a cap made from magpie tail feathers with a wild turkey tail in the middle and a central plume that was dyed red, a war whistle worn around his neck, and a dewclaw rattle. The highly decorated bow, which may have been obtained in trade from Shoshonean tribes, and the wolf tails attached to the heels of his moccasins attest to his status as a prominent and influential warrior.*

far beyond theoretical restraints, stealing perfectly innocent wives of prominent members of the rival group, displaying them in public to show they had been kidnapped, marrying them for only a day or so, and then divorcing. In such cases a husband would be subject to derision and ridicule if he were to take his wife back, since her honor and reputation had been tarnished by the implication of disloyalty and her enforced 'marriage'. This practice of attempting to score points over one another was also expressed in war and, immediately after wife-stealing, the Foxes and Lumpwoods organized a war expedition in which each tried to gain first honors or to create situations in which the other would be publicly humiliated.

In one battle, where the enemy had dug pits and were prepared to defend themselves, a leading Fox, carrying a society banner, crept close to their fortifications to assess the danger; whereupon a Lumpwood, noting that the Fox seemed

unwilling to approach more closely, grabbed the banner, ran forward and struck an enemy with it, planted the banner in the ground at the enemy position, and ran back unharmed. Here he challenged the Foxes to retrieve this prestigious emblem, which was now in the enemy's possession. Since the Foxes were unable to do this, the Lumpwoods later 'stole' their songs, using the rhythms but adding new words that mocked their opponents. Such songs could only then be recovered if the Foxes struck the first blow in another engagement.

The deep humiliation felt by the Foxes in the above tale was because their 'banner' was one of the lances by which the lance-bearer indicated his vow to take the lead. Most societies usually honored either two or four of their members in this way, their bravery being further emphasized by carrying the long lances wrapped in otter fur and decorated with feathers into battle where they acted as conspicuous markers of the bearer's status and courage. Such men obviously became targets in a fight, since it was more honorable to strike or kill a leading warrior than a member of the rank and file.

A Skidi Pawnee tradition, told to James Murie by Known-the-Leader in 1902, tells of the lances in the Two-Lance or Horse Society, claiming that these have been there 'since the beginning' and reflecting the importance of the lance-bearers as leaders and protectors. In this tale, the Stars sent the wonder-being, Paruxti, to earth to determine whether it was time to place people there, but forgot to invite Fools-Wolves (Wolf Star) to the council at which the decision was taken. Paruxti traveled the earth, carrying a bag containing the people, and each time he stopped they came out, set up camp, and hunted buffalo. Two lance-bearers always left the bag first, leading the people to a campsite and guarding them until it was time to return to the bag, when they stood watch and entered last to ensure everyone was safely inside.

Fools-Wolves, angry at the slight he felt by not being invited to the council, schemed to disrupt these peaceful migrations of the people. He placed Wolf on the earth, who snatched the bag and ran away with it, intending to devour whatever he found inside; but when he opened it the lance-bearers jumped out, frightening him. The people, however, were innocent of deceit and did not realize that Wolf was an imposter, so they set up their camp as usual. This time they found no food, and Wolf, having been discovered, tried to get away but was killed by the lance-bearers. Paruxti told the people that as they had killed Wolf they could no longer live forever, as the gods had intended, but were to carry the wolf's

hide and be known as Skidi, or Wolf People. He also said they would always have the lances to protect them, and that those who carried the lances would be soldiers.[5]

The honor attached to lance-bearers as leaders and protectors of the tribe was common practice among the Warrior Societies; thus the Tokala lance-bearer of the Oglala rode forward of the people carrying a lance adorned with eagle feathers, kit-fox skin, and the feathers of the crow, magpie and prairie chicken, and was expected to charge the enemy before others and, if necessary, make a stand to cover a retreat. All members of the Tokala, or Kit-Foxes, were, however, noted for their exceptional courage, which is reflected in the Kit-Fox song used in battle and during society dances:

> I am a Fox.
> I am supposed to die.
> If there is anything difficult,
> If there is anything dangerous,
> That is mine to do.[6]

Above: *Sharp Nose was a sub-chief of the Northern Arapaho and is shown here in a photograph taken about 1876. He was renowned as a brave but modest warrior, and as someone whose cool judgment on the battlefield always stood him in good stead.*

Left: *Although Sharp Nose was known for his modesty, his fighting skills and determination as a warrior were reflected in his membership of a No-Flight Society. The red flannel sash shown here belonged to him, and was worn into battle by passing the arm and shoulder through the slit in the upper portion. The end was then pinned to the ground, determining the radius within which he would fight unless released by a fellow Society member.*

Right: *Satank (Sitting Bear) was a Kiowa who never succumbed to the ways of the white man. His status as a Kaitsenko, a warrior elite comprising the ten bravest men of the tribe, is shown in this William Soule photograph by the leather strap over his shoulder. The end was pinned to the ground in battle in response to his no-retreat vow.*

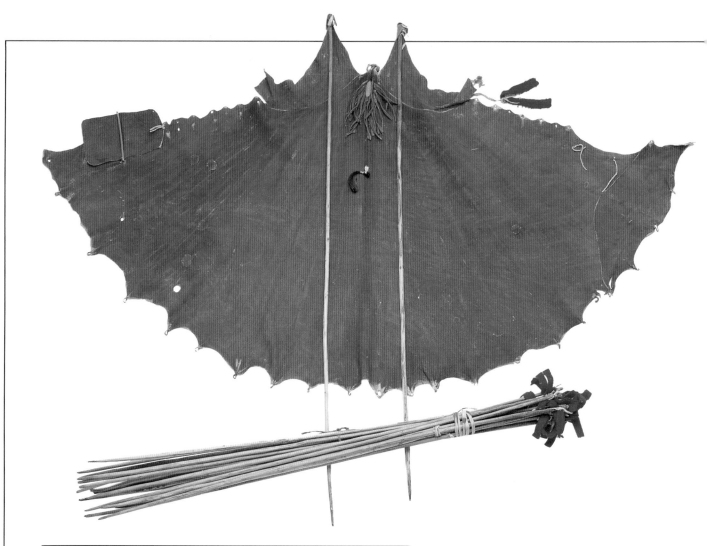

Above: *The earliest owner of this Kiowa tipi was Red Tipi Man, an important shaman who painted not only his tipi, but also his body, hair and feet a solid red. Before his death in 1873 he passed ownership of the tipi to his son Set-tain-te (Satanta, or White Bear).*

Left: *William Soule took this photograph of Satanta, who, although not the principal Kiowa chief, was renowned as an able speaker and defiant warrior during the 1860s. In the Kiowa circle camp, Satanta's red tipi occupied a prominent position in the center of the Kogui section. Whenever Satanta occupied this tipi his war shield and Society lance were displayed in front of it.*

Right: *German silver hair plates were a popular way of displaying status among the Kiowa. The example shown here, which consists of twenty-three discs cut and hammered into shape from sheet metal purchased from traders, is similar to that worn by Dohasän on the following page.*

Most Plains tribes had societies noted for being particularly brave, and usually bearing a name referring to Kit-Fox, Dog or Big Dog. Perhaps the best known of these in the historic period was the Dog Soldiers of the Southern Cheyenne, whose stubborn resistance as allies of the Arapaho, Kiowa and Comanche against United States troops earned them the grudging admiration of the Americans. Even greater honour was to be invited, or among some groups forced, to become a member of a 'No-Flight Society', known by descriptive names that detail what was expected of their members: the Not-Afraid-To-Die-Society, Those-Expecting-To-Die, Acting-Dead, Crazy-Dogs-Wishing-To-Die, and so on.

Among the Kiowa it was called the Kaitsenko (Kiowa Horses), and an invitation to join could not be refused. If someone demurred when offered the pipe that pledged him to the Kaitsenko, the members tried to persuade him; on a second attempt, they used harsh language; on the third, they became angry; and on the final attempt (the fourth, sacred, offer) they seized him by the arms and hair and forced him to touch the pipe with his lips. The Kaitsenko, limited to ten members, wore a distinguishing sash of red-dyed elk or buckskin or of red cloth which was long enough to drag on the ground, and went into battle with their face and body, clothing, moccasins and feathers painted a brilliant red. Their leader was differentiated by having a sash of black-dyed elkskin.

They were the bravest men in the tribe, who were expected to choose the most dangerous parts of the battlefield in which the heaviest fighting took place and where 'it was a member's duty to sing the song of his society, fasten his sash to the earth with a spear and thereafter stand his ground regardless of the consequences.'[7] Failure to do so would mark the man as a coward for the rest of his life. He would be forced to give up the sash and, no matter what brave deeds he performed in the future, would always be held in disdain and looked down on for the disgrace he had brought on himself and on his fellow Kaitsenko.

The eminent Kiowa warrior and chief, Sitting Bear, is said to have been the only person in the tribe to have held simultaneous membership in both the Kaitsenko and the equally powerful shamans' society known as the Eagle Shields. As emblems of these he owned the Kaitsenko war bonnet, long red sash and crooked lance, as well as the crow feather headdress and yellow shield with green bird designs of the Eagle Shield Society. When in full regalia his 'face was painted black and yellow for the Eagle Shields. He had on a yellow

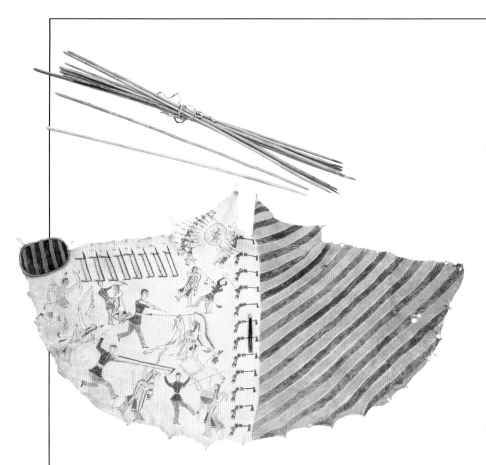

Left: *The Tipi with Battle Pictures was owned by Dohasän (Little Bluff). The stripes indicated successful war expeditions he had led, while the pictographs commemorated tribal military history. The tipi was presented to him by the Cheyenne chief, Sleeping Bear, in 1845 as a gift to seal a pact of friendship made between the two tribes five years earlier.*

Below: *Modern Kiowa maintain the tradition of the Tipi with Battle Pictures, and it was adopted in 1974 as the official tipi of the Black Leggings Society, a Veterans Society formed in 1958 to honor Kiowas who had seen active service, and named after a Warrior Society of which Dohasän was a member.*

buckskin suit with fringes so long it dragged off his leggings on the ground. He had on silver rings and bracelets, and silver chains in the holes all around the outsides of his ears. He wore his war bonnet, and he was carrying the crooked spear that went with it. He had his wildcat-skin quiver on his back, with the long bois d'arc bow sticking out of it, and his eagle shield on his arm.'[8]

Sitting Bear lavished attention on his favorite son, Young Sitting Bear, the second eldest of three sons and the one his father wished to inherit his power and to whom he wanted to entrust the care of the Grandmother Medicine Bundle. The Grandmother Bundle, one of ten in the tribe, was a major source of tribal unity; no disputes could be held in its presence, and anyone seeking refuge in one of the tipis in which these were kept was safe from all harm. Young Sitting Bear was clearly idolized by his father. When the boy joined the Rabbits, the boys' society, Sitting Bear sponsored a huge feast, and when as a youth he joined the Herders, which together with the Little Ponies, Berries, and Black Leggings formed a group of equally ranked Warrior Societies, Sitting Bear provided him with a tipi that would serve as the Herders meeting lodge and gave him the design to be painted on its cover.

Unfortunately, Sitting Bear's wish was not granted. Young Sitting Bear never had a vision entitling him to receive power, and when he and Wolf Lying Down, the favorite son of Lone Wolf, led a war party to the south the two youths never returned. Both Sitting Bear and Lone Wolf were distraught; but whereas Lone Wolf left his son's remains

Right: *Dohasän, the 'greatest Kiowa chief', was painted by Catlin while visiting the Comanche village in 1844. He was a renowned diplomat who later negotiated the successful peace with Sleeping Bear, but was equally respected for his ability as a warrior and as a member of the Kaitsenko. He was head chief of the Kiowa from 1833 until his death in 1866, having succeeded Island Man who was deposed after failing to protect the village.*

228

buried under rocks on the battlefield – the traditional means of giving last honors to a warrior – Sitting Bear was unable to control his grief. Leading the Herders south in the footsteps of the war party led by his son, he collected the bones, painted them yellow, the colors of the Herders' Society, and wrapped them in a blanket which was carried on a pack horse whenever the camp moved and placed in Young Sitting Bear's empty tipi when camp was made.

A year later, in 1871, Sitting Bear was to meet his own death. In an attempt to protect some young warriors who had killed a white farmer, Sitting Bear, White Bear, and Big Tree, all prominent but elderly chiefs, surrendered themselves to the U.S. military. As the wagon taken them to confinement approached a pecan tree, Sitting Bear, talking in Kiowa to his dead son, swore he would not pass the tree alive and that they would soon be re-united. His voice, clear, sharp and happy, rose in the defiant song of the Kaitsenko:

I live, but I will not live forever.
Mysterious moon, you only remain.
Powerful sun, you alone remain.
Wonderful earth, you remain forever[9]

Right: *This Kiowa model shield was made for James Mooney in 1904 and depicts the shield design of Tsonkiada, its original owner. The central circle, radiating horizontal lines, and border closely resemble those of a shield sketched by William Bollaert which had been taken from a Comanche war party that raided Corpus Christi in 1844. Since the Kiowa had fraternities of warriors who could be identified by the similarity of their shield designs, it is possible that the Comanche shield indicates a link with a group of warriors from this allied tribe.*

Left: *As a powerful supernatural animal the Bear was considered capable of warding off danger by deflecting the weapons of an enemy, and a bear paw might be included as part of a shield design. The painting here is on a shield cover dating from the 1840s. After the introduction of firearms, covers might be carried into battle for supernatural protection. The meanings of the designs were personal to their owners and cannot be interpreted accurately unless the original vision in which they were received is known.*

Right: *The Kiowas collaborated in the making of the 1917 silent film **Daughters of the Dawn** in which the Tipi with Battle Pictures shown on the preceding pages was featured. Charley Buffalo, the grand-nephew of Dohasän, painted the tipi cover used in the film. In this still Hunting Horse is shown inside the tipi, which has been accurately set out according to Kiowa tradition. Note in particular the placement of the shield above Hunting Horse's head in the honorific place at the rear of the tipi and its similarity to the model shield above.*

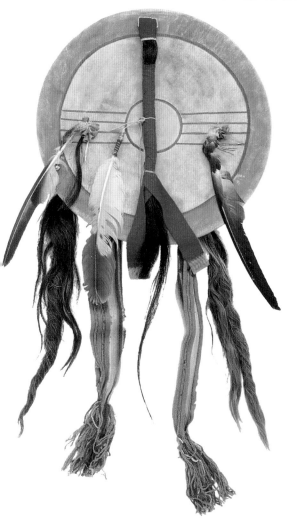

Coughing four times, he used the shaman's power of the Eagle Shields to bring a crow feather from his throat and turn it into a knife, with which he attacked the guard sitting next to him. The guard's rifle discharged as he fell from the wagon, hitting and mortally wounding Sitting Bear who died propped against the trunk of the pecan tree he had sworn not to pass.

The Kaitsenko, in common with other No-Flight Societies, indicated their promise to die in battle by using backward speech in war and during their dances, thereby echoing the voices of the dead whom they were pledged to join. In backward talking, No-Flight warriors said the opposite of what they meant. If one of their comrades was wounded they would gather around and proclaim loudly, 'Don't get well. I hope he dies soon', which was a certain means to ensure his recovery. Similarly, the Yellow Noses of the Shoshone, if requested by the chief not to charge the enemy would reply, "'No, we shall not charge', but at the same time would do so; and a Crow Crazy Dog would remain mounted watching a battle if the Crow were winning, but if the Crow fled he would dismount, turn his horse loose, and stake his sash to the ground before the advancing enemy.

An interesting account is given of a battle fought by the Windigokan, or No-Flight Contraries, of the Plains Ojibwa. They danced in front of the chief's lodge to announce their intention of going out as a war party by singing 'I am not going to war. I shall not kill the Sioux. I shall not scalp four and let the rest escape. I shall go in the daytime..' The following night they left, wearing ridiculous costumes made from old sacks and rags, plastered with mud, and with hideous masks bearing an enormous crooked beak-like nose, acting in a manner contrary to that of a war party, which would have divested itself of any unnecessary encumbrances. They stumbled along, since they were unable to see very well through the masks, until they came across a large Sioux war party, when instead of fleeing for cover or attempting to protect themselves they began to perform a grotesque dance in front of the enemy.

The astonished Sioux, not knowing who or what these strange apparitions were, sat down to watch their crazy antics, until the Windigokan drew quite close and their leader shouted 'Don't shoot!' Immediately, they drew weapons con-

Far left: *Tatanka Ptecela (Short Bull) was a Sioux shaman who, at the turn of the century, provided James R. Walker and Friedrich Weygold with information about Oglala ritual concepts. He wears the stripe facepaint which relates to the Hunka and Akicita of the Hunka ceremony associated with stone.*

Right: *When he was a boy, the Iowa Shauhauapotinia (The Man Who Killed Three Sioux) had a Hunka brother relationship with another boy in his village. They dreamed of when they would go to war together, but his friend was killed by the Sioux while they were still in their teens. Shauhauapotinia trailed the Sioux for 100 miles, then raced in to the village and killed and scalped a Sioux warrior. Before the enemy realized what was happening, he had ridden to the outskirts of the village where he killed two more Sioux.*

Left: *An Oglala man who dreamed of stone became a powerful Yuwipi shaman and maker of Wotaye (war medicines). The Stone-Dreamer Miwakan (George Sword) explained the medicine shields he had made to Weygold in 1909. From top to bottom they are: Wi wanyang wackipi (Sun Dance) shield. The shield refers to the origin of the Four Winds, and has Yuwipi dots which indicate the tracks of animals coming into camp. Yuwipi shield, with red zig-zag Yuwipi Lightnings. The Yuwipi stones on the border were said to fly at night, glowing, as messengers of the shaman. Hexaka (Wapiti) shield, with a figure of the Wapiti beneath one of Iktomi, the Spider, and with a Yuwipi stone border. Wasu (Hail) shield, in which the stones appear as hail beneath Lightning. Changaleshka (Medicine Hoop) shield, which George Sword copied after an original made by Pama, an older shaman, and where the power of the flying Yuwipi stones is concentrated within the painted circle.*

cealed beneath their clothing and killed four of the Sioux while the rest fled in terror. They scalped these four and danced back over the top of a low rise, where the leader announced 'Now, old men (they were all youths) you must walk home slowly; whereupon they all ran away as quickly as they could and escaped..'[10]

In this account of the Windigokan, power to defeat the Sioux derived from the Thunderers, formidable supernaturals, appearing in the form of birds, who demanded contrary action as a means of protecting the warriors under their influence. Without observation of this taboo at a time of crisis the Windigokan would become 'crazy' and likely to turn the uncontroled destructive force of the Thunderers against themselves' considering each other as 'enemies' and starting a fight in which several of them might be killed. Undoubtedly, the strange beaked masks indicate a link with the bird intermediaries, and the sudden and unexpected discharge of concealed weapons links with the power of Lightning, the weapon of the Thunderers, to strike when least expected.

A similar vision among the Siouan tribes turns the warrior into a Heyoka, who also exhibits the clown-like behavior of the Windigokan, the use of sacking as a war shirt, and plastering the body with mud. A Heyoka becomes so only through a vision of the Thunderbird, and is associated with Iktomi, who is the Spider or Trickster. Because of this such a warrior is immune to the trickery of Iktomi, who delights in disrupting the normal life of the people and laughs at the efforts the other supernaturals make to control his devious scheming. A warrior possessed by this power was compelled by his vision to kill, and only the Hunka, the protective power for good, was effective against the Heyoka, the destructive force of evil.

The Heyoka was feared because, although a Contrary like the No-Flight warriors, he was bound by no codes of bravery or honor. His opposite character is reflected in this inversion of the warrior ideal that emphasized the importance of noble deeds, but is indicated further by the fact he owed no alliegance other than to Iktomi and might even work against a fellow-Heyoka, yet was under the unusual obligation to obey the demands of other members of the tribe. Anyone could go to a Heyoka and say 'Don't dance for me', when he would be forced to stop immediately whatever he was doing and begin a performance. It was, however, unwise to test the patience of a Heyoka too far, since his compulsion to kill might be directed toward the person offending him rather than against an enemy.

Below left to right: *The paintings on hide depicted below are unique in the historical documentation of North America. They were sent to Switzerland in 1758 by Father Philipp von Segesser von Brunegg, a Jesuit priest with the Mission at Ures, Sonora, but have been reliably identified as recording the ill-fated Villasur expedition which the Spanish sent from the Presidio in Santa Fe in 1720 to prevent French incursions into Spanish held territories. It is also evident that the paintings were made by settlers who were either involved in the expedition or intimately associated with others who were. The scene depicted here is of a carefully prepared ambush by Pawnee and Oto warriors, assisted by the French, which completely routed the Spanish. By the end of a bitter day of fighting, thirty-three of the forty-three Spaniards who had embarked on the expedition, including Villasur, were dead, and their Pueblo Indian allies had fled. The paintings were made as wall hangings and were purchased by the Palace of the Governors in the 1980s, returning, ironically, to the very same building from which Villasur had set out nearly 300 years earlier.*

Above: *Conflict with the Spanish is also reflected in the oral history of the Skidi Pawnee, who told the Duke of Württemberg that the Spanish drove them from their homelands in the south and that the Skidi 'would drink the Spaniards blood'. La-wah-ee-coots-la-shaw-no (Brave Chief) was painted by George Catlin in 1832 at Fort Leavenworth. The hands painted on his upper chest are war honors, signifying that he had struck his enemies in close combat.*

No man chose to become a Heyoka. The vision was an involuntary one which condemned the warrior to spend his life outside the normal framework of life in the camps. At rituals he ridiculed them in a mocking burlesque of their most sacred aspects; at feasts he ate alone, and when happy or pleased with something painted his face black as a sign of mourning; laughing when he was sad and crying when he was happy. He was barred from the Warrior Societies, prevented from marrying, and although he feigned terror at the most harmless things was often one of the bravest men of the tribe, since he was unafraid of anything that would strike fear into another man.

Psychologically the Heyoka was of immense importance, as were similar characters among numerous other tribes. During periods of happiness and plenty he saw only gloom and despair, and could be goaded into providing hours of harmless amusement when he gorged himself on buffalo ribs while complaining there was no food in the camp, or declared he was dirty and proceeded to wash in a bath of mud; but when life really did seem hopeless and difficult, the Heyoka's inversion of everything normal helped lift people's spirits. In bitter winter conditions, when the tipis were frozen in and game was unavailable, a Heyoka might remind the people of better times by venturing out clad only in a breechclout and complaining of the heat, or by claiming to have just feasted on fresh meat and berries.

Yet behind this benign face of the Heyoka there lurked the

ever-present fear that he was possessed by the spirit of Iktomi, and was therefore unpredictable and potentially dangerous. He, after all, was the only person who dared challenge the supernaturals even if he was in dread of a common camp dog and would run screaming in fright if one approached too close. Thus he made a mockery of the pretensions of some of the warriors, but at the same time emphasized the fact that the powers which guided and protected them in battle were of such strength that only a Heyoka might oppose them.

Below: *This superb buffalo robe is from the Friedrich Köhler collection and dates to about 1830. It is said to have belonged to a 'Sioux chief' and depicts various battle scenes of its owner with different enemies, as well as an encounter on foot with a buffalo. The row of figures to the right of the buffalo carry pipes rather than weapons, although it has been suggested this represents the departure of a war party.*

Right: *Many of the tribes of North America
believed in the sacred circle as a symbol that
contained power within itself, and which
could therefore generate power of itself. The
hair ornament shown here is from the
Cheyenne and shows the classic division
into the four world quarters created by the
crossed bands of braided leather. The
collection notes suggest that it was a
talisman employed by a shaman.*

In many ways the Heyoka, although human, competed with the supernaturals on their own terms, and it is evident they possessed shamanic power that enabled them to do so. One of the indications of this was their ability to handle live coals and to take food from boiling kettles with their bare hands without suffering any ill consequence. This ability was also a feature of the Pawnee Iruska, or Medicine-Men's Society; although here the power is so immense that the culture hero, Crow-Feather, originates not only the ability to handle fire with impunity but also the roached headdress and the crow belt (dance bustle) In fact, the symbolic meaning of the Iruska, 'I can extinguish the life in fire', suggests even greater significance than this, since it implies an opposition to the 'eternal fire' kept in the temples of the Mississippians and maintained by other Caddoan-speaking groups.

Crow-Feather exhibits contrary behavior in that he never marries and takes no part in ceremonies, spending most of his time contemplating the nature of the powers that dwell in the skies. Eventually he is taken to the animal lodge where, after a series of trials in which he is burned and blistered, he is taught the secrets of the Iruska by Scalped-Man. This leader, who is human, had been scalped and left for dead, and since his soul had thereby been taken was unable to return to his people. The animal powers took pity and rescued him, giving him the roached headdress which they said was even more powerful than the scalplock. 'The deer furnished the hair for weaving; the turkey, feathers from his breast to edge the deer hair; and the eagle a single feather for the centre of the headdress.'[11] They also gave him deerskin, crow feathers and a wolf tail to make the crow belt.

Scalped-Man was, however, unable to wear the roach, since he lacked the scalplock by which it was fastened to the head, but gave this and the crow belt to Crow-Feather to take back to the people, where he was to build the first sweat-lodge and test the medicine men, initiating those into the Iruska who were able to demonstrate they possessed the ability 'for overpowering fire'. He told them to make headdresses and bustles similar to those he had received from Scalped-Man, telling them that although theirs was a medicine men's society, in public performances 'all must bring spears, bows and arrows, war clubs, and shields so that you can imitate the attack on an enemy. It shall be known as Iruska (fire inside of you). The red headdress represents fire, the black hair fringe represents smoke.' [12]

Warrior power derived from essentially the same sources as that of the Iruska, except that it only conferred the ability to appeal for spirit help and protection rather than permitting the direct intervention of which shamans were capable.

Below: *Games of skill were important to all North American Indian tribes, and often conducted with a fervor that equalled that of war. Often games and gaming were actually called by names that referred to war and warfare. The game of Chunkey was played by the historic tribes of the Southeast, but is clearly of great antiquity. In this a shaped stone was hurled along a cleared alley with tremendous force while two players threw lances toward it. Points were gained according to the closeness of the lance to the stone when it came to rest.*

Right: *In a variation of Chunkey, points could be gained by scoring a direct hit in a hole through the center of the stone or by the second player throwing his spear in such a manner that it could catch the spear of his opponent in mid-flight and deflect it from its course. Although the spears were remade regularly, the stones were often of great age.*

Below: *The antiquity of Chunkey is apparent from this engraved shell disc depicting a Mississippian Death Cult member wearing ceremonial costume playing the game. The line drawing helps delineate the main forms contained in the photograph, and reveals the warrior adopting a conventionalized pose immediately prior to hurling the stone.*

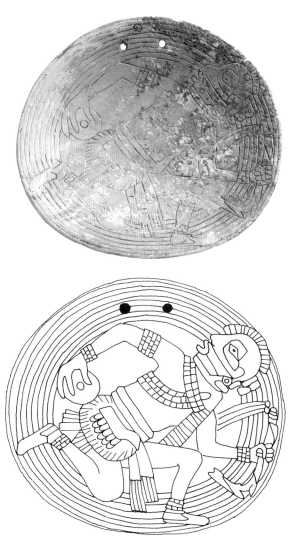

Power was usually obtained in visions, although in some tribes it could be purchased by approaching an Elder who had been a successful warrior in his youth and asking him to transfer the rights; such a request might, however, need supernatural sanction before it could be met, as in the example of Sitting Bear's favorite son who was unable to receive the sacred bundles from his father because he had not been granted power in a vision which would ensure he could handle them responsibly.

Once power had been granted it provided protection in adverse situations. Without power, a man was simply a mortal human being subject to overwhelming spiritual forces against which he had little chance of success; with it, he was transformed into a warrior who could call on the assistance of intermediaries such as Hawk to enable him to strike swiftly, Wolf to help locate enemy camps, Bear to give him courage, and even Gnuska, the humble grasshopper, who, while possessing no ability to destroy or overcome his opponents, was able to forewarn someone he protected of the approach of an enemy and the direction from which they came. Ritual preparation before a fight activated the beneficial effect of these powers and gave a warrior confidence that he could carry through a difficult encounter with success.

Each of these animals gave 'tokens' by which they could be recognized and through which their assistance could be requested, usually in the form of a facepaint, song and amulet. Associated with them was the the acquisition of the appropriate animal skin to make a medicine bundle, in which

Left: *This De Bry engraving shows Florida youths at their games. Like Chunkey, these involved skills that were required by warriors. Three different games are depicted: arrow practice, running, and one in which a thatch of twigs is set on a pole and balls are thrown at it.*

Below: *As well as having significance in war medicines and in the ritual aspects of games such as Chunkey, the hoop was a potent life symbol. This scalp contains the 'soul' of the deceased within a hoop and is a mark of honor and respect shown an enemy. Note the Morning Star cross on the reverse.*

the paints and other items deriving from the vision were contained, together with feathers and other small objects that could be tied in the hair or attached to the bridle or tail of the horse when the warrior went into battle. Elements from the vision were also painted on the warrior's pony and indicated on the weapons he carried with him.

Among the most important of his weapons was the shield. In the early days of Plains warfare, before the introduction of repeating rifles, the shield was made from the shrunken skin of the buffalo's neck and had a practical purpose in being an effective means of warding off arrows and bullets fired from muzzle-loading muskets, since its convex surface would deflect these when held at an oblique angle. Tribes of the southern Plains developed the double-layered shield in which the center space was packed with feathers, grass, or, following European contact, paper. Many pioneers were mystified by the Apache and Comanche obsession for books until they realized the purpose to which they were being put; one Comanche shield is said to have contained the entire history of Rome! Such shields were almost impenetrable, and were tested by firing arrows and bullets at them from a distance of fifty yards; if these passed through the shield it was discarded.

Much of their efficacy was, however, credited to the spiritual power they were thought to possess. The Comanche even took their shields on vision quests, holding them up each morning to the Sun whose life-giving rays were believed to harden the shield's surface and protect the bearer by granting him a long life. More frequently they bore attachments such as feathers, small bird and animal skins, or other objects revealed to the vision-seeker when power was granted,

Above: A cornhusk ring and corncob darts, flighted with two feathers and having a sharp wooden point, were the essential equipment for a throwing game played by boys at the Hopi villages. Although there appears to be no restriction on when this game might be played, it is significant that it was felt to be particularly beneficial to do so when the ceremonial season came to a close after the harvests. At this time, too, the women's dances featured the hoop and darts in rituals that formally closed the old season and opened the new. Among the Zuni this game was dedicated to the Twin War Gods and played at the winter solstice.

or they carried painted decorations depicting elements of the vision. In some tribes, such as the Blackfoot, they could be transferred, or purchased, in much the same way as the warrior purchased his membership in one of the societies, which resulted in the original owner losing its supernatural protection; whereas elsewhere a powerful shaman, who was noted for his influence over the war birds, might paint elements from his own vision on shields belonging to others if requested to do so. Several warriors might, therefore, own shields whose protective spirit derived from a single shamanic vision, and although the shaman was well paid for carrying out this service, his powers were not diminished by doing so.

An extension of the transference of shamanic power to a series of shields is found among the Kiowa, where the power of the society, which ultimately traces back to a supernatural origin, is vested in identical shields carried by all the members as a part of their society regalia, a practice that was pre-

sumably taken over from them by the Shield Bearers of the Comanche. This was an informal association of young warriors, consisting primarily of brothers and friends, who decided to indicate their solidarity by carrying shields that all bore the same markings.

After the introduction of more powerful rifles, against which the shield offered little physical protection, warriors frequently carried a miniature copy of the original tied to their hair or used a hoop with rawhide lacing that served no practical purpose but which still provided assistance from the animal powers. Others took the soft buckskin covers, used to protect shields when not in use, into battle instead of carrying the heavy shield itself, and transferred the painting through which power was granted to the cover; thus plain, undecorated shields might have highly elaborate painted covers.

All these representations were intended to act as a means whereby the supernaturals could be contacted; in a sense, the spirits dwelt within the image that depicted an aspect of the power they granted, and through the correct performance of the associated ritual this could be re-activated and brought from the spirit world into the human realm. Failure to carry

Above: Many tribes in North America played a form of ball game similar to lacrosse, but which was said to have a cosmic significance reflecting the alternating struggle between night and day or between the creatures of the air and those of the earth. George Catlin witnessed one game among the Choctaw in which there were several hundred participants, and where the ritual importance was indicated by the fact that four respected shamans both started and judged the game. In this view of the preliminaries to the contest the shamans can be seen seated at center, while between them and the two teams the women of each group sing songs asking for the spirits to bless the players.

*Above: Catlin's painting of Sioux and Choctaw ball-players shows the elaborate attention given to details of costume in the 1830s. In writing about Tullock-chish-ko (He-who-drinks-the-juice-of-a-stone), at the left of the painting, Catlin said he was 'the most distinguished ball-player of the Choctaw nation, represented in his ball-play dress, with his ball-sticks in his hands. In every ball-play of these people, it is a rule of the play, that no man shall wear moccasins on his feet . . . [he has] a beautiful bead belt, and a "tail", made of white horsehair or quills, and a "**mane**" on the neck, of horsehair dyed of various colors' (**Letters and Notes**, vol.II, pp. 124–5). His name is of interest in that it links the greatest ball-player, who is therefore also considered the greatest warrior, with the power of the stone, which among the Sioux is also linked to warriors through the medicine power of the Yuwipi stone shamans.*

out the rite exactly, or indeed failure to observe closely any of the numerous taboos and restrictions that usually attached to medicine objects, might render the power ineffective, or, in extreme cases, even turn it back against its owner.

The realization of power, as in defeating an opponent or capturing horses, could, however, be shown in a more direct manner through the use of pictographic imagery. Rather than being a means whereby success could be achieved, these were records of achievement having been accomplished. In a sense, of course, they also indicated the possession of power, for without it superiority over an opponent was impossible, and they therefore tended to become part of the cumulative expression of spirit force that marked any martial endeavor. In this way records of successes might be applied to medicine objects with sacred significance, or even be incorporated as part of an image depicting the character of a vision.

A wavy line terminating in a dot, representing the flight of a bullet, could therefore appear on a shield with an image of, say, the Bear; when it might indicate the Bear's ability to safeguard the shield owner by deflecting the path of bullets. The same line on a tipi cover, however, could be used to indicate the number of enemies the warrior had killed using this weapon. Similarly, horseshoe marks on a war pipe indicated a desire to capture horses, but on the tipi showed how many had actually been captured.

Warriors frequently applied these stylized representations of their war honors to painted buffalo robes. These showed not only what deeds had been accomplished, such as the number of horses taken, how many times he had struck an enemy, and so on, but usually contained specific information about the manner in which they had been carried out. This could be surprisingly detailed. Thus an image could contain footprints to show he had traveled on foot; triangles representing tipis and set in a circle indicated he entered the enemy camp; a horseshoe beside a line and a knife showed he had used a knife to cut free a picketed war pony; several ponies ridden by warriors meant he was pursued, and these warriors might have distinctive haircuts to identify the tribe; and an image of himself holding a gun and facing the enemy, with one of his opponents shown as a body without legs (that is, a man who no longer has the power of movement), indicated he had killed one of his pursuers.

The accuracy of these records was paramount. Dorsey tells us that at the permanent Wichita villages 'over the bed and hanging down in front, is a long curtain of buffalo hide, which can be raised or lowered at will; this is often painted with war scenes [and that] war records were usually depicted in detail on the robe, or the more salient features of the record might be indicated on the [travelling] tipi. The significance of the marks describing these war records was always supposed to be known by the other warriors of the tribe, and when an individual misrepresented his record, either on his robe or on his tipi, he was at once proclaimed a liar throughout the camp, and his robe or tipi might be destroyed.'[13]

Disputed war records were, however, more likely to arise from confusion over who struck which blow during the heat of the battle than they were from deliberate misrepresentation. The practice of counting as honors only those deeds that had been witnessed by others mitigated against this, as did the relatively small size of Indian bands and villages which meant that most people would be well aware of what deeds any particular warrior had a right to claim, and 'it would not be reputable, or even safe to life, for a warrior to wear upon his back the representations of battles he had never fought.'[14] There was also a feeling that false statements were an affront to the powers that safeguarded the warriors and that these might subsequently demonstrate their anger by causing misfortune to befall the individual, his family, or, in serious breaches, even the whole community.

Above: *Tooan Tuh's (Spring Frog) name passed into the legends of the Cherokee and was recorded in their songs for his skill as a ball-player, which was given the greatest praise even though he was also renowned as one of the tribe's most prominent warriors.*

Above right: *These ball-play sticks show a method of construction in which the handle is split to accommodate the head and then wound with a decorative binding. The netting was traditionally made from Indian hemp or twisted squirrel skin.*

Right: *Catlin called this a scene when the ball is 'up' and 'where hundreds are running together and leaping, actually over each other's heads, and darting between their adversaries' legs, tripping and throwing, and foiling each other in every possible manner, and every voice raised to the highest key, in shrill yelps and barks!'* (**Letters and Notes**, *vol.II, p.120*).

A belief in personal integrity and supernatural intervention was carried over into other activities which are not directly connected with warfare but nevertheless carry war symbolism. Prominent among these is gambling, which most American Indians thought of as a parallel to warfare in that it offered opportunities for challenge and for taking risk, and which also depended on elements of luck that could be manipulated through appeals to the animal spirits. Thus gambling songs and war songs are often indistinguishable, and call on the same spirit forces for help.

This originates in myths where the first warriors and the first gamblers are identical, and during which the division between day and night was decided in a gambling game between the animal intermediaries that assisted warriors. Coyote, the Trickster, is also implicated however. By trickery and subterfuge he often gains the better of his foes, through which he provides the necessities people need to live; but his inordinate vanity and disregard for social norms ultimately brings about his downfall.

In a typical Crow tale, Coyote, transformed into a handsome young warrior who parades before the admiring glances

of the young women of the tribe, is startled by a gambler's shout of victory, whereupon his horse shies and throws Coyote into the mud. This sudden upset is sufficient to make his 'horse' turn back into a hare, and for all of Coyote's finery to revert to the bark and leaves from which he made it. He is thereby exposed as a charlatan who pretends to be something he is not. The link between war and gambling is further emphasized in this story; Coyote rode into the village because he thought from the noise and commotion that a war was taking place and that he, being indestructible, would be able to gain honors, only to find the people engaged in gambling and games for which he is unprepared.

This tale carries the moral that warfare and gambling are acceptable if carried out with honorable intent and not taken to extremes, and it is Coyote's excesses that bring him into disrepute rather than the principles he expounds. Thus, if he had attempted through his display to win the affections of a 'sweetheart' he might have been successful, but to attract the attention of all the young women suggests that he failed to recognize the principle of restraint. It is also a cautionary tale, in that it implies if Coyote had taken the trouble to find out what the people were doing instead of thinking only of himself that he may not have experienced such an ignominious fall from grace.

Among the greatest gambling games of North American Indian tribes, in terms of sheer spectacle, were the ball games of the Creek, Choctaw and Cherokee, which were conducted with all the ritual and apparent emotions of war with enemy tribes and described as 'battles'. The Creek taking this to the

Above: *In spite of their modern appearance, these ball-game trunks were worn during Cherokee games in the 1880s after they had been allocated a reservation in North Carolina. Shorts replaced the breechclout formerly worn by ball-players, although James Mooney, who collected these, noted that at this date not all men chose shorts.*

Right: *On the evening before a game, rival Cherokee teams conducted the ball-play dance in their own settlements to give courage to the players. During this the men, dressed as for the game, danced in a circle while seven women, representing the seven Cherokee clans, danced to and fro in a line and sang in accompaniment to a drum and rattle rhythm. The songs used on this occasion predicted the defeat of their 'enemies', and various medicine tokens, such as the wing of a bat, were fastened to the rack holding the ball-sticks to ensure this had supernatural sanction. The conductor of this ceremony, who was also the trainer of the ball-players, was always a shaman, reinforcing the ritual aspect of the game. In this photograph from 1898 the central ball-player is wearing the pair of star-patterned shorts shown in the photographs above.*

Above: This shows the back of the trunks in the photograph on the facing page. The pair on the right were worn by Rope Twister, captain of the Wolftown team, and show him holding a ball in one hand and the various goods he is betting against the stakes held by the second figure in the other.

point where preliminary war dances were held by the opposing teams from the Red and White towns prior to the match, and during which they called on the animals to lend their strength, speed, and cunning to enable them to defeat their enemies. Such games often involved several hundred players, whose purpose was to catch a ball in a form of 'lacrosse' stick and pass it safely between two upright posts that served as a goal. Although the game of these three tribes was vir-

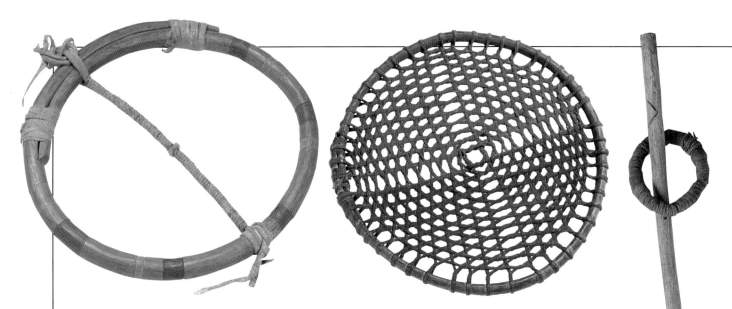

tually identical, different versions of the 'stick game' were widespread throughout North America.

Its direct connection with the animal powers that inspired warriors is evident from a Cherokee myth which describes its origin in a contest between the creatures of the earth and those of the sky. 'On the side of the animals were the bear, whose ponderous weight bore down all opposition; the deer, who excelled all others in running; and the terrapin, who was invulnerable to the stoutest blows. On the side of the birds were the eagle [and] the hawk ... noted for their swiftness and power of flight.' [15] The bat, because of his elusiveness, and the flying squirrel, which was capable of gliding soundlessly and effortlessly over great distances without being detected, were also called into service on behalf of the birds.

George Catlin called it 'this wonderful game', and made it a rule never to miss a ball play if it was being held within thirty miles. He wrote an evocative description of one he witnessed among the Choctaw, telling us that 'in these struggles, every mode is used that can be devised, to oppose the progress of the foremost, who is likely to get the ball ... there are times, when the ball gets to the ground, and such a confused mass rushing together around it, and knocking their sticks together, without the possibility of any one getting or seeing it, for the dust that they raise, that the spectator loses his strength, and everything else but his senses; when the condensed mass of ball-sticks, and shins, and bloody noses, is carried around the different parts of the ground, for a quarter of an hour at a time, without any one of the mass being able to see the ball; and which they are often thus scuffling for, several minutes after it has been thrown off, and played over another part of the ground.' [16]

The great players in these games, those who scored the highest points for their teams, were feted and lauded in much the same way as warriors returning from an exceptionally successful foray against an enemy. Victory dances were held in their honor, feasts prepared and a whole crowd

Above: *Hoop and pole was played by rolling the hoop and two players casting lances at it. The relationship between markings on the hoop and the lance decided the score of each player. The photograph shows San Carlos Apaches, but the game was widespread.*

Left: *This hoop and spear belong to the Koyemshi (Mud Heads) of Zuni Pueblo, who appeared in late fall to announce the beginning of Shalako, the Zuni festival which re-enacts the Zuni emergence and migration myth and when the spirits of the deceased are honored and the Pueblo blessed.*

Left: *Game hoops varied considerably in construction and detail. Those shown here are, from the top, a bent twig ring with sinew lashing from the Chiricahua Apache; a Cheyenne hoop filled by interlacing a single cord; a bead decorated ring made by the Ute; a large slender ring from the Sioux.*

turned out to sing their praises. But this was slight compared with the honors lavished upon the man who scored the winning point. The status of a chief, a powerful shaman, or that of a prominent warrior whom the young men tried to emulate, pale in comparison with the adulation bestowed on the champion ball player. Tooan Tuh, or Spring Frog, a Cherokee warrior who once trailed an Osage war party over hundreds of miles after they attacked his village, and then surprised and killed them, was a terrifying man of war; yet the tribe remembered him in their songs and legends for his skill on the ball field rather than for those on the battlefield.

Another game of tremendous importance was the hoop and pole, which is clearly linked with war and gambling and was distributed across the entire North American continent. In principle it is a simple game of skill. A marked hoop was rolled along the ground and contestants cast lances or arrows at it, the positions of the markings relative to the lance giving a score by which the winner could be identified. The significance of the game is, however, much deeper. Among the southern Plains tribes the hoop is equated with the netted rawhide lacing of war shields, and the Zuni claim this represents power derived from the Twin War Gods. Such power

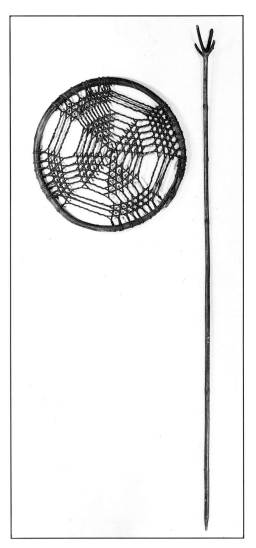

was never used as a physical means of defence, but was an adaptation of the web woven by Spider Woman, the mother of the War Twins, and was therefore a symbol of her protection and of the defeat of the Monsters that threatened human existence.

Its link with gambling is clear from the Kwakiutl, who used four stone rings which were called the 'mist-covered gambling stone', the 'rainbow gambling stone', the 'cloud-covered gambling stone', and the 'carrier of the world';[17] but its connection with creation and war is also evident, since the first game was played by Thunderbird and the animals of the upper world in a contest with the mythic people, who were helped by Woodpecker. Because Woodpecker's team defeated Thunderbird, the hoops were given to the people when they separated from the supernaturals, whose power could later be called back whenever the gambling stones were used.

Hopi Indians considered the hoop to be the protective power of the Lesser War God, who carried this symbol upon his back and at which the Kachin Manas, or Kachina Mothers, cast their corn cob darts, expressing the primacy of female reproductive power over masculine destructive power. The Oglala say the hoop represents day and night, and the lances the four winds; and in this respect we need to note that the four winds traveled the earth before the creation of the people, destroying the monsters and creating a suitable environment for people to occupy. Arapaho groups claim the wheel is the Sun, and the markings placed on it are symbols of the harmless water snake, but that all snakes represent a body of water surrounding the earth and are equivalent to the Four-Old-Men who represent the four world quarters. They are ever-present sentinels who guard and watch over the people, keeping them safe from harm or injury.

Game hoops, with or without their associated lances, might also be used by shamans during cures, when the hoop was touched to various parts of the patient's body to 'make them strong', and Stewart Culin takes its significance a lit-

Above: *Kiowa gaming arrows are painted with designs that relate to aspects of their cosmology as well as to colors identified with the war standard and shield. The set shown here were thrown like a javelin, the objective being to see who could throw furthest, but they may also have been used with a hoop.*

tle further by saying 'the hoop or ring stands as the feminine symbol, as opposed to the dart or arrows, which are masculine. The implements of the game together represent the shield and the bows or darts of the War Gods.'[18]

In this sense the hoop and pole game, which is deceptively simple when viewed superficially, becomes a representation of all the vital forces: of feminine and masculine, peace and war, defence and offence, health and sickness. It also brings together widely varying beliefs and attitudes toward war, since elements from the game are found among tribes as diverse as the warlike Kwakiutl and the peaceful Pomo, but links all of these to the sacred circle which, unlike any other of the mysterious forces, possesses both power and will whereby it is self-motivating and self-perpetuating. Black Elk, the renowned Oglala shaman, spoke of the life of the individual as a hoop, protected within the hoop of the tribe, which is surrounded by the hoop of the spirits. It is the purpose of the Twin War Gods to ensure these hoops remain unbroken.

Above: *Gaming rings were often adapted into dance rings as a link with the powers of the sacred circle, as in this Cree example. It is wrapped with red wool and sinew, has sinew strings forming the central cross, and hawk feather pendants.*

Left: *This early gaming ring and pole was collected from the Mandan in the 1830s by Maximilian, and is said to represent the unification of the male and female principles. The ring, for the female, was rolled between two warriors who tried to catch it on the male pole.*

Right: *Among the widely scattered Athapascan-speaking Carrier Indians of British Columbia the ring and pole game was the major diversion for young warriors whenever distant bands met. The example shown here is a model of the ring but is made using traditional methods. It consists of a bundle of small twigs which are lashed together with strips of willow bark.*

BIBLIOGRAPHY

Amsden, Charles Avery, *Navaho Weaving: Its Technic and History*, Fine Arts Press, Southwest Museum, 1934; Rio Grande Classics, Glorietta, New Mexico, 1971

Axtell, James, *The European and the Indian: Essays on the Ethnohistory of Colonial North America*, Oxford, 1981

Ball, Eve, *In the Days of Victorio*, University of Arizona Press, Tucson, 1970

Bancroft-Hunt, Norman, *Head and Hair Trophies* (ms), 1989
North American Indians, Brian Trodd Publishing, London, 1991
Indians of North America, Apple Press, London, 1992

Bancroft-Hunt, Norman and Forman, Werner, *People of the Totem*, Orbis Publishing, London, 1979; University of Oklahoma, Norman, 1988
Indians of the Plains, Orbis Publishing, London, 1981; University of Oklahoma, Norman, 1992

Bandi, Hans-Georg, *Eskimo Prehistory*, Methuen & Co., London, 1964

Barlowe, Arthur,, *The First Voyage Made to the Coasts of America*, Hakluyt Society, 1589

Barnard, Herwanna Becker, *The Comanche and his Literature*; MA thesis, University of Oklahoma, Norman, 1941

Battey, Thomas C, *The Life and Adventures of a Quaker Among the Indians*, Boston, 1889

Benedict, Ruth Fulton, The Concept of the Guardian Spirit in North America, *Memoir 29, American Anthropological Association*, Menasha, Wis., 1924
Patterns of Culture, Houghton Mifflin, 1934;Boston, Mass., 1989

Benndorf, Helga and Speyer, Arthur, *Indianer Nordamerikas 1700–1800*, Deutsches Ledermuseum, Offenbach, 1968

Berlandier, Jean-Louis, *The Indians of Texas in 1830*, John C Ewers (ed), Smithsonian Press, Washington D.C., 1969

Birket-Smith, Kaj, Contributions to Chipewyan Ethnology, *Report of the 5th Thule Expedition, Copenhagen*, 1930
The Eskimos, London, 1936

Boas, Franz, *Indianische Sagen von der Nord-Pacifischen Küste Amerikas*, Berlin, 1895
The Social Organisation and Secret Societies of the Kwakiutl Indians, Annual Report 1895, U.S. National Museum, Washington D.C., 1897
Bella Bella Tales, *Memoir, American Folk-Lore Society*, N.Y., 1932
Race, Language and Culture, MacMillan, N.Y., 1948
Primitive Art, H. Aschehoug & Co, Oslo, 1927; Dover Publications, N.Y., 1955
Kwakiutl Ethnography, Helen Codere (ed), Chicago, 1966

Boas, Franz and Hunt, George, *Kwakiutl Texts*, Publication of Jesup North Pacific Expedition, vol. 3, Leiden, 1905

Bodmer Karl, *Karl Bodmer's America*, Joslyn Art Museum and University of Nebraska, Lincoln, 1984

Bourke, John G, *On the Border with Crook*, N.Y., 1891

Brown, Joseph Epes, *The Sacred Pipe: Black Elk's Account of the Seven Rites of the Oglala Sioux*, Penguin Books, Middx., 1971

Brown, Mark H and Felton, W R (eds), *The Frontier Years: L A Huffman, Photographer of the Plains*, Bramhall House, N.Y., 1955

Burch, Ernest and Forman, Werner, *The Eskimo*, Macdonald Orbis, London, 1988

Burns, Louis F, *Osage Indian Customs and Myths*, Ciga Press, Fallbrook, California, 1984

Burt, Struthers, *Powder River, Let 'er Buck*, N.Y., 1938

Bushnell, David I Jr, Evidence of Indian Occupancy in Albemarle County, Virginia, *Miscellaneous Collections*, Smithsonian Institution, vol. 89, no. 7, Washington D.C., 1933

Cartier, Jaques, *Bref Récit et Succincte Narration de la Navigation*, Paris, 1863

Catlin, George, *Letters and Notes on the Manners, Customs, and Condition of the North American Indians*, 2 vols., London, 1841; Ross and Haines, Minn., 1965
Life Among the Indians, Gall and Inglis, London, 1897
O-Kee-Pa: A Religious Ceremony and Other Customs of the Mandans, John C Ewers (ed), Yale University Press, New Haven, 1967

Clark, A McFadyen, *Strangers of the North*, National Museum of Man, Ottawa, 1974

Clark, LaVerne Harrell, *They Sang for Horses*, University of Arizona Press, 1966, third printing 1983

Clark, W P, *The Indian Sign Language*, Phil., 1885

Cloutier, David, *Spirit, Spirit, Shaman Songs*, Copper Beech Press, Brown University, Rhode Island, 1980

Codere, Helen, Fighting with Property; *Monograph XVIII*, American Ethnological Society, 1950

Coe, Michael; Snow, Dean; Bensen, Elizabeth, *Atlas of Ancient America*, Facts on File, Oxford, 1986

Cremony, John C, *Life Among the Apaches*, A Roman & Co, San Francisco, 1868; University of Nebraska, Lincoln, 1983

Culin, Stewart, Games of the North American Indians, *24th Annual Report 1902-1903, Bureau of American Ethnology*, Smithsonian Institution, Washington D.C., 1907; Dover Publications, N.Y., 1975

Curtis, Edward S, *The North American Indian*, 20 vols., 1908; Johnson Reprint Corporation, N.Y., 1970

Cushing, Frank Hamilton, Zuni Fetiches, *2nd Annual Report 1880-1881, Bureau of American Ethnology*, Smithsonian Institution, Washington D.C., 1883; K. C. Publications, Las Vegas, Nevada, 1990 (9th printing)

de Bry, Theodore, *Discovering the New World*, Michael Alexander (ed), London Editions, London, 1976

de Laguna, Frederica, *Under Mount St. Elias: The History and Culture of Yakutat Tlingit*, 3 vols., Smithsonian Press, Washington D.C., 1972

de Laudonnière, René, *A Notable Historie*, Hakluyt Society, 1587

de Smet, Father Pierre Jean, *Life, Letters, and Travels*, Francis Harper, 1905; Hiram Martin Chittenden and Alfred Talbot Richardson (eds), 4 vols., Kraus Reprints, N.Y., 1969

Dixon, R B, The Shasta, *Bulletin*, American Museum of Natural History, vol. xvii, pt. v, N.Y.

Dodge, Richard Irving, *Our Wild Indians: Thirty Three Years Personal Experience among the Red Men of the Great West*. Hartford, 1882

Dorsey, George A, Mythology of the Wichita, *Publication 21*, Carnegie Institute of Washington, 1904
Traditions of the Arikara, *Publication 47*, Carnegie Institute of Washington, 1904
Traditions of the Skidi Pawnee, *Memoir, American Folk-Lore Society*, vol. viii, Boston, 1904
The Cheyenne, *Publication 99, Anthropological Series IX*, No. 1, Field Columbian Museum, Chicago, 1905
Pawnee Mythology, *Publication 59*, Carnegie Institute of Washington, 1906

Dorsey, George A and Kroeber, A L, Traditions of the Arapaho, *Anthropological Series 81*, Field Columbian Museum, Chicago, 1903

Dorsey, George A and Murie, James, Traditions of the Caddo, *Publication 41*, Carnegie Institute of Washington, 1905

Dorsey, J Owen, An Account of the War Customs of the Osages, *American Naturalist*, vol. xviii, no. 2, 1884

Driver, Harold, *Indians of North America*, Chicago, 1964

Drucker, Philip, Northern and Central Nootkan Tribes, *Bulletin 144, Bureau of American Ethnology*, Smithsonian Institution, Washington D.C., 1951
Cultures of the North Pacific Coast, San Francisco, 1965

Drummond, Don E, *The Eskimos and Aleuts*, Thames and Hudson, London, 1977; revised edition, Thames and Hudson, London, 1987

Dunbar, J B, *The Pawnee Indians: A Sketch*, Morrisania, N.Y., 1882

Eggan, Fred, *Social Organization of the Western Pueblos*, Chicago, 1950

Ewers, John C, The Horse in Blackfoot Culture, *Bulletin 159, Bureau of American Ethnology*, Smithsonian Institution, Washington D.C., 1955
The Blackfeet: Raiders on the Northwestern Plains, University of Oklahoma Press, Norman, 1958
Intertribal Warfare as the Precursor of Indian-White Warfare on the Northern Great Plains, *Western Historical Quarterly*, 4:4, 1975

Feest, Christian, *The Indians of Northeastern North America*, Institute of Religious Iconography, State University, Groningen, Section X North America, Fascicle seven, Leiden, 1980

Ferg, Alan, *Western Apache Material Culture: The Goodwin and Guenther Collections*, University of Arizona, (2nd Printing) 1988

Fewkes, Jesse Walter, *Hopi Snake Ceremonies*, Awanyu Publishing, New Mexico, 1986

Fletcher, Alice and La Flesche, Francis, The Omaha Tribe, *Bulletin 27, Bureau of American Ethnology*, Washington D.C., 1911

Fletcher, Alice and Murie, James, The Hako: a Pawnee Ceremony, *22nd Annual Report, Bureau of American Ethnology*, Smithsonian Institution, Washington D.C., 1904

Friederici, Georg, *Skalpieren und Ähnliche Kriegsbebräuche in Amerika*, University Leipzig, Braunschweig, 1906

Fundaburk, Emma Lila, *Southeastern Indians: Life Portraits 1564-1860*, Scarecrow Reprint Corporation, New Jersey, 1969

Gatschet, A S, The Klamath Indians of Southwestern Oregon, *Contributions to North American Ethnology*, vol. II, Washington, 1890

Goddard, Pliny Earle, Chipewyan Texts, *Anthropological Papers*, American Museum of Natural History, vol. X, pt. i, N.Y., 1912
Dancing Societies of the Sarsi Indians, *Anthropological Papers*, American Museum of Natural History, vol. XI, 1914
The Beaver Indians, *Anthropological Papers*, American Museum of Natural History, vol. IX, pt. iv, N.Y., 1916
Beaver Texts, *Anthropological Papers*, American Museum of Natural History, vol. X, pt. v, N.Y., 1917
Sarsi Texts; University of California Publications in *American Archaeology and Ethnology*, vol. 11, no. 3

Greene, Candace C, The Tepee with Battle Pictures, *Natural History Magazine*, American Museum of Natural History, 1993

Grinnell, George Bird, *Blackfoot Lodge Tales: The Story of a Prairie People*, N.Y., 1892
Pawnee Hero Stories and Folk Tales, N.Y., 1899
Coup and Scalp among the Plains Indians, *American Anthropologist*, n.s., 12, 1910
The Fighting Cheyennes, N.Y., 1915
Two Great Scouts and their Pawnee Battalion, Arthur H Clark Co., 1928; University of Nebraska, Lincoln, 1973

Gunther, Erna, Northwest Coast Indian Art, in *Anthropology and Art, American Museum Sourcebooks in Anthropology*, Natural History Press, N.Y., 1971
Indian Life on the Northwest Coast, Chicago, 1972

Haberland, Wolfgang, *Oglala: Pine Ridge Reservation*, 1909; Wegweiser zur Völkerkunde, Heft 31, Hamburg, 1988

Hallowell, A I, Bear Ceremonialism in the Northern Hemisphere, *American Anthropologist*, vol. xxviii, 1926

Hartmann, Horst, *Kachina Figuren der Hopi Indianer*, Berlin, 1978
Die Plains-und Prärieindianer Nordamerikas; Berlin, 1987

Hassrick, Royal B, *The Sioux: Life and Customs of a Warrior Society*, University of Oklahoma Press, Norman, 1964

Hill, Ruth Beebe, *Hanta Yo*, Doubleday & Co., 1979

Hill, W W, *Navaho Warfare*, Yale University Publications in *Anthropology 5*, New Haven, 1936

Hill-Tout, Charles, *The Salish People*, 4 vols., Talonbooks, Vancouver, 1978

Hodge, Frederick Webb, *Handbook of Indians North of Mexico; Bulletin 30, Bureau of American Ethnology*, Smithsonian Institution, Washington D.C., 1906

Hoebel, E Adamson, Associations and the State in the Plains, *American Anthropologist*, vol. XXXVIII, n.s., Menasha, Wis., 1936
The Cheyenne: Indians of the Great Plains, Holt, Rinehart and Winston, N.Y., 1960

Holder, Preston, *The Horse and the Hoe on the Plains*; University of Oklahoma Press, Norman, 1970

Holloway, David, *Lewis and Clark and the Crossing of North America*, Weidenfeld and Nicolson, London, 1974

Horgan, James D, *The McKenny-Hall Portrait Gallery of American Indians*, Crown Publishing, N.Y., 1972

Horgan, John, Early Arrivals: Scientists Argue over how Old the New World is, *Scientific American*, February 1992

Howard, Edgar B, An Outline of the Problem of Man's Antiquity in North America, *American Anthropologist*, vol. XXXVIII, n.s., Menasha, Wis., 1936

Hyde, George E, *The Pawnee Indians*, Denver, 1951; Oklahoma University, Norman, 1973

Irrving, John Treat Jr, *Indian Sketches: Taken During an Expedition to the Pawnee Tribes*, 1833; Philadelphia, 1835; University of Oklahoma, Norman, 1955

Jacobsen N, Johan Adrian, *Reise an der Nordwestkste Amerikas, 1881-83*, Leipzig, 1884
Alaskan Voyage 1881–1883, Erna Gunther (trans), Chicago, 1977

James, Edwin, *Account of an Expedition from Pittsburgh to the Rocky Mountains Performed in the Years 1819 and 1820*, 2 vols., Phil., 1823

Jones, Strachan, The Kutchin Tribes, *Annual Report 1866*, Smithsonian Institution, Washington D.C., 1872

Josephy, Alvin M Jr (ed), *American Heritage Book of Indians*, American Heritage, 1961

King, J C H, *Portrait Masks from the Northwest Coast of America*, British Museum Publications, London, 1974
Artificial Curiosities from the Northwest Coast of America, British Museum Publications, London, 1981
Thunderbird and Lightning, British Museum Publications, London, 1982

Krause, Aurel, *Die Tlinkit Indianer*, Jena, 1885, Erna Gunther (trans), *Monograph 26, American Ethnological Society*, University of Washington, 1976 (4th printing)

Krech, Shepard III, *A Victorian Earl in the Arctic, 1888–1889*, British Museum Publications, London, 1989

Kroeber, A L, The Arapaho, *Bulletin*, American Museum of Natural History, vol. 18, pt. 1, N.Y., 1902

Kroeber, Theodora and Heizer, Robert F, *Almost Ancestors: The First Californians*, Sierra Club, N.Y., 1968

La Flesche, Francis, The Osage Tribe, *36th Annual Report 1914–1915, Bureau of American Ethnology*, Smithsonian Institution, Washington D.C., 1921

Lamb, W Kay (ed), *The Letters and Journals of Sir Alexander Mackenzie*, Hakluyt Society, Cambridge, 1970

Landes, Ruth, *The Mystic Lake Sioux*, University of Wisconsin, Madison, 1968

Le Moyne, *Narrative of Le Moyne*, Boston, 1875

Levernier, James and Cohen, Hennig, *The Indians and their Captives*, Contributions in American Studies, Greenwood Press, Conn., 1977

Lewis, Meriwether and Clark, William, *Original Journals of the Lewis and Clark Expedition, 1804–1806*, Reuben Gold Thwaites (ed), 8 vols., Dodds, Mead and Co., N.Y., 1904

Loeb, E M, The Blood Sacrifice Complex, *Memoir 30, American Anthropological Association*, Menasha, Wis., 1923

Lowie, Robert H, The Northern Shoshone, *Anthropological Papers, American Museum of Natural History*, vol. II, pt. ii, N.Y., 1909
Chipewyan Tales, *Anthropological Papers*, American Museum of Natural History, vol. X, pt. ii, N.Y., 1912
Dance Associations of the Eastern Dakota, *Anthropological Papers*, American Museum of Natural History, vol. IX, N.Y.,

1913
Military Societies of the Crow Indians, *Anthropological Papers*, American Museum of Natural History, vol. XI, N.Y., 1913
Societies of the Hidatsa and Mandan Indians, *Anthropological Papers*, American Museum of Natural History, vol. XI, pt. iii, N.Y., 1913
Societies of the Arikara Indians, *Anthropological Papers*, American Museum of Natural History, vol. XI, N.Y., 1915
Dances and Societies of the Plains Shoshone, *Anthropological Papers*, American Museum of Natural History, vol. XI, N.Y., 1916
Plains Indian Age Societies: A Historical and Comparative Summary, *Anthropological Papers*, American Museum of Natural History, vol. XI, pt. xiii, N.Y., 1916
Societies of the Kiowa, *Anthropological Papers*, American Museum of Natural History, vol. XI, N.Y., 1916
Myths and Traditions of the Crow Indians, *Anthropological Papers*, American Museum of Natural History, vol. XXV, pt. i, N.Y., 1918
Primitive Society, Boni and Liveright, N.Y., 1920
Shoshonean Ethnography, *Anthropological Papers*, American Museum of Natural History, vol. XX, pt. iii, N.Y., 1924
The Crow Indians, Farrar and Rinehart, N.Y., 1935
Indians of the Plains, American Museum of Natural History, N.Y., 1954; Bison Books, University of Nebraska, Lincoln, 1982
Macgowan, Kenneth and Hester, Joseph, *Early Man in the New World*, American Museum of Natural History, N.Y., 1962
Mackenzie, Sir Alexander, *Voyages from Montreal*, University Microfilms, 1966
Macneish, R S, Early Man in the New World, *American Scientist*, vol. 63, no. 3, New Haven, 1976
Mandelbaum, David C, The Plains Cree, *Anthropological Papers*, American Museum of Natural History, vol. XXXVII, N.Y., 1940; *Canadian Plains Studies 9*, Canadian Plains Research Center, University of Regina, 1979
Marriott, Alice, *The Ten Grandmothers*, University of Oklahoma, Norman, 1945
Mason, Michael H, *The Arctic Forests*, London, 1924
Maximilian, Prinz zu Wied, *Travels in the Interior of North America*, London, 1843
McAllister, J G, Kiowa-Apache Social Organization, in Fred Eggan (ed), *Social Anthropology of North American Tribes*, Chicago, 1935
McClintock, Walter, *The Old North Trail*, MacMillan and Co., London, 1910
McCoy, Ronald, Circles of Power, *Plateau*, vol. 55, no. 4, Museum of Northern Arizona, Arizona, 1988
McKenny, Thomas and Hall, James, *History of the Indian Tribes of North America*, Phil., 1854
Melody, Michael E, *The Apache*, Chelsea House, N.Y., 1989
Merriam, C Hart, *Ethnographic Notes on California Indian Tribes*; Robert F Heizer (comp. and ed), University of California Archaeological Research Facility, Berkeley, 1966–67
Michelson, Truman, Narrative of a Southern Cheyenne Woman, *Smithsonian Miscellaneous Collections*, vol. 87, no. 5, Smithsonian Institution, Washington D.C., 1932
Mishkin, Bernard, Rank and Warfare among the Plains Indians, *Monograph 3, American Ethnological Society*, 1966
Mooney, James, Calendar History of the Kiowa Indians, *17th Annual Report, Bureau of American Ethnology*, Smithsonian Institution, Washington D.C., 1898; Smithsonian Institution Press, Washington D.C., 1979
Morgan, William, *Human-Wolves Among the Navaho*, Yale University Publications in Anthropology 11, New Haven, 1936
Morice, Father A G, *A First Collection of Minor Essays, Mostly Anthropological*, Stuart's Lake Mission, Quesnel, B.C., 1902
The Canadian Déné, *Annual Archaeological Report*, Toronto, 1905
Murdock, George Peter, *Rank and Potlatch Among the Haida*, Yale University Publications in Anthropology 13, New Haven, 1936
Murie, James, Pawnee Societies, *Anthropological Papers*, American Museum of Natural History, vol. XI, pt. vii, N.Y., 1914
Nadeau, Gabriel, Indian Scalping: Technique in Different Tribes, *The New England Journal of Medicine*, 1937
Neihardt, John G, *Black Elk Speaks*, W. Morrow, N.Y., 1932
Newcomb, W W, *The Indians of Texas*, University of Texas, Austin, 1961; 1990 (10th printing)
Nye, Wilbur Sturtevant, *Plains Indian Raiders*, University of Oklahoma, Norman, 1968; 1987 (4th printing)
Oberg, Kalervo, The Tlingit, *Monograph 55, American Ethnological Society*, Washington, 1933
Olson, Ronald,Social Organisation of the Haida of British Columbia, *Anthropological Records 12*, University of California Press, 194
Opler, Morris Edward, Three Types of Variation and their Relation to Culture Change, in *Language, Culture, and Personality: Essays in Honour of Edward Sapir*, n.d.
A Summary of Jicarilla Apache Culture, *American Anthropologist*, n.s., vol. XXXVIII, Menasha, Wis., 1936
Dirty Boy: A Jicarilla Tale of Raid and War, *Memoir 52, American Anthropological Association*, Menasha, Wis., 1938
Opler, Morris Edward and Hoijer, Harry, The Raid and Warpath Language of the Chiricahua Apache, *American Anthropologist*, n.s., vol. 42, Menasha, Wis., 1940
Osgood, Cornelius, *Contributions to the Ethnography of the Kutchin*, Yale University Publications in Anthropology 14, New Haven, 1936
The Ethnography of the Tanaina, Yale University Publications in Anthropology 16, New Haven, 1937
Ingalik Material Culture, Yale University Publications in Anthropology 22, New Haven, 1940
Ingalik Social Culture, Yale University Publications in Anthropology 53, New Haven, 1958
Ingalik Mental Culture, Yale University Publications in Anthropology 56, New Haven, 1959
The Han Indians: A Compilation of Ethnographic and Historical Data on the Alaska-Yukon Boundary Area, Yale University Publications in Anthropology 74, New Haven, 1971
Pakes, Fraser J, Making War Attractive, *English Westerners' Brand Book*, vol. 26, no. 2, London, 1989
Park, Willard Z, Culture Succession in the Great Basin, in *Language, Culture, and Personality: Essays in Honour of Edward Sapir*, n.d.
Parks, Douglas R, Bands and Villages of the Arikara and Pawnee, *Nebraska History*, vol. 60, no. 2, Summer 1979
Parsons, Elsie Clews, The Scalp Ceremonial of Zuni, *Memoir 31, American Anthropological Association*, Menasha, Wis., 1924
Kiowa Tales, *Memoirs of the American Folk-Lore Society*, vol. XXII, 1929
Hopi and Zuni Ceremonialism, *Memoir 39, American Anthropological Association*, Menasha, Wis., 1933
Pike, Zebulon M, An Account of Expeditions to the Sources of the Mississippi and through the Western Parts of Louisiana to the Sources of the Arkansaw, Kans, La Platte, and Pierre Juan, Rivers, Performed by Order of the Government of the United States during the Years 1805, 1806 and 1807. And a Tour through the Interior Parts of New Spain, when Conducted through these Provinces by Order of the Captain General, in the Year 1807; Phil., 1810
Powell, Father Peter, *Sweet Medicine: The Continuing Role of the Sacred Arrows, the Sun Dance, and the Sacred Buffalo Hat in Northern Cheyenne History*, 2 vols., University of Oklahoma, Norman, 1969; Harper and Row, N.Y., 1981
Provinse, J H, The Underlying Sanctions of Plains Indian Society, in Fred Eggan (ed) *Social Anthropology of North American Tribes*, Chicago, 1937
Reichard, Gladys A, *Navaho Religion*, Bollingen Foundation, N.Y., 1950; Princeton University Press, 1974
Ritzenthaler, Robert E, *Prehistoric Indians of Wisconsin*, Milwaukee Public Museum, 1985
Roberts, Helen H, *Musical Areas in Aboriginal North America*, Yale University Publications in Anthropology 12, New Haven, 1936
Roe, Frank, *The Indian and the Horse*, University of Oklahoma, Norman, 1955
Schoolcraft, Henry Rowe, Historical and Statistical Information Respecting the History, Condition, and Prospects of the Indian Tribes of the United States, pts. i–iv, Phil., 1851-1857
Scientific American, Early Man in America, San Francisco, 1973
Scott, Hugh Lennox, Notes on the Kado: or Sun Dance of the Kiowa, *American Anthropologist*, n.s., vol. 13, no. 3, 1911
Secoy, Frank R, Changing Military Patterns on the Great Plains, *Monograph of the American Ethnological Society*, vol. 21, N.Y., 1953
Siebert, Anna and Forman, Werner, *Indianerkunst*, Verlag Werner Dausien, Hanau, 1967
Skinner, Alanson B, The Eastern Cree, *Anthropological Papers*. American Museum of Natural History, vol. IX, N.Y., 1911
Political Organization, Cults and Ceremonies of the Plains Cree, *Anthropological Papers*, American Museum of Natural History, vol. XI, N.Y., 1914
Political and Ceremonial Organization of the Plains Ojibway, *Anthropological Papers*, American Museum of Natural History, vol. XI, N.Y., 1914
Societies of the Iowa, *Anthropological Papers*, American Museum of Natural History, vol. XI, N.Y., 1915
Kansa Organizations, *Anthropological Papers*, American Museum of Natural History, vol. XI, N.Y., 1915
Ponca Societies and Dances; *Anthropological Papers*, American Museum of Natural History, vol. XI, N.Y., 1915
Smith, Marion W, The War Complex of the Plains Indians, *Proceedings LXXVIII, American Philosophical Society*, 1938
Snow, Dean and FormanN, Werner, *North American Indians: Their Archeology and Prehistory*, Thames and Hudson, London, 1976
Speck, Frank G, *Naskapi: The Savage Hunters of the Labrador Peninsula*, University of Oklahoma, Norman, 1935
Spier, Leslie, *Klamath Ethnography*, University of California Press, Berkeley, 1930
Cultural Relations of the Gila River and Lower Colorado Tribes, Yale University Publications in Anthropology 3, New Haven, 1936
Stands-In Timber, John and Liberty, Margot, *Cheyenne Memories*, Yale University Press, New Haven, 1967; University of Nebraska, Lincoln, 1972
Strickland, Rennard, *Fire and the Spirits: Cherokee Law from Clan to Court*, University of Oklahoma, Norman, 1975
Sturtevant, William C and Taylor, Colin, *The Native Americans*, Salamander Books, London, 1991
Swanton, John R, Contributions to the Ethnology of the Haida, Publication of Jesup North Pacific Expedition, vol. V, pt. 1, Leiden, 1905–9
Indian Tribes of the Lower Mississippi Valley and Adjacent Coast of the Gulf of Mexico, *Bulletin 43, Bureau of American Ethnology*, Smithsonian Institution, Washington D.C., 1911
Early History of the Creek Indians and Their Neighbours, *Bulletin 73, Bureau of American Ethnology*, Smithsonian Institution, Washington D.C., 1922
Modern Square Grounds of the Creek Indians, *Smithsonian Miscellaneous Collections*, vol. 85, no. 8, Smithsonian Institution, Washington D.C., 1931
Source Material on the History and Ethnology of the Caddo Indians, *Bulletin 132, Bureau of American Ethnology*, Smithsonian Institution, Washington D.C., 1942
The Indians of the Southeastern United States, *Bulletin 137, Bureau of American Ethnology*, Smithsonian Institution, Washington D.C., 1946
Tanner, John, *Narrative of the Captivity and Adventures of John Tanner during Thirty Years Residence among the Indians in the Interior of America*, N.Y., 1830
Thomas, Davis and Ronnefeldt, Karin, *People of the First Man*, Dutton, N.Y., 1976
Thwaites, Reuben Gold (ed), *Jesuit Relations 1610–1791*, 73 vols., Paegent, N.Y., 1959
Trigger, Bruce, *Children of Aataentsic: a History of the Huron People to 1660*, McGill-Queen's University Press, 1976
von Champlain, *Oeuvres de Champlain, 1603, Laverdiére (ed)*, Quebec, 1870
Voegelin, C F, *The Shawnee Female Deity*, Yale University Publications in Anthropology 11, New Haven, 1936
Walker James R, *Lakota Belief and Ritual*, Raymond J De Mallie and Elaine A Jahner (eds), University of Nebraska, Lincoln, 1980
Lakota Myth, Elaine A Jahner (ed), University of Nebraska, Lincoln, 1983
Walker, Winslow, The Troyville Mounds, Catahoula Parish, La, *Bulletin 113, Bureau of American Ethnology*, Smithsonian Institution, Washington D.C., 1936
Wallace, E and Hoebel, E Adamson, *The Comanches: Lords of the Southern Plains*, University of Oklahoma, Norman, 1954
Waters, Frank, *Book of the Hopi*, Viking Press, 1963; Ballantine Books, N.Y., 1971 (5th printing)
Wedel, Waldo R, An Introduction to Pawnee Archeology; *Bulletin 112, Bureau of American Ethnology*, Smithsonian Institution, Washington D.C., 1936
Culture Sequences in the Central Great Plains, in *Essays in Historical Anthropology of North America*, Smithsonian Miscellaneous Publications, vol. 100, Washington, 1940
Archeological Remains in Central Kansas and their Possible Bearing on the Location of Quivira, *Smithsonian Miscellaneous Collections*, vol. 101, no. 7, Smithsonian Institution, Washington D.C., 1942
Prehistoric Man on the Great Plains, University of Oklahoma, Norman, 1961 (reprinted 1970)
Weltfish, Gene, *The Lost Universe: Pawnee Life and Culture*, N.Y., 1965; University of Nebraska, Lincoln, 1977
Weygold, Frederick, Die Hunkazeremonie, *Archiv für Anthropologie 39*, N.F., Bd. XI, 1912
White, Leslie A, The Pueblo of San Felipe, *Memoir 38, American Anthropological Association*, Menasha, Wis., 1932
Wildschut, William, Crow Indian Medicine Bundles, John C Ewers (ed), *Contributions from the Museum of the American Indian, Heye Foundation*, vol. XVII, N.Y., 1975
Wissler, Clark, Social Organization and Ritualistic Ceremonies of the Blackfoot Indians, *Anthropological Papers*, American Museum of Natural History, vol. VII, N.Y., 1911
Ceremonial Bundles of the Blackfoot Indians, *Anthropological Papers*, American Museum of Natural History, vol. VII, pt. ii, N.Y., 1912
Societies and Ceremonial Associations in the Oglala Division of the Teton-Dakota, *Anthropological Papers*. American Museum of Natural History, vol. XI, N.Y., 1912
Societies and Dance Associations of the Blackfoot Indians; *Anthropological Papers*, American Museum of Natural History, vol. XI, N.Y., 1913
Shamanistic and Dancing Societies, *Anthropological Papers*, American Museum of Natural History, vol. XI, N.Y., 1916
North American Indians of the Plains, American Museum of Natural History, N.Y., 1937
Indians of the United States, American Museum of Natural History, N.Y., 1940; Anchor Books, 1966
Wissler, Clark and Duvall, D C, Mythology of the Blackfoot Indians, *Anthropological Papers*, American Museum of Natural History, vol. II, pt. i, N.Y., 1908
Württemberg, Paul Wilhelm Herzog von: Reise nach dem Nördlichen Amerika, 1822-1824; Verlag Lothar Borowsky, München

INDEX

Page numbers in **bold** indicate illustrations or mentions in captions

254

REFERENCES

INTRODUCTION

1 Catlin, George: *Letters and Notes on the Manners, Customs, and Condition of the North American Indians*, Letter No. 2

CHAPTER ONE

1 Fundaburk, Emma Lila, *Southeastern Indians: Life Portraits 1504–1800*, p. 96
2 Fundaburk, p. 111
3 Fundaburk, p. 99
4 Fundaburk, p. 99
5 Josephy, Alvin M Jr (ed), *American Heritage Book of Indians*, p. 149
6 Swanton, John R, *The Indians of the Southeastern United States*, pp. 700-701
7 Swanton, John R, *Indian Tribes of the Lower Mississippi Valley and Adjacent Coast of the Gulf of Mexico*
8 Josephy, p. 152
9 Axtell, James, *The European and the Indian: Essays on the Ethnohistory of Colonial North America*, p. 23
10 Trigger, Bruce, *Children of Aataentsic: A History of the Huron People to 1000*, p. 70
11 Trigger, p. 70
12 Horan, James D, *The McKenny-Hall Portrait Gallery of American Indians*, p. 43
13 Josephy, p. 163

CHAPTER TWO

1 Dorsey, George A, *Traditions of the Arikara*, p. 18
2 Württemberg, Paul Wilhelm Herzog von, *Reise nach dem Nördlichen Amerika 1822–1824*, pp. 401-2
3 Irving, John Treat Jr, *Indian Sketches: Taken During an Expedition to the Pawnee Tribes, 1833*, pp. 122–3
4 Fletcher, Alice and Murie, James, *The Hako: A Pawnee Ceremony*, p. 21
5 Fletcher, Alice and La Flesche, Francis, *The Omaha Tribe*, p. 404
6 Fletcher and La Flesche, p. 47
7 Dorsey, George A, *Pawnee Mythology*, p. 116
8 Irving, p. 59
9 Catlin, George, *Letters and Notes on the Manners, Customs, and Condition of the North American Indians*, vol. 2, p. 6
10 James, Edwin, *Account of an Expedition from Pittsburgh to the Rocky Mountains Performed in the Years 1819 and 1820*, pp. 232-3
11 Fletcher and La Flesche, p. 36
12 Burns, Louis F, *Osage Indian Customs and Myths*, p. 125
13 Burns, p. 126
14 Dorsey, George A, *Mythology of the Wichita*, pp. 15–16
15 Author in discussion with Osage tribal historian
16 Grinnell, George Bird, *Two Great Scouts and their Pawnee Battalion*, p. 133
17 Hyde, George E, *The Pawnee Indians*, pp. 254–5
18 Fletcher and La Flesche, pp. 407–8

CHAPTER THREE

1 Burt, Struthers, *Powder River, Let 'er Buck*, p. 198
2 Catlin, George, *Letters and Notes on the Manners, Customs, and Condition of the North American Indians*, vol. 1, p. 51
3 Hill, Ruth Beebe, *Hanta Yo*, p. 109
4 Author in conversation with Blackfoot Elder
5 Landes, Ruth, *The Mystic Lake Sioux*, p. 214
6 Wissler, Clark, *Social Organization and Ritualistic Ceremonies of the Blackfoot Indians*, p. 41
7 Newcomb, W W, *The Indians of Texas*, p. 181

8 Hoebel, E Adamson, *The Cheyenne: Indians of the Great Plains*, p. 432
9 Smith, Marion W, *The War Complex of the Plains Indians*, p. 432
10 Dodge, Richard Irving, *Our Wild Indians: Thirty Three Years Personal Experience among the Red Men of the Great West*, pp. 401–2
11 Catlin, George, *O-Kee-Pa: A Religious Ceremony and Other Customs of the Mandans*, p. 67
12 Catlin; ibid. p. 47
13 Walker, James R, *Lakota Myth*, pp. 142–3
14 Kroeber, A L, *The Arapaho*, p. 8
15 Berlandier, Jean-Louis, *The Indians of Texas in 1830*, p. 64
16 Mooney, James, *Calendar History of the Kiowa Indians*, p. 174
17 Mooney, p. 258
18 Catlin: op. cit. *Letters and Notes*, vol. 2, p. 65
19 Newcomb, p. 180

CHAPTER FOUR

1 Opler, Morris Edward, *A Summary of Jicarilla Apache Culture*, p. 211–2
2 Cremony, John C, *Life Among the Apaches*, p. 215
3 Josephy, Alvin M Jr, *American Heritage Book of Indians*, p. 386
4 Josephy, p. 386
5 Cremony, p. 189
6 Cremony, p. 180
7 Reichard, Gladys A, *Navaho Religion*, p. 248
8 Clark, Laverne Harrell, *They Sang for Horses*, p. 85
9 Reichard, p. 580
10 Melody, Michael E, *The Apache*, p. 31
11 Waters, Frank, *Book of the Hopi*, pp. 313–14
12 Waters, p. 225
13 White, Leslie A, *The Pueblo of San Felipe*, pp. 53–4
14 Benedict, Ruth Fulton, *Patterns of Culture*, p. 114
15 Cushing, Frank Hamilton, *Zuni Fetiches*, p. 41
16 Parsons, Elsie Clews, *The Scalp Ceremonial of Zuni*, p. 6
17 Josephy, p. 112
18 Benedict, p. 115
19 Cremony; pp. 91–2
20 Spier, Leslie, *Cultural Relations of the Gila River and Lower Colorado Tribes*, p. 5
21 Kroeber, Theodora and Heizer, Robert F, *Almost Ancestors: The First Californians*, p. 44
22 Reid, 1926; quoted in Spier.
23 Josephy, p. 151
24 Josephy, p. 304
25 Kroeber and Heizer, p. 29
26 Kroeber and Heizer, p. 29

CHAPTER FIVE

1 Merriam, C Hart, *Ethnographic Notes on California Indian Tribes*, p. 210
2 Driver, Harold, *Culture Element Distribution*, no. 2332
3 Spier, Leslie, *Klamath Ethnography*, pp. 24–5
4 Spier, p. 31
5 Merriam, p. 199
6 Merriam, p. 265
7 Spier, p. 31
8 Holloway, David, *Lewis and Clark and the Crossing of North America*, pp. 144–5
9 Holloway, p. 149
10 Hill-Tout, Charles, *The Salish People*, vol. II, p. 49

11 Codere, Helen, *Fighting With Property*, p. 92
12 Boas, Franz, *The Social Organisation and Secret Societies of the Kwakiutl Indians*, p. 571
13 Codere, p. 97
14 Benedict, Ruth Fulton, *Patterns of Culture*, p. 216
15 Boas, Franz, *Kwakiutl Ethnography*, pp. 110–15
16 Boas, op. cit. *Social Organisation*, p. 602
17 Boas, ibid. p. 356
18 Boas, ibid. p. 356
19 Benedict, pp. 197–9
20 Drucker, Philip, *Northern and Central Nootkan Tribes*, p. 377
21 Gunther, Erna, *Northwest Coast Indian Art*, p. 338
22 King, JCH, *Portrait Masks from the Northwest Coast of America*, p. 43
23 Cloutier, David, *Spirit, Spirit, Shaman Songs*, p. 59
24 de Laguna, Frederica, *Under Mount St. Elias: The History and Culture of Yakutat Tlingit*, p. 581

CHAPTER SIX

1 Burch, Ernest and Forman, Werner, *The Eskimo*, p. 39
2 Osgood, Cornelius, *Contributions to the Ethnography of the Kutchin*, p. 86
3 Osgood, p. 86
4 Jones, Strachan, *The Kutchin Tribes*, p. 325
5 Mason, Michael H, *The Arctic Forests*, p. 60
6 Krech, Shepard III, *A Victorian Earl in the Arctic, 1888–1889*, pp. 51–2
7 Roberts, Helen H, *Musical Areas in Aboriginal North America*, p. 9
8 Goddard, Pliny Earle, *The Beaver Indians*, p. 227
9 Goddard, p. 229
10 Mackenzie, Sir Alexander, *Voyages from Montreal*, p. lxxii
11 Mackenzie, pp. cxxv–cxxvi
12 Goddard, Pliny Earle, *Chipewyan Texts*, p. 193
13 Harmon, pp. 143-4, quoted in Speck, Frank G, *Naskapi: The Savage Hunters of the Labrador Peninsula*, p. 46
14 Speck, p. 44

CHAPTER SEVEN

1 Wissler, Clark, *Social Organization and Ritualistic Ceremonies of the Blackfoot Indians*, p. 411
2 Grinnell, George Bird, *Blackfoot Lodge Tales: The Story of a Prairie People*, p. 262
3 Wissler, Clark, *Societies and Ceremonial Associations in the Oglala Division of the Teton-Dakota*, p. 14
4 Wissler, ibid. p. 20
5 Murie, James, *Pawnee Societies*, pp. 561–3
6 Wissler, Clark, op. cit. *Oglala Societies*, p. 20
7 Lowie, Robert H, *Societies of the Kiowa*, p. 348
8 Marriott, Alice, *The Ten Grandmothers*, pp. 117–18
9 Marriott, p. 124
10 Skinner, Alanson B, *Political and Ceremonial Organization of the Plains Ojibway*, pp. 501–2
11 Murie, p. 610
12 Murie, p. 616
13 Dorsey, George A, *Mythology of the Wichita*, pp. 5 and 7
14 Catlin, George, *Letters and Notes on the Manners, Customs, and Condition of the North American Indians*, vol. 1, p. 148
15 Culin, Stewart, *Games of the North American Indians*, p. 578
16 Catlin, vol. 2, pp. 123–6
17 Boas, Franz and Hunt, George, *Kwakiutl Texts*, p. 295
18 Culin, p. 441

PICTURE CREDITS

Kiowa